250
must-have
slow
cooker
recipes

MURDOCH BOOKS

Contents

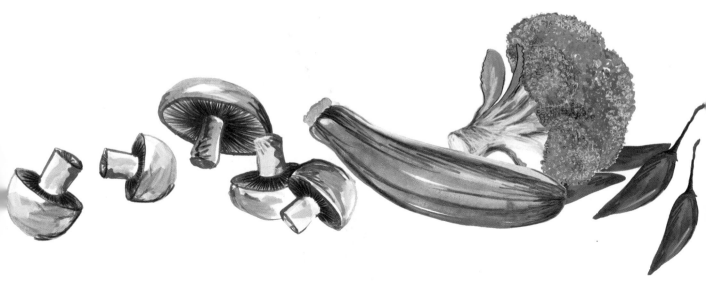

Introduction

Trends come and go, and when it comes to kitchen gadgetry, we've possibly seen them all. From omelette makers, ice-cream machines and bread makers to plug-in tagines and electric tin openers, it seems there's been an electrical appliance invented for every culinary situation imaginable.

Yet how many of us have succumbed to the latest, greatest gizmo, only to discover that it takes up too much space in our cupboards or is annoyingly hard to clean?

Having said that, there are some machines and appliances we'd rather not live without. Food processors, blenders and electric beaters have removed a great deal of tedious chopping, beating and whisking from much of our cooking, and many of us would be hard-pressed to cook successfully without them.

Slow cookers are another indispensable kitchen device that no busy household should be without. They've been around since the 1960s and have always had their devotees, but more and more cooks are wising up to the time- and budget-saving capabilities of the slow cooker.

Cooks like magic

Slow cookers transform many foods — particularly those tougher, tastier cuts of meat — from their raw state to melting tenderness, often with little more exertion required than flicking a switch.

They can be plugged in anywhere, they use less electricity than your oven, and there is only one bowl to wash up afterwards. You don't need to stir or hover over a meal that is simmering in a slow cooker, and it's almost impossible to burn anything — there's such latitude in cooking times that an hour or two more usually isn't going to make much difference.

In a slow cooker, meals practically cook themselves and they taste incredible — every last drop of the food's natural flavour is captured inside the cooker. From hearty soups to creamy chicken curry, country beef stew and lamb shanks in red wine, the hardest thing about using your slow cooker will be deciding what to make in it.

Slow cookers are also called 'Crock Pots'; Crock Pot is a brand name that was conjured

up in America in 1971. Essentially, a slow cooker is an electrical appliance, comprising a round, oval or oblong cooking vessel made of glazed ceramic or porcelain. This cooking vessel is surrounded by a metal housing, which contains a thermostatically controlled heating element. The lid is often transparent, making it easy to keep an eye on how things are bubbling along inside.

Slow cookers come in a variety of sizes, with the largest having a capacity of about 7 litres (245 fl oz/28 cups). Note that slow cookers work best when they are at least half — and preferably three-quarters — full; the operating manual that comes with your slow cooker will advise you on this.

Tricks of the trade

Most slow cookers have a number of temperature settings — typically 'low', 'medium' and 'high'. The 'low' setting cooks food at around 80°C (175°F), and 'high' at around 90°C (195°F). 'Medium' falls in between these two temperatures; the slow cooker cooks for around an hour at 'high', then automatically clicks to 'low' and continues cooking at that temperature.

As a general rule, cooking on 'low' doubles the cooking time from a 'high' setting, and you can tweak the cooking times of recipes to make them longer or shorter. Recipe cooking times vary from 3 to 12 hours.

At its simplest, to use your slow cooker all you need to do is prepare and chop your ingredients, add liquid (water, wine or stock) and turn the slow cooker on, leaving the contents to murmur away until cooked to lush tenderness. Time-strapped cooks can put ingredients in the slow cooker in the morning before leaving for work and return home at night to a dinner ready-to-go; alternatively, meals can be cooked overnight.

The cooking environment in a slow cooker is very moist, making it perfect for tough cuts of meat, such as beef blade, pork belly, or lamb or veal shanks. Such cuts contain a great

quantity of connective tissue that can only be broken down with long, slow cooking. When preparing meat, it is important that you trim fatty meat well, as the fat tends to settle on top of the cooking juices.

The slow cooker requires less liquid than normal stovetop or oven cookery, as there is no chance for the liquid to evaporate. In fact, many foods, including some meats, release moisture of their own during cooking — up to 250 ml (9 fl oz/1 cup) per average recipe — so bear this in mind when you think a recipe doesn't have enough liquid in it, or when adapting recipes for the slow cooker. (When adapting standard recipes for a slow cooker, reduce the liquid by 50 per cent.)

Resist the urge to lift the lid during cooking, particularly at the beginning, as the slow cooker takes a while to heat up, and always cook with the lid on unless the recipe instructs otherwise — perhaps when thickening a sauce. If you need to remove the lid to stir or to check the food is cooked, replace the lid quickly so the slow cooker doesn't lose too much heat.

It is difficult to overcook tougher meats, but it is still possible (the meat will turn raggedy and fall apart into thin shreds), so you still need to stick to the suggested cooking times for each recipe. Keep in mind,

however, that cooking times may vary, depending on the brand and size of slow cooker you are using.

While most recipes use the slow cooker as a true one-pot solution, where everything goes in together at the start, other recipes use the cooker as the primary mode of cooking but incorporate other steps along the way. Sometimes ingredients such as onions, spices and meats are cooked briefly on the stovetop first, either in the insert pan of the slow cooker or in a frying pan to develop flavours. Meat gains extra flavour when browned, as the outside surfaces caramelise over high temperatures (about 100°C/210°F), and this cannot be achieved in a slow cooker.

Hard vegetables such as root vegetables can take a very long time to cook, so cut them into smallish pieces and push them to the base

of the cooker or around the side, where the heat is slightly greater. Green vegetables can lose some nutrients if cooked for prolonged periods, so blanch them first (if required) and add them at the end of cooking to heat through. Seafood and dairy products should also be added to the slow cooker near the end of cooking.

Food safety

In the past there have been concerns about food safety issues with slow cookers, namely whether harmful bacteria that are present in foods, particularly in meats, are killed at such low temperatures. However, bacteria are killed off at around 68°C (155°F), so users of slow cookers need not be concerned about bacteria.

One rule here though is to never place meats that are still frozen, or partially frozen, in a slow cooker, as this scenario can cause food-poisoning bacteria to flourish; ALWAYS have meats thawed fully before cooking. And never use the ceramic insert after it has been frozen or refrigerated as the sudden change in temperature could cause it to crack.

Another caveat is that you cannot cook dried red kidney beans from their raw state in the slow cooker because the temperature is not high enough to destroy the natural toxins found in these beans. Dried red kidney beans,

and other dried beans, need to be boiled for 10 minutes first to destroy these toxins. Tinned beans, however, are safe for immediate use. To prepare dried beans, soak them in water for 8 hours or overnight. Discard the water, then rapidly boil the beans in fresh water for 10 minutes to destroy the toxins.

Make sure you read the manufacturer's instructions for the safe use of your slow cooker. This will ensure you get the best results from your slow cooker for many years to come.

Breakfast

Cinnamon porridge with winter fruit compote

Serves **8**   Preparation time **15 minutes**   Cooking time **4 hours 30 minutes**

Winter fruit compote
1 kg (2 lb 4 oz) dried fruit salad mix
600 ml (21 fl oz) orange juice
2 tablespoons brown sugar
2 orange zest strips
2 slices of lemon
1 cinnamon stick
1 star anise

Cinnamon porridge
300 g (10½ oz/3 cups) rolled
   (porridge) oats
500 ml (17 fl oz/2 cups) milk, plus
   extra, for serving
1½ cinnamon sticks
Brown sugar, for sprinkling (optional)

1 Place all the winter fruit compote ingredients in a 5 litre (175 fl oz/20 cup) slow cooker. Stir in 400 ml (14 fl oz) water. Cover and cook on high, stirring occasionally, for 2–2½ hours, or until the fruit is plump. Transfer to a container and refrigerate until required.

2 To make the cinnamon porridge, combine the oats, milk, cinnamon sticks and 1 litre (35 fl oz/4 cups) water in the slow cooker. Cover and cook on high for 2 hours, stirring occasionally, until the porridge is thick and creamy.

3 Stir some extra milk into the porridge, if desired. Serve hot, topped with the compote, and sprinkled with brown sugar, if desired.

⚙ *Tip: The fruit compote is great to make on the weekend – keep it in the fridge and it will last you all through the week.*

Apple and rhubarb breakfast crumble with hazelnuts

Serves **6**   Preparation time **30 minutes**   Cooking time **2 hours 20 minutes**

4 granny smith apples, peeled,
cored and cut into wedges
1 bunch rhubarb, about 750 g
(1 lb 10 oz), trimmed and roughly
chopped
100 g (3½ oz/½ cup, lightly packed)
brown sugar
2 tablespoons plain (all-purpose)
flour
2 teaspoons ground cinnamon
1 teaspoon mixed spice
Greek-style vanilla yoghurt,
to serve (optional)

Crumble topping
150 g (5½ oz/1 cup) plain
(all-purpose) flour
100 g (3½ oz/½ cup, lightly packed)
brown sugar
1 teaspoon ground cinnamon
½ teaspoon sea salt
150 g (5½ oz) chilled butter, diced
100 g (3½ oz/1 cup) rolled
(porridge) oats
30 g (1 oz/¼ cup) chopped hazelnuts

1 Place the apple, rhubarb, sugar, flour and spices, in a 5 litre (175 fl oz/20 cup) slow cooker. Stir to coat the fruit evenly, then set aside.

2 To make the crumble topping, place the flour, sugar, cinnamon and salt in a bowl and stir together well. Add the diced butter and rub in with your fingertips until combined. Stir in the oats and hazelnuts. Scatter the mixture over the fruit in the slow cooker.

3 Cover and cook on high for 2–2 hours 20 minutes, or until the fruit is tender when tested with a skewer. Serve warm, with a dollop of yoghurt, if desired.

Homemade breakfast beans

Serves **6**   Preparation time **15 minutes (+ 8 hours soaking)**   Cooking time **8 hours 15 minutes**

400 g (14 oz/2 cups) dried navy
    or haricot beans
1 tablespoon olive oil
1 brown onion, finely chopped
2 garlic cloves, chopped
2–3 long fresh red chillies, chopped
    (optional)
60 g (2¼ oz/¼ cup) tomato paste
    (concentrated purée)
375 ml (13 fl oz/1½ cups) tomato
    passata (puréed tomatoes)
400 g (14 oz) tin chopped tomatoes
2 tablespoons worcestershire sauce
45 g (1½ oz/¼ cup, lightly packed)
    brown sugar
1 tablespoon dijon mustard
950 g (2 lb 2 oz) ham hock (ask
    your butcher to cut it into 4 cm
    (1½ inch) chunks) (see Tip)
2 tablespoons chopped flat-leaf
    (Italian) parsley
Hot, buttered sourdough toast,
    to serve

1 Soak the beans for 8 hours or overnight in plenty of cold water. Drain the beans, discarding the water, then place in a large saucepan. Cover with fresh water and bring to the boil. Boil rapidly for 10 minutes. Rinse the beans and drain again.

2 Heat the olive oil in the insert pan of a 5 litre (175 fl oz/ 20 cup) slow cooker or a frying pan over medium–low heat. Add the onion, garlic and chilli, if using, and cook for 3–4 minutes, or until softened. Return the insert pan, if using, to the slow cooker or transfer the onion mixture to the slow cooker.

3 Add the tomato paste, passata, tomatoes, worcestershire sauce, sugar, mustard and beans. Stir well to combine, then add the ham hock pieces, submerging them into the liquid.

4 Cover and cook on low for 8 hours, or until the beans are tender and the ham falls off the bone.

5 Use tongs to remove the bones and skin from the ham. Stir to break up the ham pieces and distribute them through the beans. Season to taste with sea salt and freshly ground black pepper, then stir through the parsley. Serve on hot, buttered sourdough toast.

⚙ *Tip: Getting the butcher to cut the ham hock ensures that the pieces will be small enough to be submerged in the beans and liquid during cooking. This is a great dish to prepare during the day and then put on before going to bed, so you can wake up to the smell of baked beans!*

Chorizo, chilli and tomato baked eggs

Serves **6**   Preparation time **20 minutes**   Cooking time **2 hours 35 minutes**

2 tablespoons olive oil

3 chorizo sausages, coarsely chopped

2 red onions, cut into thin wedges

4 fresh red or green banana chillies (long, thin peppers), coarsely chopped

4 garlic cloves, thinly sliced

400 g (14 oz) tin chopped or cherry tomatoes

1 tablespoon red wine vinegar or sherry vinegar

6 eggs

2 tablespoons chopped flat-leaf (Italian) parsley

Hot, buttered toast, to serve

1 Heat the olive oil in the insert pan of a 5 litre (175 fl oz/ 20 cup) slow cooker or a frying pan over medium–high heat. Add the chorizo and cook for 2–3 minutes, or until it starts to colour. Add the onion and chilli and cook for 5–6 minutes, stirring occasionally, until starting to soften. Add the garlic, tomatoes and vinegar.

2 Return the insert pan, if using, to the slow cooker, or transfer the mixture to the slow cooker. Cover and cook on high for 1 hour, or until the vegetables are tender.

3 Remove the lid and cook for a further 45–60 minutes, or until the sauce has reduced slightly.

4 Make six indentations in the sauce using a large spoon, then carefully crack the eggs into the holes. Season with sea salt and freshly ground black pepper. Cover and cook for a further 20–25 minutes, or until the eggs are cooked. Sprinkle with the parsley and serve with hot, buttered toast.

Corned beef hash

Serves **8–10**   Preparation time **30 minutes**   Cooking time **4 hours 10 minutes**

4 whole cloves
1 brown onion
1 kg (2 lb 4 oz) piece of corned beef
18 small new potatoes, peeled
1 carrot, coarsely chopped
1 fresh bay leaf
1 teaspoon whole black peppercorns
½ cup finely chopped, flat-leaf
   (Italian) parsley
2 tablespoons dijon mustard
3 eggs, lightly beaten
2 tablespoons plain (all-purpose)
   flour
60 ml (2 fl oz/¼ cup) olive oil
Rocket (arugula) leaves, soft-poached
   eggs and cornichons, to serve

1 Press the cloves into the onion and place in a 7 litre (245 fl oz/28 cup) slow cooker. Add the corned beef, potatoes, carrot, bay leaf and peppercorns. Pour in enough water to just cover the beef. Cover and cook on high for 3–4 hours, or until the beef is very tender and the potatoes are cooked.

2 Transfer the beef and potatoes to a plate and set aside to cool. Discard the stock and vegetables. Coarsely shred the beef, then place in a large bowl with the parsley and mustard. Season to taste with sea salt and freshly ground black pepper and stir to combine.

3 Coarsely crush the potatoes using a fork, then add to the beef mixture with the eggs and flour. Stir to combine and set aside.

4 Heat half the olive oil in a large frying pan over high heat. Add half beef mixture and cook for 3–4minutes, or until golden, turning occasionally. Set aside and keep warm. Repeat with the remaining oil and beef mixture.

5 Transfer the hash to serving plates. Top with rocket, poached eggs and cornichons, season to taste and serve.

Chicken congee with corn and mushrooms

Serves **7–8**   Preparation time **25 minutes**   Cooking time **3 hours 20 minutes**

2 litres (70 fl oz/8 cups)
   good-quality chicken stock
5 cm (2 inch) piece fresh ginger,
   peeled and thinly sliced
4 spring onions (scallions), green
   tops chopped and the white
   stems thinly sliced diagonally
2 tablespoons Chinese rice
   wine or medium–dry sherry
2 skinless chicken breast fillets,
   about 300 g (10½ oz) each
200 g (7 oz/1 cup) long-grain
   white rice
1 tablespoon sesame oil
300 g (10½ oz) mixed mushrooms,
   thinly sliced
2 corn cobs, kernels removed
2 garlic cloves, finely chopped

1 Combine the stock, ginger, green spring onion tops and Chinese rice wine in a large saucepan over medium heat. Bring to a simmer and add the chicken. Reduce the heat to low and cook for 10–15 minutes, or until the chicken is cooked through. Strain the mixture through a sieve, reserving the stock. Set the chicken aside. When it is cool enough to handle, coarsely shred the meat and set aside. Cover and put in the refrigerator until needed.

2 Combine the rice and reserved chicken stock in a 5 litre (175 fl oz/20 cup) slow cooker, then season to taste with sea salt and freshly ground black pepper. Cover and cook on high for 2½–3 hours, or until the rice is very tender, stirring occasionally. Stir through the shredded chicken and season to taste.

3 Heat the sesame oil in a large frying pan over high heat. Add the mushrooms, corn kernels and garlic and cook for 4–5 minutes, or until the mixture is golden.

4 Serve the congee topped with the corn mixture and scattered with the white spring onion slices.

Soups

Herb tomato soup

Serves **6**   Preparation time **20 minutes**   Cooking time **6 hours**

2 kg (4 lb 8 oz) mixed tomatoes
  (see Tip)
½ cup flat-leaf (Italian) parsley
  leaves, chopped
½ cup whole basil leaves
2 tablespoons oregano leaves
5 garlic cloves, peeled and halved
1 long fresh red chilli, halved
  lengthways
1 red onion, cut into wedges
1 dried bay leaf
375 ml (13 fl oz/1½ cups) tomato
  juice
1½ tablespoons brown sugar
1 tablespoon red wine vinegar
  or sherry vinegar
1 teaspoon sea salt
½ teaspoon freshly ground black
  pepper
80 ml (2½ fl oz/⅓ cup) olive oil
4 thick sourdough bread slices

1 Using a sharp knife, cut a cross in the base of each
   tomato, except for any cherry tomatoes. Working
   in batches, blanch the tomatoes in boiling water for
   30 seconds, until their skins loosen. Drain the tomatoes
   and leave until cool enough to handle, then peel the skins
   away from the cross. Cut each tomato into quarters and
   remove the core.

2 Arrange the herbs in a 7 litre (245 fl oz/28 cup) slow
   cooker. Scatter eight of the garlic clove halves, the chilli
   and onion over the top, then top with the tomatoes and
   bay leaf. Mix together the tomato juice, sugar, vinegar,
   salt, pepper and 60 ml (2 fl oz/¼ cup) of the olive oil,
   then pour over the tomatoes.

3 Cover and cook on low for 6 hours, or until the onion
   is very soft. Remove the bay leaf.

4 Purée the mixture to a rough consistency, using a hand-
   held stick blender or food processor.

5 Brush the bread slices with the remaining olive oil and
   chargrill on both sides for 2 minutes. Rub with the
   remaining garlic clove halves and serve with the soup.

*Tip: Use whatever tomatoes are in season and are at their ripest.
If you use some cherry tomatoes there is no need to peel them.*

Leek and potato soup with herb salsa

Serves **5–6** Preparation time **25 minutes** Cooking time **3 hours 5 minutes**

2 tablespoons olive oil
3 leeks, white part only, chopped
3 garlic cloves, chopped
1.125 litres (39 fl oz/4½ cups)
    good-quality chicken or
    vegetable stock
1 kg (2 lb 4 oz) all-purpose potatoes,
    peeled and coarsely chopped
    into 2 cm (¾ inch) dice
250 ml (9 fl oz/1 cup) milk or cream

Herb salsa
⅔ cup chopped flat-leaf (Italian)
    parsley
⅓ cup chopped mint
1 tablespoon finely snipped chives
Finely grated zest of 1 lemon
80 ml (⅓ cup) extra virgin olive oil,
    plus extra, for drizzling

1 Heat the olive oil in the insert pan of a 5 litre (175 fl oz/20 cup) slow cooker or a large frying pan over low heat. Add the leek and garlic and cook for 5–6 minutes, or until softened.

2 Return the insert pan, if using, to the slow cooker, or transfer the leek mixture to the slow cooker. Add the stock and potatoes. Cover and cook on high for 3 hours, or until the potato is very tender.

3 Near serving time, combine the herb salsa ingredients in a bowl and mix to combine well.

4 Add the milk to the slow cooker. Purée the mixture until smooth, using a hand-held stick blender or food processor. Season to taste with sea salt and freshly ground black pepper.

5 Ladle into bowls and top with the herb salsa. Drizzle with extra virgin olive oil and serve sprinkled with extra pepper.

Chickpea and sweet potato soup

Serves **7–8**   Preparation time **20 minutes (+ 8 hours soaking)**   Cooking time **5 hours 20 minutes**

200 g (7 oz/1 cup) dried chickpeas
2½ tablespoons olive oil
20 g (¾ oz) butter, chopped
3 leeks, white part only, sliced
3 garlic cloves, chopped
1 teaspoon ground cumin
1 teaspoon ground coriander
2 litres (70 fl oz/8 cups)
    good-quality chicken stock
1 teaspoon sea salt
850 g (1 lb 14 oz) sweet potato,
    peeled and cut into 2 cm
    (¾ inch) chunks
100 g (3½ oz/2 cups) baby English
    spinach leaves, trimmed

1 Soak the chickpeas for 8 hours or overnight in plenty of cold water. Drain the chickpeas, discarding the water, then place in a large saucepan. Cover with fresh water and bring to the boil. Boil rapidly for 10 minutes. Rinse the chickpeas and drain again.

2 Heat the olive oil and butter in the insert pan of a 7 litre (245 fl oz/28 cup) slow cooker or a frying pan over medium–low heat. Add the leek and cook for 5 minutes, or until softened. Add the garlic and spices and cook, stirring, for 1–2 minutes.

3 Return the insert pan, if using, to the slow cooker, or transfer the leek mixture to the slow cooker. Stir in the stock, salt, chickpeas, sweet potato and 500 ml (17 fl oz/2 cups) water.

4 Cover and cook on low for 5 hours, or until the chickpeas are tender. Season well with freshly ground black pepper.

5 Add the spinach leaves and stir until they wilt. Ladle into bowls and serve.

Spiced carrot and cumin soup

Serves **4**   Preparation time **20 minutes**   Cooking time **6 hours 10 minutes**

1 tablespoon vegetable oil
1 brown onion, chopped
2 garlic cloves, chopped
1 kg (2 lb 4 oz) carrots, halved
    lengthways and cut into 1 cm
    (½ inch) pieces
1 potato, peeled and cut into
    2 cm (¾ inch) chunks
3 teaspoons ground cumin
1 teaspoon ground coriander
1 teaspoon sea salt
375 ml (13 fl oz/1½ cups)
    good-quality chicken stock
2 teaspoons honey
5 cm (2 inch) piece of fresh ginger,
    peeled
⅓ cup shredded mint

1 Heat the oil in the insert pan of a 5 litre (175 fl oz/ 20 cup) slow cooker or a frying pan over medium heat. Add the onion, garlic, carrot and potato and cook for 10 minutes, or until the vegetables have softened, stirring occasionally. Add the spices and salt and cook for 1 minute.

2 Return the insert pan, if using, to the slow cooker, or transfer the vegetable mixture to the slow cooker. Add the stock, honey and 125 ml (4 fl oz/½ cup) water. Season well with freshly ground black pepper and stir to combine.

3 Cover and cook on low for 6 hours, or until the carrot is very tender.

4 Purée the mixture until smooth, using a hand-held stick blender or food processor. Finely grate the ginger, then squeeze it over a small bowl to extract the juice. Stir the ginger juice through the soup, then season to taste.

5 Ladle into bowls and serve sprinkled with the mint.

Split pea soup

Serves **5–6**   Preparation time **20 minutes**   Cooking time **6 hours 10 minutes**

1 tablespoon olive oil
400 g (14 oz) bacon slices, trimmed
    and cut into 1 cm (½ inch) strips
1 large brown onion, finely diced
2 carrots, finely diced
2 celery stalks, finely diced
2 garlic cloves, chopped
2 litres (70 fl oz/8 cups)
    good-quality chicken stock
500 g (1 lb 2 oz/2¼ cups) dried
    green split peas, rinsed
Sour cream and shredded mint,
    to serve

1 Heat the olive oil in the insert pan of a 5 litre (175 fl oz/ 20 cup) slow cooker or a large frying pan over medium– high heat. Add the bacon and cook, stirring occasionally, for 3 minutes, or until golden. Reduce the heat to medium–low. Add the onion, carrot, celery and garlic and cook, stirring, for 3 minutes, or until softened.

2 Return the insert pan, if using, to the slow cooker, or transfer the bacon mixture to the slow cooker. Add the stock and split peas and stir to combine. Cover and cook on low for 6 hours or until the split peas are very tender.

3 Ladle half the soup into a blender and blend until smooth. Return the blended soup to the slow cooker and stir to combine. Season to taste with sea salt and freshly ground black pepper.

4 Ladle into bowls and serve topped with a dollop of sour cream and a sprinkling of mint.

⚙ Tip: If you'd like a smoother finish, you can blend the entire quantity of soup in step 3, rather than just a portion.

Thai-style pumpkin soup

Serves **4–6**   Preparation time **25 minutes**   Cooking time **3 hours**

2 butternut pumpkins (squash),
   about 3 kg (6 lb 12 oz) peeled,
   seeded and chopped
1 brown onion, finely chopped
2 makrut (kaffir lime) leaves, torn
1 lemongrass stem, bruised
1 teaspoon finely grated fresh ginger
1 tablespoon fish sauce
270 ml (9½ fl oz) tin coconut cream
1 tablespoon purchased mild red
   curry paste
875 ml (30 fl oz/3½ cups)
   good-quality chicken or
   vegetable stock
2 teaspoons lime juice
2 tablespoons Thai sweet chilli
   sauce
Coriander (cilantro) leaves, to garnish
1 long fresh red chilli, thinly sliced

1 Put the pumpkin and onion in a 5.5 litre (192 fl oz/ 22 cup) slow cooker with the lime leaves, lemongrass, ginger and fish sauce. Reserve 2 tablespoons of the coconut cream, then mix the curry paste with the remaining coconut cream until smooth. Pour over the pumpkin mixture, then pour in the stock and gently mix together.

2 Cover and cook on high for 3 hours, or until the pumpkin is tender. Set aside to cool slightly. Remove the lime leaves and lemongrass stem.

3 Purée the mixture until smooth, using a hand-held stick blender or food processor. Stir in the lime juice and sweet chilli sauce.

4 Ladle into bowls and drizzle with the reserved coconut cream. Serve garnished with the coriander and chilli.

⌘ *Tip: This soup can be frozen. Allow the soup to cool, then transfer to an airtight container. Label and date the container and freeze for up to 6 months.*

Tunisian chickpea and silverbeet soup

Serves **4**   Preparation time **15 minutes**   Cooking time **3 hours 40 minutes**

1 tablespoon olive oil
1 brown onion, thinly sliced
1 teaspoon ground white pepper
1 teaspoon freshly grated nutmeg
½ teaspoon ground cumin
¼ teaspoon ground cloves
¼ teaspoon ground cinnamon
2 x 400 g (14 oz) tins chickpeas, drained and rinsed
1 bunch silverbeet (Swiss chard), about 900 g (2 lb)
625 ml (21½ fl oz/2½ cups) good-quality chicken or vegetable stock
Greek-style yoghurt, crusty bread and lemon wedges, to serve

1 Heat the olive oil in the insert pan of a 5.5 litre (192 fl oz/ 22 cup) slow cooker or a frying pan over medium–high heat. Add the onion and cook for 3 minutes, or until it starts to brown, stirring occasionally. Reduce the heat to low and cook for another 5 minutes, or until soft.

2 Add the pepper, nutmeg, cumin, cloves and cinnamon and cook, stirring, for another 30 seconds. Add the chickpeas and stir until well coated. Return the insert pan, if using, to the slow cooker, or transfer the chickpea mixture to the slow cooker.

3 Wash the silverbeet leaves well and shake dry. Remove the stem below the leaf and discard. Slice across the leaves, cutting the silverbeet into 2 cm (¾ inch) ribbons.

4 Add the silverbeet to the slow cooker and pour in the stock. Gently mix together. Cover and cook on low for 2½–3½ hours, or until the silverbeet is just tender.

5 Using a hand-held stick blender, process the mixture in a few short bursts, just to blend a portion of the soup — most of the chickpeas should still be whole. Season to taste with sea salt and freshly ground black pepper.

6 Ladle into bowls and top with a small dollop of yoghurt. Serve with crusty bread and lemon wedges.

Tip: If you're in a hurry, cook the soup on high for 1½–2 hours. Once the soup has been cooked, the flavours will continue to improve if the soup is left to rest for 30 minutes or more.

Ribollita

Serves **7–8**   Preparation time **25 minutes (+ 8 hours soaking)**   Cooking time **6 hours 20 minutes**

150 g (5½ oz/¾ cup) dried cannellini
    beans
2 tablespoons olive oil
1 large brown onion, chopped
2 carrots, cut into 1 cm (½ inch) dice
3 celery stalks, cut into 1 cm (½ inch)
    dice
3 garlic cloves, chopped
400 g (14 oz) tin chopped tomatoes
1 tablespoon thyme leaves
650 g (1 lb 7 oz) large waxy
    potatoes, peeled and cut into
    1.5 cm (⅝ inch) dice
175 g (6 oz) cavolo nero, trimmed
    and coarsely shredded (see Tip)
1 loaf of rustic bread, such as
    ciabatta or sourdough, thickly
    sliced
Finely grated parmesan, to serve
Extra virgin olive oil, for drizzling

1 Soak the beans for 8 hours or overnight in plenty of cold water. Drain the beans, discarding the water, then place in a large saucepan. Cover with fresh water and bring to the boil. Boil rapidly for 10 minutes. Rinse the beans and drain again.

2 Heat the olive oil in the insert pan of a 5 litre (175 fl oz/ 20 cup) slow cooker or a large frying pan over low heat. Add the onion, carrot and celery and cook for 8 minutes, or until softened, stirring occasionally. Add the garlic and cook for 2 minutes, stirring frequently.

3 Return the insert pan, if using, to the slow cooker, or transfer the vegetable mixture to the slow cooker. Add the beans, tomatoes, thyme, potato and 2 litres (70 fl oz/ 8 cups) water. Cover and cook on low for 5 hours, or until the beans and potato are nearly tender.

4 Stir the cavolo nero through the soup. Cover, increase the heat to high and cook for a further 1 hour. Season to taste with sea salt and freshly ground black pepper.

5 Tear the bread slices into chunks and place in bowls. Ladle the soup over the top. Sprinkle with parmesan and some more black pepper, drizzle with extra virgin olive oil and serve.

Tip: Instead of cavolo nero (also called Tuscan black cabbage or Tuscan kale), you can use silverbeet (Swiss chard) if desired.

Curried yellow split pea and coconut soup

Serves **6–8**   Preparation time **20 minutes**   Cooking time **3 hours 40 minutes**

2 tablespoons olive oil
2 brown onions, finely diced
3 garlic cloves, thinly sliced
1 leek, white part only, thinly sliced
1 carrot, diced
3 tablespoons purchased korma
    curry powder
660 g (1 lb 7 oz/3 cups) yellow
    split peas, rinsed
2 litres (70 fl oz/8 cups)
    good-quality vegetable or
    chicken stock
300 ml (10½ fl oz) coconut milk
45 g (1½ oz/1 cup) baby English
    spinach leaves
Juice of 2 limes, or to taste
1 long fresh red chilli, thinly sliced
    diagonally, Greek-style yoghurt
    and coriander (cilantro) leaves,
    to serve

1 Heat the olive oil in the insert pan of a 5 litre (175 fl oz/ 20 cup) slow cooker or a frying pan over medium heat. Add the onion, garlic, leek and carrot and sauté for 5–7 minutes, or until tender. Add the curry powder and stir for 30 seconds, or until aromatic.

2 Return the insert pan, if using, to the slow cooker, or transfer the vegetable mixture to the slow cooker. Add the split peas and stock. Cover and cook on high for 3½ hours, or until the split peas are very tender.

3 Stir the coconut milk through. Purée the mixture to a rough consistency, using a hand-held stick blender or food processor, leaving some of the soup un-puréed if desired. (You may need to add a little extra coconut milk to reach your desired consistency.)

4 Stir in the spinach and lime juice, to taste. Season with sea salt and freshly ground black pepper.

5 Ladle into bowls and serve topped with chilli, yoghurt and coriander.

Minestrone with pesto crostini

Serves **8**   Preparation time **20 minutes (+ 8 hours soaking)**   Cooking time **4 hours 20 minutes**

390 g (13¾ oz/2 cups) dried
　cannellini beans
60 ml (2 fl oz/¼ cup) olive oil
200 g (7 oz) mild flat pancetta, diced
3 zucchini (courgettes), diced
2 celery stalks, diced
2 carrots, diced
2 brown onions, diced
4 garlic cloves, crushed
1 piece of parmesan rind
400 g (14 oz) tin chopped
　or cherry tomatoes
2 litres (70 fl oz/8 cups) good-quality
　chicken or vegetable stock
3 basil stalks, plus some extra basil
　leaves, to garnish
260 g (10 oz/2 cups) small dry pasta
　shapes

Pesto crostini
1 baguette, cut diagonally into 2 cm
　(¾ inch) slices
1½ cups, firmly packed basil leaves
40 g (1½ oz/¼ cup) pine nuts,
　lightly toasted
100 g (3½ oz/¾ cup) finely grated
　parmesan
60 ml (2 fl oz/¼ cup) olive oil

1 Soak the beans for 8 hours or overnight in plenty of cold water. Drain the beans, discarding the water, then place in a large saucepan. Cover with fresh water and bring to the boil. Boil rapidly for 10 minutes. Rinse the beans and drain again.

2 Heat the olive oil in the insert pan of a 7 litre (245 fl oz/ 28 cup) slow cooker or a frying pan over medium heat. Add the pancetta and cook for 3–4 minutes, stirring occasionally, until the fat renders. Add the zucchini, celery, carrot, onion and garlic and cook for 3–4 minutes, or until the vegetables start to soften, stirring occasionally.

3 Return the insert pan, if using, to the slow cooker, or transfer the vegetable mixture to the slow cooker. Add the beans, parmesan rind, tomatoes, stock and basil stalks, season to taste with sea salt and freshly ground black pepper. Cover and cook on high for 4 hours, or until the beans are very tender.

4 Meanwhile, cook the pasta in a saucepan of boiling salted water for 7–8 minutes, or until al dente. Drain, then stir it through the minestrone. Season to taste and keep warm.

5 To make the pesto crostini, preheat the grill (broiler) to high. Place the bread slices on a baking tray and grill for 1–2 minutes on each side, or until golden. Meanwhile, process the basil, pine nuts, parmesan and oil in a food processor until combined. Season to taste, then spread over the toasted bread slices.

6 Ladle the soup into bowls and garnish with basil leaves. Serve with the warm crostini.

French onion soup

Serves **4**   Preparation time **20 minutes**   Cooking time **6 hours**

20 g (¾ oz) butter
1 tablespoon olive oil
1 kg (2 lb 4 oz) brown onions,
   thinly sliced
250 ml (9 fl oz/1 cup) dry white wine
2 tablespoons brandy (optional)
750 ml (26 fl oz/3 cups) good-
   quality beef stock
4 thyme sprigs
2 tablespoons finely chopped
   flat-leaf (Italian) parsley
Crusty bread, to serve

1 Put the butter, olive oil and onion in a 4.5 litre (157 fl oz/
   18 cup) slow cooker. Cover and cook on low for 4 hours,
   stirring occasionally.

2 Add the wine, brandy, if using, stock, thyme and
   250 ml (9 fl oz/1 cup) water. Cover and cook on high
   for a further 2 hours.

3 Season to taste with sea salt and freshly ground black
   pepper. Remove the thyme sprigs. Ladle into bowls,
   sprinkle with the parsley and serve with crusty bread.

Cream of mushroom soup

Serves **4**   Preparation time **20 minutes (+ 20 minutes soaking)**   Cooking time **2 hours 5 minutes**

10 g (¼ oz) dried porcini
   mushrooms
1 leek, white part only, thinly sliced
100 g (3½ oz) pancetta or bacon,
   chopped
200 g (7 oz) Swiss brown
   mushrooms, coarsely chopped
300 g (10½ oz) large mushroom
   flats, coarsely chopped
125 ml (4 fl oz/½ cup) Madeira
   (see Tip)
1 litre (35 fl oz/4 cups) good-quality
   chicken or vegetable stock
2 teaspoons chopped marjoram,
   plus extra leaves, to garnish
85 g (3 oz/⅓ cup) light sour cream
   or crème fraîche
Crusty bread, to serve

1 Soak the porcini in 250 ml (9 fl oz/1 cup) boiling water
for 20 minutes. Drain, reserving the soaking water.

2 Put the porcini and their soaking water in a 4.5 litre
(157 fl oz/18 cup) slow cooker. Add the leek, pancetta,
Swiss brown and mushroom flats, Madeira, stock and
half the chopped marjoram. Cover and cook on high
for 2 hours.

3 Purée the mixture until smooth, using a hand-held
stick blender or food processor.

4 Stir the sour cream through and cook for a further
5 minutes. Stir in the remaining chopped marjoram.

5 Ladle into bowls, garnish with marjoram leaves and
serve with crusty bread.

*Tip: Madeira is a fortified wine made in Portugal. Malmsey
is the richest and fruitiest of the Madeiras and can also be
enjoyed as an after-dinner drink. If unavailable, use sherry.*

Cauliflower and almond soup

Serves **4**   Preparation time **20 minutes**   Cooking time **3 hours**

1 large leek, white part only,
   chopped
2 garlic cloves, crushed
1 kg (2 lb 4 oz) cauliflower, cut
   into small florets
2 all-purpose potatoes, such as
   desiree, about 375 g (13 oz),
   peeled and diced
1.5 litres (52 fl oz/6 cups)
   good-quality chicken stock
80 g (2¾ oz/½ cup) blanched
   almonds, chopped
⅓ cup snipped chives
Pouring cream, to serve

1 Put the leek, garlic, cauliflower, potato and stock in a 4.5 litre (157 fl oz/18 cup) slow cooker. Cover and cook on high for 3 hours, or until the potato and cauliflower are tender.

2 Add the almonds to the slow cooker. Purée the mixture until smooth, using a hand-held stick blender or food processor. Stir in half the chives and season to taste with sea salt and freshly ground black pepper.

3 Ladle into bowls, drizzle with cream and serve garnished with the remaining chives.

Tip: This soup will thicken on standing. Stir in some extra stock to thin the soup if desired.

Butternut pumpkin soup

Serves **4**   Preparation time **15 minutes**   Cooking time **3 hours**

1.25 kg (2 lb 12 oz) butternut
   pumpkin (squash), peeled,
   seeded and chopped into
   even-sized chunks
1 all-purpose potato, such as
   desiree, peeled and chopped
1 brown onion, chopped
1 carrot, chopped
2 teaspoons ground cumin
1 teaspoon freshly grated nutmeg
750 ml (26 fl oz/3 cups) good-quality
   chicken or vegetable stock
60 ml (2 fl oz/¼ cup) pouring
   cream
1 tablespoon chopped flat-leaf
   (Italian) parsley

1 Put the pumpkin, potato, onion and carrot in a 4.5 litre
   (157 fl oz/18 cup) slow cooker. Sprinkle the cumin and
   nutmeg over and season with sea salt and freshly ground
   black pepper. Stir to coat the vegetables in the spices.

2 Pour in the stock. Cover and cook on high for 3 hours,
   or until the pumpkin is tender.

3 Purée the mixture until smooth, using a hand-held stick
   blender or food processor.

4 Ladle into bowls, drizzle with the cream and serve
   sprinkled with the parsley.

Tomato, spinach and risoni soup

Serves **4**   Preparation time **15 minutes (+ 10 minutes soaking)**   Cooking time **3 hours 30 minutes**

1 leek, white part only, thinly sliced
1 garlic clove, crushed
½ teaspoon ground cumin
500 ml (17 fl oz/2 cups) tomato
   passata (puréed tomatoes)
750 ml (26 fl oz/3 cups)
   good-quality chicken or
   vegetable stock
200 g (7 oz/1 cup) risoni (see Tip)
200 g (7 oz) smoked ham, chopped
   (optional)
500 g (1 lb 2 oz) English spinach,
   trimmed, leaves sliced
1½ tablespoons lemon juice
Crusty bread, to serve

1 Put the leek, garlic, cumin, passata, stock and 500 ml (17 fl oz/2 cups) water in a 4.5 litre (157 fl oz/18 cup) slow cooker. Cover and cook on low for 3 hours.

2 Place the risoni in a heatproof bowl and cover with boiling water. Leave to soak for 10 minutes, then drain. Add the risoni to the slow cooker along with the ham, if using. Cover and cook for a further 30 minutes, or until the risoni is al dente.

3 Remove the lid and stir the spinach and lemon juice through the soup. Cook, stirring, until the spinach has wilted. Season to taste with sea salt and freshly ground black pepper.

4 Ladle into bowls and serve with crusty bread.

⚙ *Tip: Risoni looks like rice but is actually a type of pasta, often used in soups and stews. If unavailable, use any type of small soup pasta.*

Pasta and bean soup

Serves 6   Preparation time **30 minutes**   Cooking time **6 hours 30 minutes**

1 brown onion, finely chopped
1 small celery stalk, finely chopped
1 carrot, finely chopped
1 smoked ham hock, about 500 g
   (1 lb 2 oz), skin scored
400 g (14 oz) tin chopped tomatoes
750 ml (26 fl oz/3 cups) good-quality
   chicken stock
1 dried bay leaf
1 large rosemary sprig
400 g (14 oz) tin red kidney beans,
   drained and rinsed
155 g (5½ oz/1 cup) macaroni
2 tablespoons chopped flat-leaf
   (Italian) parsley

1 Put the onion, celery and carrot in a 4.5 litre (157 fl oz/ 18 cup) slow cooker. Add the ham hock, tomatoes, stock, bay leaf, rosemary and 1.5 litres (52 fl oz/6 cups) water. Cover and cook on low for 6 hours.

2 Remove the ham hock and set aside to cool slightly. Add the beans and macaroni to the slow cooker and increase the heat to high. Cover and cook for a further 30 minutes, or until the pasta is al dente.

3 When the ham hock is cool enough to handle, remove the meat from the bone, discarding the fat and bone. Cut the meat into small pieces and return to the slow cooker.

4 Stir the parsley through. Season to taste with sea salt and freshly ground black pepper and serve.

Tip: This Italian-style soup is very thick. If you prefer, you can stir in a little more stock at the end of the cooking time to thin it.

Cream of parsnip soup

Serves **4–6**   Preparation time **20 minutes**   Cooking time **4 hours 20 minutes**

1 kg (2 lb 4 oz) parsnips, peeled
   and chopped
200 g (7 oz) all-purpose potatoes,
   such as sebago, peeled and
   chopped
1 granny smith apple, peeled, cored
   and chopped
1 brown onion, finely chopped
1 garlic clove, chopped
750 ml (26 fl oz/3 cups) good-quality
   chicken stock
A pinch of saffron threads
250 ml (9 fl oz/1 cup) pouring cream
Snipped chives, to serve

1 Place the parsnip and potato in a 5.5 litre (192 fl oz/
   22 cup) slow cooker with the apple, onion and garlic.
   Stir in the stock and saffron threads. Cover and cook
   on high for 4 hours.

2 Purée the mixture until smooth, using a hand-held stick
   blender or food processor. Season to taste with sea salt,
   then stir in the cream. Cover and cook for a further
   20 minutes.

3 Ladle into bowls and serve sprinkled with chives and
   plenty of freshly ground black pepper.

⚙ *Tips: For a vegetarian soup, replace the chicken stock with vegetable
stock. For a sensational dinner party starter, serve this soup topped
with pan-fried scallops.*

Cauliflower and red lentil soup

Serves **6–8**   Preparation time **15 minutes**   Cooking time **3 hours**

1 kg (2 lb 4 oz) cauliflower
1 large brown onion
2 celery stalks
100 g (3½ oz/½ cup) red lentils
1½ tablespoons purchased mild
   curry paste
400 ml (14 fl oz) tin coconut milk
1 litre (35 fl oz/4 cups) good-quality
   vegetable stock
2 tablespoons finely shredded mint
Lime wedges, to serve

1 Cut the cauliflower, onion and celery into 2 cm (¾ inch) chunks. Place in a 5.5 litre (192 fl oz/22 cup) slow cooker with the lentils.

2 In a small bowl, mix the curry paste with the coconut milk until smooth. Pour into the slow cooker, then pour in the stock. Cover and cook on high for 3 hours, or until the vegetables are tender.

3 Remove and reserve a large ladleful of the cooked cauliflower. Purée the remaining mixture until smooth, using a hand-held stick blender or food processor. Season to taste with sea salt and freshly ground black pepper.

4 Ladle into bowls, top with the reserved cauliflower florets and mint and serve with lime wedges.

⚙ *Tips: This soup is delicious served with warmed naan bread, with some chopped cooked chicken stirred through. You could also serve it with a dollop of minted yoghurt, made by mixing 2 tablespoons finely chopped mint through 200 g (7 oz) yoghurt.*

White bean and rocket soup with basil pesto

Serves **6**   Preparation time **15 minutes**   Cooking time **8 hours 20 minutes**

1 large brown onion, chopped
2 garlic cloves, crushed
2 x 400 g (14 oz) tins cannellini
  beans, drained and rinsed
300 g (10½ oz/2 bunches) rocket
  (arugula), trimmed and chopped
2 litres (70 fl oz/8 cups) good-
  quality chicken stock
125 ml (4 fl oz/½ cup) pouring
  cream
Crusty bread, to serve

Basil pesto
2 tablespoons pine nuts, toasted
1 garlic clove, crushed
125 g (4½ oz/1 bunch) basil, leaves
  picked
35 g (1¼ oz/⅓ cup) grated
  parmesan
60 ml (2 fl oz/¼ cup) olive oil

1 Place the onion, garlic, beans, rocket and stock in
   a 5.5 litre (192 fl oz/22 cup) slow cooker. Gently mix
   until well combined. Cover and cook on low for 8 hours.

2 Purée the mixture until smooth, using a hand-held
   stick blender or food processor. Stir the cream through.
   Cover and cook for a further 20 minutes, or until
   warmed through.

3 Meanwhile, make the basil pesto. Place the pine nuts,
   garlic and basil in a food processor and blend until
   smooth and combined. Add the parmesan and process
   for a further 1 minute. With the motor running, add the
   olive oil in a slow steady stream until the pesto is smooth
   and of a sauce consistency. Season to taste with sea salt
   and freshly ground black pepper.

4 Ladle the soup into bowls and sprinkle generously with
   freshly ground black pepper. Add a generous dollop of
   the basil pesto and serve with crusty bread.

⚙ *Tips: This soup can be frozen. Allow the soup to cool, then transfer
to an airtight container. Label and date the container and freeze for
up to 6 months. When making the pesto, toasting the pine nuts helps
bring out their flavour. Gently cook them in a frying pan over medium-
low heat, without any oil, for 3–4 minutes, or until golden brown,
keeping a close eye on them and shaking the pan frequently so they
don't burn.*

Sweet corn soup with chicken dumplings

Serves **6 as a starter, 4 as a main**   Preparation time **30 minutes (+ 10 minutes soaking)**
Cooking time **3 hours 20 minutes**

1 tablespoon peanut oil
1 brown onion, finely chopped
1 garlic clove, finely chopped
1½ tablespoons finely shredded
    fresh ginger
4 coriander (cilantro) roots, well
    rinsed and finely chopped
1 teaspoon sea salt
80 ml (2½ fl oz/⅓ cup) Chinese rice
    wine or dry sherry
4 sweet corn cobs, kernels removed
400 g (14 oz) tin creamed corn
1 litre (35 fl oz/4 cups) good-quality
    chicken stock
2–3 teaspoons light soy sauce
A pinch of ground white pepper
2 eggs, lightly beaten

Dumplings
3 dried shiitake mushrooms
400 g (14 oz) minced (ground) chicken
1 tablespoon finely chopped fresh
    ginger
1 garlic clove, finely chopped
2 spring onions (scallions), white
    stems finely chopped and the
    green tops sliced diagonally
    and reserved
½ teaspoon sesame oil
½ teaspoon sea salt
2 teaspoons soy sauce
1 tablespoon coriander (cilantro)
    leaves, finely chopped
A pinch of ground white pepper

1 To make the dumplings, soak the mushrooms in hot
   water for 10 minutes. Drain, reserving 2 tablespoons
   of the water. Squeeze out the excess water, then finely
   chop the mushrooms. Place in a bowl with the remaining
   dumpling ingredients and mix well. Using wet hands, roll
   half-tablespoons of the mixture into small balls and place
   on a tray lined with baking paper. Chill in the refrigerator
   while preparing the soup ingredients.

2 Heat the peanut oil in the insert pan of a 5 litre
   (175 fl oz/20 cup) slow cooker or a frying pan over
   medium–high heat. Fry the dumplings for 4–5 minutes,
   or until golden on all sides. Remove with a slotted spoon.

3 Reduce the heat to medium. Add the onion, garlic, ginger,
   coriander root and salt and sauté for 7–8 minutes, without
   colouring. Increase the heat to medium–high, add the
   Chinese rice wine and cook for 1–2 minutes, or until the
   liquid has reduced by two-thirds.

4 Return the insert pan, if using, to the slow cooker,
   or transfer the vegetable mixture to the slow cooker.
   Add the corn kernels, creamed corn, stock, soy sauce
   and reserved mushroom liquid. Season with white pepper
   and stir to combine. Add the dumplings, then cover and
   cook on high for 3 hours, or until the dumplings are
   cooked through.

5 Remove the lid and push the dumplings to one side.
   Quickly pour in the egg, in a slow stream, while stirring
   with a fork, until the egg creates small ribbons. Add half
   the reserved spring onion and season to taste. Serve
   garnished with the remaining reserved spring onion.

Thai chicken and galangal soup

Serves **4**   Preparation time **20 minutes**   Cooking time **2 hours**

2 x 5 cm (¾ x 2 inch) piece fresh galangal, thinly sliced
500 ml (17 fl oz/2 cups) coconut milk
250 ml (9 fl oz/1 cup) good-quality chicken stock
1 tablespoon finely chopped coriander (cilantro) root, well rinsed
1–2 teaspoons finely chopped fresh red chilli, or to taste
4 makrut (kaffir lime) leaves, torn
500 g (1 lb 2 oz) skinless chicken breast fillets
2 tablespoons fish sauce
1½ tablespoons lime juice
3 teaspoons grated palm sugar (jaggery) or brown sugar
Coriander (cilantro) leaves, to garnish

1 Put the galangal, coconut milk and stock in a 4.5 litre (157 fl oz/18 cup) slow cooker with the coriander root, chilli and half the lime leaves. Cover and cook on low for 1 hour 45 minutes.

2 Trim the chicken of any fat. Cut the chicken into thin strips and add to the slow cooker with the fish sauce, lime juice and sugar. Stir to combine, then cover and cook for 5–10 minutes, or until the chicken is cooked through. Stir in the remaining lime leaves.

3 Ladle into bowls, garnish with coriander leaves and serve.

Chicken laksa

Serves **4**   Preparation time **30 minutes (+ 10 minutes soaking)**   Cooking time **2 hours 30 minutes**

3 tablespoons purchased laksa paste
500 ml (17 fl oz/2 cups) coconut milk
750 ml (26 fl oz/3 cups) good-quality
    chicken stock
200 g (7 oz) rice vermicelli noodles
8 fried tofu puffs, halved diagonally
100 g (3½ oz) bean sprouts, tails
    trimmed
2 tablespoons shredded Vietnamese
    mint
3 tablespoons coriander (cilantro)
    leaves
Lime wedges, to serve

Chicken dumplings
500 g (1 lb 2 oz) minced (ground)
    chicken
1 small fresh red chilli, finely
    chopped
2 garlic cloves, finely chopped
½ small red onion, finely chopped
1 lemongrass stem, white part only,
    finely chopped
2 tablespoons chopped coriander
    (cilantro) leaves

1 To make the chicken dumplings, put the chicken, chilli, garlic, onion, lemongrass and coriander in a food processor and blend until just combined. Using wet hands, roll tablespoons of the mixture into balls.

2 Put the chicken dumplings in a 4.5 litre (157 fl oz/ 18 cup) slow cooker. Mix the laksa paste with some of the coconut milk until smooth, then add to the slow cooker with the remaining coconut milk and stock. Cover and cook on high for 2½ hours.

3 Near serving time, put the noodles in a heatproof bowl, cover with boiling water and leave to soak for 10 minutes, or until softened. Drain well.

4 Divide the noodles, tofu puffs and bean sprouts among bowls. Ladle the soup over the top, dividing the chicken dumplings evenly. Garnish with the mint and coriander and serve with lime wedges.

Curried chicken and peanut soup

Serves 4   Preparation time **25 minutes (+ 10 minutes soaking)**   Cooking time **8 hours 20 minutes**

2 tablespoons fish sauce
2 garlic cloves, crushed
1 tablespoon lime juice
1 tablespoon brown sugar
2 small fresh red chillies, seeded
   if desired, finely chopped
1.5 kg (3 lb 5 oz) whole chicken,
   rinsed
270 ml (9½ fl oz) tin coconut cream
250 g (9 oz) rice vermicelli noodles
Chopped salted peanuts, and
   coriander (cilantro) sprigs,
   to garnish

Spice paste
3 tablespoons chopped coriander
   (cilantro) leaves
½ small onion, chopped
3 spring onions (scallions), chopped
1 teaspoon grated fresh galangal
1 teaspoon ground turmeric
1 teaspoon ground coriander
2 tablespoons salted peanuts

1 Combine the fish sauce, garlic, lime juice, sugar and chilli in a 5.5 litre (192 fl oz/22 cup) slow cooker. Pour in 750 ml (26 fl oz/3 cups) water and stir until the sugar has dissolved. Add the chicken, placing it breast side down. Cover and cook on low for 8 hours.

2 When the chicken is nearly done, put the spice paste ingredients in a food processor or blender with 2 tablespoons water. Process to a smooth paste.

3 Remove the chicken to a board. Pour the cooking stock from the slow cooker through a sieve into the food processor, then blend with the spice paste until smooth. Return the stock to the slow cooker.

4 Discard the skin and bones of the chicken, then shred the meat. Stir the chicken meat through the soup with the coconut cream. Cover and cook for a further 20 minutes, or until the soup is heated through.

5 Meanwhile, place the noodles in a large heatproof bowl. Cover with boiling water and leave to soak for 10 minutes, or until softened.

6 Drain the noodles and divide among bowls. Ladle the soup over the top. Serve garnished with chopped peanuts and coriander sprigs.

Simple chicken soup

Serves **6**   Preparation time **20 minutes**   Cooking time **8 hours 5 minutes**

1.6 kg (3 lb 8 oz) whole chicken,
   rinsed
1 leek, white part only, sliced
2 celery stalks, sliced
1 large carrot, chopped
1 parsnip, chopped
1 tablespoon chopped dill

1 Put the chicken in a 4.5 litre (157 fl oz/18 cup) slow cooker with the leek, celery, carrot and parsnip. Pour in 2.5 litres (87 fl oz/10 cups) water.

2 Cover and cook on low for 8 hours, or until the chicken meat is falling off the bones.

3 Remove the chicken to a board. When cool enough to handle, discard the skin of the chicken, then remove the meat from the bones.

4 Add the chicken meat to the slow cooker, then cover and cook for a further 5 minutes, or until heated through.

5 Ladle into bowls and serve sprinkled with the dill.

Tip: If desired, you can transfer the soup to a container and refrigerate it overnight, then skim the congealed fat from the top the next day, before reheating and serving.

Mulligatawny soup

Serves **4**   Preparation time **30 minutes**   Cooking time **4 hours**

2 tablespoons tomato chutney
1 tablespoon purchased mild Indian
 curry paste
2 teaspoons lemon juice
½ teaspoon ground turmeric
1.25 litres (44 fl oz/5 cups)
 good-quality chicken stock
375 g (13 oz) skinless chicken
 thigh fillets, trimmed of fat
 and cut into small dice
1 brown onion, finely chopped
1 all-purpose potato, such
 as sebago, peeled and diced
1 carrot, diced
1 celery stalk, diced
65 g (2¼ oz/⅓ cup) basmati rice
2 tablespoons chopped coriander
 (cilantro) leaves

1 Put the chutney, curry paste, lemon juice and turmeric in a 4.5 litre (157 fl oz/18 cup) slow cooker and mix in some of the stock. Add the remaining stock, then add the chicken, onion, potato, carrot, celery and rice.

2 Cover and cook on high for 3–4 hours, or until the chicken, vegetables and rice are cooked.

3 Season to taste with sea salt and freshly ground black pepper. Ladle into bowls and serve sprinkled with the coriander.

Tip: Add a little more curry paste if you prefer a stronger curry flavour.

Hearty chicken noodle soup

Serves **4–6**   Preparation time **15 minutes**   Cooking time **7 hours**

800 g (1 lb 12 oz) skinless chicken
　breast fillets
500 ml (17 fl oz/2 cups) good-quality
　chicken stock
2 celery stalks, diced
1 brown onion, diced
2 carrots, diced
1 parsnip, diced
2 cm (¾ inch) piece fresh ginger
3 black peppercorns
220 g (7¾ oz) fresh rice noodles
2 zucchini (courgettes), diced
½ cup flat-leaf (Italian) parsley,
　finely chopped

1 Trim the chicken of any fat and place in a 5.5 litre (192 fl oz/22 cup) slow cooker. Add the stock, celery, onion, carrot, parsnip, ginger, peppercorns and 250 ml (9 fl oz/1 cup) water. Cover and cook on low for 6 hours.

2 Remove the chicken from the slow cooker and allow to cool slightly. When cool enough to handle, shred the chicken into bite-sized pieces. Return to the slow cooker and stir in the noodles and zucchini.

3 Turn the slow cooker setting to high. Cover and cook for a further 1 hour. Discard the ginger and season to taste with sea salt and freshly ground black pepper.

4 Ladle into bowls and serve sprinkled with the parsley.

⚙ *Tips: Instead of sprinkling chopped parsley over the finished soup, try some chopped basil or coriander (cilantro). You can also stir some chopped chilli through for a spicy kick. If preparing the soup ahead, leave out the rice noodles. Without the noodles, the soup can be frozen for up to 3 months.*

Canja

Serves **6**   Preparation time **20 minutes**   Cooking time **3 hours 20 minutes**

3 tomatoes
200 g (7 oz/1 cup) long-grain
    white rice
2.5 litres (87 fl oz/10 cups)
    good-quality chicken stock
1 brown onion, cut into thin wedges
1 celery stalk, finely chopped
1 teaspoon finely grated lemon zest
1 mint sprig
2 skinless chicken breast fillets
2 tablespoons lemon juice
2 tablespoons shredded mint

1 Score a cross in the base of each tomato. Put the tomatoes in a heatproof bowl and cover with boiling water. Leave for 30 seconds, then transfer to cold water, drain and peel the skin away from the cross. Cut the tomatoes in half, scoop out the seeds and chop the flesh.

2 Place the tomato in a 4.5 litre (157 fl oz/18 cup) slow cooker. Stir in the rice, stock, onion, celery, lemon zest and mint sprig. Cover and cook on high for 3 hours, or until the rice is tender.

3 Trim the chicken of any fat, then cut into thin slices. Add the chicken to the slow cooker with the lemon juice. Cover and cook, stirring occasionally, for 10 minutes, or until the chicken is cooked through.

4 Season to taste with sea salt and freshly ground black pepper. Stir in shredded mint, ladle into bowls and serve.

Creamy chicken and corn soup

Serves **4–6**   Preparation time **20 minutes**   Cooking time **2 hours 15 minutes**

4 sweet corn cobs
500 g (1 lb 2 oz) skinless
    chicken thigh fillets
2 garlic cloves, chopped
1 leek, white part only, chopped
1 large celery stalk, chopped
1 dried bay leaf
½ teaspoon thyme
1 litre (35 fl oz/4 cups) good-quality
    chicken stock
60 ml (2 fl oz/¼ cup) sherry
1 large floury potato, such as russet,
    peeled and cut into 1 cm
    (½ inch) dice
185 ml (6 fl oz/¾ cup) pouring cream
Snipped chives, to garnish

1 Using a large knife, remove the corn kernels from the cobs and place in a 4.5 litre (157 fl oz/18 cup) slow cooker. Trim the chicken of any fat, then add to the slow cooker with the garlic, leek, celery, bay leaf, thyme, stock, sherry and potato. Cover and cook on high for 2 hours.

2 Remove the chicken to a board and allow to cool. Discard the bay leaf.

3 Purée the vegetable mixture until smooth, using a hand-held stick blender or food processor. When the chicken is cool enough to handle, shred the meat and return it to the slow cooker. Stir in the cream.

4 Cover and cook for a further 10–15 minutes, or until the chicken is heated through.

5 Ladle into bowls and serve garnished with chives.

Curried chicken noodle soup

Serves **6**   Preparation time **25 minutes (+ 10 minutes soaking)**   Cooking time **1 hour 50 minutes**

1 small fresh red chilli, seeded and finely chopped
1 tablespoon finely chopped fresh ginger
2 tablespoons purchased Indian curry powder
750 ml (26 fl oz/3 cups) good-quality chicken stock
2 x 400 ml (14 fl oz) tins coconut milk
120 g (4¼ oz) rice vermicelli noodles
300 g (10½ oz) baby bok choy (pak choy)
2 x 250 g (9 oz) skinless chicken breast fillets
¼ cup torn basil leaves

1 Put the chilli, ginger, curry powder, stock and coconut milk in a 4.5 litre (157 fl oz/18 cup) slow cooker. Stir together, then cover and cook on high for 1½ hours.

2 When the stock is nearly ready, place the noodles in a large heatproof bowl, cover with boiling water and leave to soak for 10 minutes, or until softened.

3 Separate the bok choy leaves and slice the large leaves in half lengthways. Trim the chicken of any fat, then cut into thin slices.

4 Drain the noodles and stir through the soup with the bok choy and chicken. Cover and cook for a further 20 minutes, or until the chicken is tender and cooked through.

5 Stir in the basil, ladle into bowls and serve.

Lamb shank, lentil and pumpkin soup

Serves **8–10**   Preparation time **25 minutes**   Cooking time **8 hours 15 minutes**

2 tablespoons olive oil

3 lamb shanks, about 400 g (14 oz) each

2 carrots, diced

1 brown onion, finely diced

1 celery stalk, diced

3 garlic cloves, thinly sliced

2 tablespoons ground coriander

2 tablespoons ground cumin

1 tablespoon smoked paprika

2 litres (70 fl oz/8 cups) good-quality chicken stock

800 g (1 lb 12 oz) pumpkin (winter squash), peeled and cut into 3 cm (1¼ inch) wedges

400 g (14 oz) tin chopped or cherry tomatoes

210 g (7½ oz/1 cup) puy lentils or tiny blue-green lentils

2 tablespoons purchased harissa, or to taste (see Tip)

Greek-style yoghurt, coriander (cilantro) leaves and lemon wedges, to serve

1 Heat the olive oil in the insert pan of a 7 litre (245 fl oz/ 28 cup) slow cooker or a large frying pan over medium–high heat. Add the lamb shanks, season with sea salt and freshly ground black pepper and cook, turning occasionally, for 3–4 minutes, or until golden brown. Remove and set aside.

2 Reduce the heat to medium, add the carrot, onion, celery and garlic and cook for 5–7 minutes, or until tender, stirring occasionally. Add the spices and stir to combine.

3 Return the insert pan, if using, to the slow cooker, or transfer the vegetable mixture to the slow cooker. Add the stock, pumpkin, tomatoes, lentils and lamb shanks. Season to taste. Cover and cook on low for 7–8 hours, or until the lamb is very tender and falling off the bone.

4 Carefully remove the lamb shanks and set aside to cool slightly. When cool enough to handle, roughly shred the meat, then stir it through the soup with the harrisa.

5 Ladle into bowls and add a dollop of yoghurt. Garnish with coriander and serve with lemon wedges.

Tip: Harissa is a hot, spicy chilli paste widely used in North African cooking. You'll find it in larger supermarkets and gourmet shops.

Harira

Serves **8**   Preparation time **30 minutes (+ 8 hours soaking)**   Cooking time **5 hours 15 minutes**

150 g (5½ oz/¾ cup) dried chickpeas
2 tablespoons vegetable oil
500 g (1 lb 2 oz) boneless lamb leg
   or shoulder, trimmed of excess
   fat and cut into 1.5 cm (⅝ inch)
   chunks
2 celery stalks, diced
1 brown onion, diced
1 carrot, diced
2 tablespoons tomato paste
   (concentrated purée)
1 tablespoon ground cumin
1 teaspoon ground cinnamon
4 garlic cloves, finely chopped
2 cm (¾ inch) piece fresh ginger,
   peeled and finely grated
110 g (3¾ oz/½ cup) green lentils
2 x 400 g (14 oz) tin whole tomatoes
1.5 litres (52 fl oz/6 cups) good-
   quality chicken stock
90 g (3¼ oz/1 bunch) coriander
   (cilantro), leaves picked and
   coarsely chopped
150 g (5½ oz/1 bunch) flat-leaf
   (Italian) parsley, leaves picked
   and coarsely chopped
Juice of 1 lemon, or to taste
Warmed pitta breads, to serve
   (see Tip)

1 Soak the chickpeas for 8 hours or overnight in plenty of cold water. Drain the chickpeas, discarding the water, then place in a large saucepan. Cover with fresh water and bring to the boil. Boil rapidly for 10 minutes. Rinse the chickpeas and drain again.

2 Heat the oil in the insert pan of a 5 litre (175 fl oz/20 cup) slow cooker or a frying pan over medium heat. Brown the lamb for 3–5 minutes, turning occasionally, then remove with a slotted spoon. Cook the celery, onion and carrot for 4–6 minutes, or until tender. Add the tomato paste and cook, stirring, for 1 minute. Add the spices, garlic and ginger and stir for 30 seconds, or until aromatic.

3 Return the insert pan, if using, to the slow cooker, or transfer the mixture to the slow cooker. Add the lamb, chickpeas, lentils, tomatoes and stock. Cover and cook on high for 4–5 hours, or until the meat is very tender. Stir in the herbs and lemon juice and season to taste with sea salt and freshly ground black pepper. Serve with pitta breads.

Tip: Instead of pitta, try yoghurt flatbreads. Place 450 g (1 lb/3 cups) plain (all-purpose) flour in a large bowl and make a well in the centre. Combine 3 teaspoons (10 g/¼ oz) dried yeast and 150 ml (5 fl oz) warm water and stand for 10 minutes, or until foamy. Slowly work the yeast mixture into the flour. Add 3 tablespoons Greek-style yoghurt and 60 ml (2 fl oz/¼ cup) olive oil; knead on a floured surface until smooth. Cover and rest in an oiled bowl for 30 minutes. Divide into 8 pieces, then roll out to 20 cm (8 inch) circles. Heat some oil in a large frying pan over medium–high heat. Fry one bread at a time for 1–2 minutes each side, until golden, adding oil as needed. Rub with cut garlic and serve hot.

Korean short rib soup with glass noodles

Serves **4–6**   Preparation time **15 minutes (+ 1 hour soaking)**   Cooking time **5 hours 25 minutes**

6 beef short ribs, about 2 kg
    (4 lb 8 oz)
½ daikon, about 200 g (7 oz),
    peeled and halved
1 brown onion, coarsely chopped
6 spring onions (scallions),
    3 coarsely chopped, 3 thinly sliced
125 ml (4 fl oz/½ cup) light soy
    sauce
1 tablespoon sesame oil
5 garlic cloves, finely grated
1½ tablespoons finely grated
    fresh ginger
300 g (10½ oz) glass noodles

1 Soak the ribs in a bowl of cold water for 1 hour.

2 Drain the ribs and place in a large saucepan. Cover with cold water and bring to the boil over medium–high heat. Reduce the heat to low and simmer for 15 minutes, then skim the surface to remove the impurities. Drain the ribs and rinse under cold running water.

3 Transfer the ribs to a 7 litre (245 fl oz/28 cup) slow cooker. Add the daikon, onion and the coarsely chopped spring onions, then cover with 3 litres (105 fl oz/12 cups) cold water. Cover and cook on high for 4½–5 hours, or until the ribs are tender.

4 Meanwhile, combine the soy sauce, sesame oil, garlic and ginger in a large bowl and set aside.

5 Use tongs to transfer the ribs to the soy mixture and toss to combine. Transfer the daikon to a chopping board, thinly slice, then add to the rib and soy mixture. Strain the remaining stock through a sieve into a large saucepan, discarding the solids. Keep warm.

6 Cook the noodles in a saucepan of boiling salted water for 1–2 minutes, or until tender.

7 Drain the noodles and divide among bowls. Top with the ribs and daikon, then pour over the hot stock. Drizzle with the remaining soy mixture and serve garnished with the thinly sliced spring onions.

Vietnamese pho

Serves **8–10**   Preparation time **25 minutes**   Cooking time **12 hours 35 minutes**

1.5 kg (3 lb 5 oz) beef bones,
    cut into 5 cm (2 inch) pieces
    (ask your butcher to do this)
1 kg (2 lb 4 oz) oxtail, cut into
    5 cm (2 inch) pieces
2 tablespoons vegetable oil
2 brown onions, halved
10 cm (4 inch) piece fresh ginger,
    peeled and halved
1 whole garlic bulb, sliced in half
    crossways
4 star anise
3 whole cloves
2 cinnamon sticks
2 teaspoons coriander seeds
1 teaspoon fennel seeds
1 teaspoon whole black peppercorns
125 ml (4 fl oz/½ cup) fish sauce,
    or to taste
2 tablespoons caster (superfine)
    sugar, or to taste
400 g (14 oz) fresh rice noodles
800 g (1 lb 12 oz) beef fillet, thinly
    sliced
6 spring onions (scallions), thinly
    sliced diagonally
3 long fresh red chillies, seeded and
    thinly sliced
4 cups mixed herbs, including
    coriander (cilantro), mint,
    Vietnamese mint and Thai basil
Lime wedges, to serve

1 Place the bones and oxtail pieces in a large saucepan. Cover with cold water and bring to the boil over high heat. Reduce the heat to low and simmer for 15 minutes, occasionally skimming the impurities from the surface. Drain, rinse under cold running water and set aside.

2 Heat the oil in the insert pan of a 7 litre (245 fl oz/ 28 cup) slow cooker or a frying pan over medium–high heat. Add the onion, ginger and the garlic bulb, cut side down. Cook for 5–7 minutes, or until the mixture is golden and aromatic. Remove to a plate.

3 Wipe the insert pan or frying pan with paper towel, then dry-roast the spices for 30 seconds to 1 minute, or until aromatic. Coarsely crush the spices using a mortar and pestle, then add the fish sauce and sugar.

4 Transfer the bones, oxtail, onion mixture and spice mixture to the slow cooker. Pour in enough cold water to cover the bones. Cover and cook on low for 10–12 hours, or until the stock is aromatic and well flavoured. Carefully strain the stock through a fine sieve, discarding the solids.

5 Return the stock to a clean insert pan of the slow cooker or a large saucepan. Bring to a simmer over medium heat and season to taste with extra fish sauce and sugar if needed.

6 Meanwhile, blanch the noodles in a saucepan of boiling water for 30 seconds to 1 minute. Divide among bowls, then top with the beef slices, spring onion, chilli and herbs.

7 Ladle the hot stock over and serve with lime wedges.

Beef borscht

Serves **4–6**   Preparation time **20 minutes**   Cooking time **5 hours**

1.2 kg (2 lb 10 oz) beef chuck steak
1 brown onion, cut into 2 cm
  (¾ inch) dice
2 celery stalks, cut into 2 cm (¾ inch)
  dice
2 beetroot (beets), peeled and cut
  into wedges
½ small cabbage, cut into 2 cm
  (¾ inch) dice
3 tablespoons tomato paste
  (concentrated purée)
400 g (14 oz) tin chopped tomatoes
375 ml (13 fl oz/1½ cups)
  good-quality beef stock
2 tablespoons vinegar
125 g (4½ oz/½ cup) sour cream
2 tablespoons bottled horseradish
A squeeze of lemon juice
2 tablespoons chopped flat-leaf
  (Italian) parsley

1 Trim the beef of any fat and cut it into 2 cm (¾ inch) chunks. Place in a 4.5 litre (157 fl oz/18 cup) slow cooker with the onion, celery, beetroot, cabbage, tomato paste, tomatoes, stock and vinegar. Stir to combine, then cover and cook on high for 3 hours.

2 Remove the lid and continue to cook on high for a further 1½–2 hours, or until the borscht has a thick casserole consistency. Season to taste with sea salt and freshly ground black pepper.

3 Combine the sour cream, horseradish and lemon juice in a bowl and season with sea salt.

4 Ladle the soup into bowls. Serve with a dollop of the horseradish cream and sprinkled with the parsley.

Sukiyaki soup

Serves **4–6**   Preparation time **30 minutes (+10 minutes soaking)**   Cooking time **2 hours 10 minutes**

1 teaspoon dashi granules (see Tip)
1 leek
10 g (¼ oz) sliced dried shiitake
    mushrooms
1.5 litres (52 fl oz/6 cups)
    good-quality chicken stock
125 ml (4 fl oz/½ cup) soy sauce
2 tablespoons mirin
1½ tablespoons sugar
100 g (3½ oz) Chinese cabbage
    (wong bok), shredded
300 g (10½ oz) silken firm tofu,
    cut into 2 cm (¾ inch) cubes
400 g (14 oz) rump steak, trimmed
    of excess fat and thinly sliced
100 g (3½ oz) rice vermicelli noodles
4 spring onions (scallions), sliced
    diagonally

1 Put the dashi in a heatproof bowl with 500 ml (17 fl oz/2 cups) boiling water. Stir until the granules have dissolved.

2 Leaving the root attached to the leek, cut off and discard the green top half. Slice the white stem in half lengthways, wash thoroughly under cold water to remove any grit, then drain. Thinly slice the leek, discarding the root end.

3 Put the dashi and leek in a 4.5 litre (157 fl oz/18 cup) slow cooker. Add the mushroom, stock, soy sauce, mirin and sugar. Cover and cook on low for 2 hours.

4 Stir in the cabbage, then cover and cook for 5 minutes, or until wilted. Gently mix the tofu and beef through. Cover and cook for a further 2 minutes, or until the beef is just cooked.

5 Meanwhile, put the noodles in a heatproof bowl, cover with boiling water and leave to soak for 10 minutes, or until softened. Drain well.

6 Divide the noodles among bowls. Ladle the soup over and serve garnished with the spring onion.

Tip: Dashi granules are a powdered stock used in Japanese cooking. Made from seaweed and dried flakes of a fish called bonito, it has a distinctive salty flavour. You'll find dashi in larger supermarkets and Asian grocery stores.

Pea and ham soup

Serves **8–10**   Preparation time **25 minutes**   Cooking time **7 hours 10 minutes**

2 tablespoons olive oil
2 brown onions, finely diced
2 leeks, white part only, sliced
4 garlic cloves, crushed
660 g (1 lb 7 oz/3 cups) green
   split peas, rinsed
2 litres (70 fl oz/8 cups) good-quality
   chicken or vegetable stock
1 ham hock, about 1.2 kg (2 lb 10 oz)
500 g (1 lb 2 oz) frozen green peas,
   thawed
Chopped dill and sour cream,
   to serve

1 Heat the olive oil in the insert pan of a 7 litre (245 fl oz/ 28 cup) slow cooker or a frying pan over medium heat. Add the onion, leek and garlic and cook, stirring, for 6–7 minutes, or until softened.

2 Return the insert pan, if using, to the slow cooker, or transfer the onion mixture to the slow cooker. Add the split peas, stock and ham hock. Cover and cook on low for 6–7 hours, or until the ham is falling off the bone.

3 Carefully remove the ham hock and set aside to cool slightly. When cool enough to handle, coarsely shred the meat, discarding the skin and bone, and set aside.

4 Add the thawed peas to the soup. Purée the mixture until smooth, using a hand-held stick blender or food processor. Season to taste with sea salt and freshly ground black pepper.

5 Stir the ham through the soup and reheat briefly if required. Ladle into bowls and serve garnished with dill and a dollop of sour cream.

White bean, rosemary and chorizo soup

Serves 8   Preparation time **20 minutes (+ 8 hours soaking)**   Cooking time **3 hours 45 minutes**

500 g (1 lb 2 oz) dried white beans, such as cannellini
100 ml (3½ fl oz) olive oil
3 brown onions, diced
8 garlic cloves, crushed
2 litres (70 fl oz/ 8 cups) good-quality chicken stock
2 rosemary sprigs
2 tablespoons sherry vinegar, or to taste
Finely grated zest of 1 lemon
4 chorizo sausages, thinly sliced diagonally
⅓ cup chopped flat-leaf (Italian) parsley

1 Soak the beans for 8 hours or overnight in plenty of cold water. Drain the beans, discarding the water, then place in a large saucepan. Cover with fresh water and bring to the boil. Boil rapidly for 10 minutes. Rinse the beans and drain again.

2 Heat half the olive oil in the insert pan of a 7 litre (245 fl oz/28 cup) slow cooker or a frying pan over medium heat. Add the onion and garlic and cook for 8–10 minutes, or until the onion is soft.

3 Return the insert pan, if using, to the slow cooker, or transfer the onion mixture to the slow cooker. Add the beans, stock and rosemary. Cover and cook on high for 3–3½ hours, or until the beans are very tender.

4 Remove the rosemary sprigs. Purée the mixture until smooth, using a hand-held stick blender or food processor. Add the vinegar and lemon zest and season to taste with sea salt and freshly ground black pepper. Keep warm.

5 Heat the remaining oil in a frying pan over medium–high heat. Add the chorizo and fry for 2–3 minutes, or until golden, turning occasionally.

6 Ladle the soup into bowls. Scatter the chorizo over the top, then drizzle with the oil from the pan. Serve sprinkled with the parsley.

⚙ *Tip: You'll need to begin this recipe a day ahead.*

Pancetta, mushroom and barley soup with garlic croutons

Serves **6**   Preparation time **15 minutes**   Cooking time **3 hours 15 minutes**

1 tablespoon olive oil

300 g (10½ oz) pancetta, cut into
5 mm (¼ inch) pieces

10 g (¼ oz) butter, diced

200 g (7 oz) mushroom flats,
thickly sliced

150 g (5½ oz) Swiss brown
mushrooms, quartered

2 litres (70 fl oz/8 cups) good-quality
chicken or vegetable stock

150 g (5½ oz/¾ cup) pearl barley,
rinsed under cold running water

5 thyme sprigs

100 g (3½ oz) English spinach,
trimmed and leaves coarsely
chopped

Lemon wedges, to serve

Garlic croutons

80 ml (2½ fl oz/⅓ cup) olive oil

125 g (4½ oz) crustless sourdough
bread, cut into 1 cm (½ inch)
cubes

1 garlic clove, finely chopped

1   Heat the olive oil in the insert pan of a 5 litre (175 fl oz/
20 cup) slow cooker or a frying pan over medium heat.
Add the pancetta and cook, stirring occasionally, for
3–5 minutes, or until golden. Add the butter and all the
mushrooms and cook for 5–6 minutes, or until tender,
stirring occasionally.

2   Return the insert pan, if using, to the slow cooker, or
transfer the mushroom mixture to the slow cooker. Add
the stock, barley and thyme, then season to taste with sea
salt and freshly ground black pepper. Cover and cook on
high for 3 hours, or until the barley is tender.

3   Meanwhile, make the garlic croutons. Heat the oil in
a frying pan over medium–high heat. Add the bread
and cook, stirring occasionally, for 2–3 minutes, or until
golden. Remove from the heat and stir the garlic through.
Season to taste and set aside on paper towels to drain.

4   Stir the spinach through the soup and season to taste.
Remove the thyme sprigs. Ladle into bowls, scatter
the garlic croutons over the top and serve with
lemon wedges.

Pork congee

Serves **4**   Preparation time **15 minutes**   Cooking time **5 hours**

300 g (10½ oz/1½ cups) long-grain
  white rice
1 star anise
2 spring onions (scallions), white
  part only, sliced
5 cm (2 inch) piece fresh ginger,
  peeled and thinly sliced
1 garlic clove, crushed
2 litres (70 fl oz/8 cups) good-quality
  chicken stock
400 g (14 oz) minced (ground) pork
60 ml (2 fl oz/¼ cup) light soy
  sauce
Ground white pepper, to taste
Sesame oil and fried bread sticks, to
  serve (optional; see Tip)

1 Rinse the rice thoroughly under cold running water.
Place in a 4.5 litre (157 fl oz/18 cup) slow cooker with
the star anise, spring onion, ginger, garlic, stock, pork
and 750 ml (26 fl oz/3 cups) water.

2 Cover and cook on low for 5 hours, or until the rice has
broken down and the mixture has a soupy consistency.
Stir the soy sauce through and season to taste with
white pepper.

3 Ladle into bowls and drizzle with sesame oil. Serve with
fried bread sticks, if desired.

⚙ *Tips: Fried bread sticks are sold in Asian grocery stores. They are
best eaten fresh on the day they are made. This soup will thicken
on standing, so thin it with a little water or chicken stock if desired.*

Potato and smoked ham soup

Serves **8–10**   Preparation time **20 minutes**   Cooking time **4 hours 10 minutes**

2 tablespoons olive oil
2 brown onions, finely diced
2 leeks, white part only, thinly sliced
1 celery stalk, diced
4 garlic cloves, crushed
1.5 kg (3 lb 5 oz) Dutch cream
　　potatoes, peeled and chopped
　　into 3 cm (1¼ inch) chunks
1.2 kg (2 lb 10 oz) smoked ham
　　hock
1.5 litres (52 fl oz/6 cups)
　　good-quality vegetable or
　　chicken stock
5 thyme sprigs, plus extra leaves,
　　to serve
250 ml (9 fl oz/1 cup) pouring cream
Crème fraîche or sour cream,
　　to serve

1 Heat the olive oil in the insert pan of a 7 litre (245 fl oz/ 28 cup) slow cooker or a frying pan over medium heat. Add the onion, leek, celery and garlic and cook, stirring occasionally, for 5–7 minutes, or until softened.

2 Return the insert pan, if using, to the slow cooker, or transfer the onion mixture to the slow cooker. Add the potato, ham hock, stock and thyme sprigs.

3 Cover and cook on high for 4 hours, or until the ham is tender and falling off the bone.

4 Remove the ham hock and set aside to cool. When cool enough to handle, remove the meat from the bone, discarding the skin and bone. Coarsely shred the meat and set aside.

5 Remove the thyme sprigs. Purée the mixture until smooth, using a hand-held stick blender or food processor. Stir the cream and shredded ham through, then season to taste with sea salt and freshly ground black pepper.

6 Ladle into bowls and scatter with thyme leaves. Serve topped with a dollop of crème fraîche.

Lion's head meatballs

Serves **4**   Preparation time **30 minutes (+10 minutes soaking)**   Cooking time **2 hours 10 minutes**

450 g (1 lb) minced (ground) pork
1 egg white
4 spring onions (scallions), finely
   chopped
1 tablespoon Chinese rice wine
1 teaspoon finely grated fresh ginger
1 tablespoon light soy sauce
2 teaspoons sugar
1 teaspoon sesame oil
A pinch of ground white pepper
750 ml (26 fl oz/3 cups) good-quality
   chicken stock
300 g (10½ oz) bok choy (pak choy),
   sliced
100 g (3½ oz) rice vermicelli noodles

1 Put the pork and egg white in a food processor and blend briefly to form a fluffy mixture. Alternatively, mash the pork in a large bowl and gradually stir in the egg white, beating well until the mixture is fluffy.

2 Add the spring onion, Chinese rice wine, ginger, soy sauce, sugar and sesame oil. Season with sea salt and white pepper, then process or beat again briefly. Using wet hands, roll the mixture into walnut-sized balls.

3 Place the meatballs in a 4.5 litre (157 fl oz/18 cup) slow cooker, then pour in the stock. Cover and cook on low for 2 hours.

4 Add the bok choy, then cover and cook for a further 10 minutes, or until the bok choy is wilted.

5 Meanwhile, put the noodles in a heatproof bowl, cover with boiling water and leave to soak for 10 minutes, or until softened. Drain well, then add to the slow cooker and stir to combine.

6 Divide the noodles and meatballs among bowls. Ladle some broth over the top and serve.

Seafood chowder

Serves **4–6** Preparation time **30 minutes** Cooking time **3 hours 30 minutes**

100 g (3½ oz) smoked ham, diced
3 large all-purpose potatoes, such
  as sebago, peeled and cut
  into 1 cm (½ inch) dice
2 leeks, white part only, thinly
  sliced
3 large garlic cloves, crushed
1.125 litres (39 fl oz/4½ cups)
  good-quality fish or chicken stock
1 dried bay leaf
3 thyme sprigs
500 g (1 lb 2 oz) skinless firm white
  fish fillets (see Tip)
20 scallops, about 350 g (12 oz),
  without roe
290 g (10¼ oz) tin baby clams
  (vongole), undrained
435 ml (15¼ fl oz/1¾ cups) thick
  (double/heavy) cream
2 tablespoons chopped flat-leaf
  (Italian) parsley
Crusty bread, to serve

1 Put the ham, potato and leek in a 4.5 litre (157 fl oz/ 18 cup) slow cooker. Add the garlic, stock, bay leaf and thyme sprigs. Cover and cook on high for 3 hours, or until the potato is tender.

2 Cut the fish into 2 cm (¾ inch) dice. Add the fish to the slow cooker with the scallops, as well as the clams and their liquor. Gently stir in the cream, then cover and cook for a further 30 minutes, or until the fish is cooked through and flakes when tested with a fork.

3 Season to taste with sea salt and freshly ground black pepper. Stir in the parsley, ladle into bowls and serve with crusty bread.

✦ *Tip: You can use any firm white fish for the chowder, such as ling, snapper, monkfish or gemfish.*

Bouillabaisse

Serves **6**   Preparation time **30 minutes**   Cooking time **6 hours**

2 tomatoes
1 carrot, chopped
1 celery stalk, chopped
1 leek, white part only, chopped
1 fennel bulb, coarsely chopped
250 ml (9 fl oz/1 cup) good-quality
   fish stock
100 ml (3½ fl oz) white wine or
   Pernod
2 garlic cloves, crushed
Finely grated zest of 1 orange
A pinch of saffron threads
1 tablespoon tomato paste
   (concentrated purée)
200 g (7 oz) firm white fish fillets,
   such as monkfish
200 g (7 oz) salmon fillet
12 mussels
12 raw prawns (shrimp)
Chopped flat-leaf (Italian) parsley
   and crusty bread, to serve

1 Score a cross in the base of each tomato. Put the tomatoes in a heatproof bowl and cover with boiling water. Leave for 30 seconds, then transfer to cold water, drain and peel the skin away from the cross. Cut the tomatoes in half, scoop out the seeds and coarsely chop the flesh.

2 Put the tomato in a 4.5 litre (157 fl oz/18 cup) slow cooker with the carrot, celery, leek, fennel, stock, wine, garlic, orange zest, saffron threads and tomato paste. Stir together, then cover and cook on high for 3 hours.

3 Meanwhile, prepare the seafood. Cut the white fish into 2 cm (¾ inch) pieces. Remove any bones from the salmon using your fingers or a pair of tweezers, then cut into 2 cm (¾ inch) pieces. Scrub the mussels with a stiff brush and pull out the hairy beards. Discard any broken mussels or open ones that don't close when tapped on the bench. Peel the prawns, leaving the tails intact, then gently pull out the dark vein from the pack of each prawn, starting at the head end. Refrigerate the seafood until needed.

4 After 3 hours cooking time, allow the soup base to cool slightly, then transfer to a food processor and blend until smooth. Return to the slow cooker along with the white fish and salmon and cook for a further 2 hours on low.

5 Add the mussels and prawns to the slow cooker and cook for a further 1 hour on low. When the mussels are cooked, discard any unopened mussels.

6 Ladle into bowls, sprinkle with parsley and serve with crusty bread.

Prawn gumbo

Serves **4–6**   Preparation time **30 minutes**   Cooking time **4 hours 20 minutes**

1 brown onion, finely chopped
1 garlic clove, crushed
1 red capsicum (pepper), chopped
4 bacon slices, trimmed and diced
1½ teaspoons dried thyme
2 teaspoons dried oregano
1 teaspoon sweet paprika
¼ teaspoon cayenne pepper
100 g (3½ oz/½ cup) par-cooked
    long-grain white rice
2 dried bay leaves
400 g (14 oz) tin chopped tomatoes
150 g (5½ oz) okra, sliced
60 ml (2 fl oz/¼ cup) dry sherry
1 litre (35 fl oz/4 cups) good-quality
    fish or light chicken stock
1 kg (2 lb 4 oz) raw prawns
    (shrimp), peeled and deveined,
    tails left intact

1 Put the onion, garlic, capsicum and bacon in a 4.5 litre (157 fl oz/18 cup) slow cooker with the herbs, spices, rice, bay leaves, tomatoes and okra. Stir in the sherry and stock.

2 Cover and cook on low for 4 hours, or until the rice is cooked and the okra is tender.

3 Stir in the prawns, then cover and cook for a further 15–20 minutes, or until the prawns are cooked through.

4 Ladle into bowls and serve.

Corn and crab soup

Serves **4**   Preparation time **10 minutes**   Cooking time **2 hours 5 minutes**

420 g (15 oz) tin creamed corn
2 teaspoons finely grated fresh
   ginger
2 x 170 g (6 oz) tins crabmeat
6 spring onions (scallions), thinly
   sliced diagonally, plus extra,
   to garnish
750 ml (26 fl oz/3 cups) good-quality
   chicken stock
1 tablespoon mirin (see Tip)
2 tablespoons soy sauce, plus extra,
   to serve
¼ teaspoon ground white pepper
2 egg whites, lightly beaten

1 Place the corn, ginger, crabmeat and half the spring onion in a 5.5 litre (192 fl oz/22 cup) slow cooker. Pour in the stock, mirin and 500 ml (17 fl oz/2 cups) water. Cover and cook on low for 2 hours.

2 Remove the lid. Stir in the soy sauce and white pepper. Add the egg white and remaining spring onion and stir for 1–2 minutes, or until the egg white has just cooked through.

3 Ladle into bowls and sprinkle with extra spring onion. Serve immediately, with extra soy sauce on the side.

⊙ *Tips: Mirin is a Japanese cooking wine. If unavailable, you can substitute Chinese rice wine or dry sherry in this recipe. It's important not to let the egg cook too long in this soup — serve it straight away, while the egg is still velvety and soft.*

Prawn laksa lemak

Serves **4**   Preparation time **25 minutes (+ 20 minutes soaking)**   Cooking time **2 hours 30 minutes**

4 tablespoons purchased laksa paste
545 ml (19 fl oz) coconut milk
1 tablespoon fish sauce
24 raw king prawns (shrimp), about
    600 g (1 lb 5 oz), peeled and
    deveined, tails left intact
300 g (10½ oz) rice stick noodles
1 cucumber
100 g (3½ oz) bean sprouts,
    tails trimmed
1 cup coriander (cilantro) leaves
½ cup Thai basil
Sambal oelek, to serve (see Tip)

1 In a small bowl, mix the laksa paste with the coconut milk until smooth. Pour into a 5.5 litre (192 fl oz/22 cup) slow cooker, then add the fish sauce and 500 ml (17 fl oz/ 2 cups) water. Add the prawns and gently mix. Cover and cook on low for 2½ hours. Season to taste with sea salt.

2 Near serving time, put the noodles in a large heatproof bowl and cover with boiling water. Leave to soak for 20 minutes, or until softened.

3 Meanwhile, cut the cucumber in half lengthways and scrape out the seeds. Thinly slice the cucumber into matchsticks 5 cm (2 inches) long.

4 Drain the noodles and divide among bowls. Ladle the laksa over the noodles. Top with the bean sprouts, coriander and basil and serve with the cucumber and sambal oelek.

Tip: Sambal oelek is a spicy condiment made from ground chillies. It is widely used in Indonesian and Malaysian cooking and is sold in larger supermarkets and Asian grocery stores.

Curries

Chickpea and vegetable curry

Serves **4–6**   Preparation time **30 minutes**   Cooking time **4 hours 10 minutes**

3 garlic cloves, crushed
1 long fresh red or green chilli,
    seeded and chopped
2 tablespoons purchased Indian
    curry paste
1 teaspoon ground cumin
½ teaspoon ground turmeric
400 g (14 oz) tin chopped tomatoes
250 ml (9 fl oz/1 cup) good-quality
    vegetable stock
1 red onion, cut into thin wedges
1 large carrot, sliced diagonally into
    3 cm (1¼ inch) chunks
250 g (9 oz) orange sweet potato,
    sliced diagonally into 3 cm
    (1¼ inch) chunks
250 g (9 oz) cauliflower, cut into
    florets
250 g (9 oz) broccoli, cut into florets
2 long, thin eggplants (aubergines),
    about 100 g (3½ oz), cut into
    3 cm (1¼ inch) thick slices
400 g (14 oz) tin chickpeas, drained
    and rinsed
140 g (5 oz/1 cup) frozen peas
165 ml (5¼ fl oz) tin coconut milk
Coriander (cilantro) leaves, to garnish
Steamed rice, to serve

1 Combine the garlic, chilli, curry paste, cumin, turmeric, tomatoes and stock in a 4.5 litre (157 fl oz/18 cup) slow cooker. Stir in the onion, carrot, sweet potato, cauliflower, broccoli, eggplant and chickpeas.

2 Cover and cook on high for 3–4 hours, or until all the vegetables are tender.

3 Add the peas and stir the coconut milk through. Cover and cook for a further 10 minutes, or until the peas are just cooked.

4 Sprinkle with coriander and serve with steamed rice.

⊙ *Tip: Add a little more curry paste if you prefer a stronger curry flavour.*

Yellow curry with vegetables

Serves **4**   Preparation time **30 minutes**   Cooking time **3 hours**

100 g (3½ oz) cauliflower
1 long, thin eggplant (aubergine)
1 small red capsicum (pepper)
2 small zucchini (courgettes)
150 g (5½ oz) green beans
1–2 tablespoons purchased yellow
  curry paste
500 ml (17 fl oz/2 cups) coconut
  cream
125 ml (4 fl oz/½ cup) good-quality
  vegetable stock
150 g (5½ oz) baby corn
1½ tablespoons fish sauce
2 teaspoons grated palm sugar
  (jaggery) or brown sugar
1 small fresh red chilli, seeded and
  chopped
Coriander (cilantro) leaves, to garnish
Steamed rice, to serve

1 Chop the cauliflower into florets. Cut the eggplant, capsicum and zucchini into 1 cm (½ inch) slices. Trim the beans and chop into 3 cm (1¼ inch) lengths.

2 Put the cauliflower, eggplant and capsicum in a 4.5 litre (157 fl oz/18 cup) slow cooker. Add the curry paste, coconut cream and stock. Cover and cook on low for 2 hours, or until the cauliflower is tender.

3 Stir in the zucchini, beans, corn, fish sauce and palm sugar and cook for a further 1 hour, or until all the vegetables are tender.

4 Sprinkle with the chilli and coriander and serve with steamed rice.

Indian-style vegetable curry

Serves **4**   Preparation time **15 minutes**   Cooking time **6 hours 30 minutes**

1 brown onion, finely chopped
2 teaspoons finely grated fresh
  ginger
3 tablespoons purchased mild curry
  paste (such as balti)
1 small handful curry leaves
  (see Tip)
375 ml (13 fl oz/1½ cups) good-
  quality vegetable stock
350 g (12 oz/2¾ cups) cauliflower
  florets
300 g (10½ oz) sweet potato,
  cut into 2 cm (¾ inch) chunks
1 zucchini (courgette), sliced
2 tomatoes, chopped
3 tablespoons plain yoghurt
400 g (14 oz) tin brown lentils,
  drained and rinsed
45 g (1½ oz/1 cup) baby English
  spinach leaves
140 g (5 oz/1 cup) frozen peas,
  thawed
3 tablespoons chopped coriander
  (cilantro) leaves
Steamed basmati rice, to serve

1 Put the onion, ginger, curry paste, curry leaves and stock in a 5.5 litre (192 fl oz/22 cup) slow cooker. Add the cauliflower, sweet potato, zucchini and tomato and gently mix together.

2 Cover and cook on low for 6 hours, or until all the vegetables are tender.

3 Stir in the yoghurt, lentils, spinach, peas and half the coriander. Turn the slow cooker setting to high. Cover and cook for a further 30 minutes, or until the spinach has wilted.

4 Sprinkle with the remaining coriander and serve with steamed rice.

⚙ *Tip: Curry leaves are highly aromatic and used extensively in Sri Lankan and southern Indian cooking, particularly in curries. They are available in Asian food stores, selected greengrocers and larger supermarkets.*

Green curry of tofu and vegetables

Serves **4**   Preparation time **15 minutes**   Cooking time **2 hours 30 minutes**

300 g (10½ oz) orange sweet
   potato, cut into 1 cm (½ inch)
   dice
8 baby corn
3 tablespoons purchased green
   curry paste
500 ml (17 fl oz/2 cups) coconut
   cream
300 g (10½ oz) firm tofu, cut into
   3 cm (1¼ inch) chunks
2 zucchini (courgettes), thickly sliced
60 g (2¼ oz) green beans, trimmed
   and cut into 3 cm (1¼ inch)
   lengths
250 g (9 oz/1 bunch) broccolini,
   washed and halved lengthways
1–2 tablespoons fish sauce
2 tablespoons lime juice
6 makrut (kaffir lime) leaves,
   finely shredded (see Tip)
Steamed jasmine rice, to serve

1 Place the sweet potato and baby corn in a 5.5 litre
   (192 fl oz/22 cup) slow cooker. In a small bowl, whisk
   the curry paste and coconut cream until smooth, then
   pour over the vegetables.

2 Cover and cook on high for 2 hours, or until the sweet
   potato is tender.

3 Stir in the tofu, zucchini, beans, broccolini and
   1 tablespoon of the fish sauce. Cover and cook for a
   further 30 minutes, or until all the green vegetables
   have softened.

4 Stir the lime juice and half the lime leaves through the
   curry. Check the seasoning, adding another tablespoon
   of fish sauce if the curry needs more saltiness.

5 Garnish with the remaining lime leaves and serve with
   steamed rice.

*Tips: Kaffir lime leaves are available from greengrocers or Asian
supermarkets. They are sometimes just labelled 'lime leaves', and can
be frozen for later use. To finish the soup, you could stir some Thai basil
through it and garnish with some extra Thai basil sprigs or leaves.
Alternatively, garnish the curry with long fresh green chilli halves.*

Vegetarian chilli beans

Serves **4**   Preparation time **15 minutes**   Cooking time **4 hours**

1 brown onion, chopped
1 red capsicum (pepper), chopped
400 g (14 oz) tin chopped tomatoes
1 tablespoon tomato paste
    (concentrated purée)
2 x 400 g (14 oz) tins red kidney
    beans, drained and rinsed
3 teaspoons ground coriander
2 teaspoons ground cumin
½ teaspoon chilli powder
2 garlic cloves, crushed
2 dried bay leaves
125 ml (4 fl oz/½ cup) good-quality
    vegetable stock
90 g (3¼ oz/⅓ cup) sour cream
Coriander (cilantro) sprigs, flour
    tortillas and steamed rice, to
    serve (optional)

Avocado salsa
1 avocado, peeled and diced
2 tablespoons lemon juice
1 roma (plum) tomato, seeded and
    diced
½ red onion, thinly sliced

1 Place the onion, capsicum, tomatoes, tomato paste and beans in a 5.5 litre (192 fl oz/22 cup) slow cooker. Add the ground coriander, cumin, chilli powder, garlic and bay leaves.

2 Pour in the stock and stir to combine well. Cover and cook for 4 hours on low.

3 Put all the avocado salsa ingredients in a bowl and gently stir to combine. Season to taste with sea salt and freshly ground black pepper. Cover and refrigerate until required.

4 Spoon the chilli beans into bowls. Top with a dollop of the sour cream and garnish with coriander sprigs. Serve with the avocado salsa, tortillas and steamed rice, if desired.

Green chicken curry

Serves **8**   Preparation time **35 minutes**   Cooking time **2 hours 40 minutes**

1 tablespoon vegetable oil

1 large brown onion, finely chopped

2 teaspoons finely grated fresh ginger

1 lemongrass stem, white part only, thinly sliced

1 litre (35 fl oz/4 cups) coconut cream

2 tablespoons purchased green curry paste (see Tip)

1.75 kg (3 lb 12 oz) skinless chicken thigh fillets, trimmed of fat and cut in half

1 teaspoon hot chilli sauce or sambal oelek

12 makrut (kaffir lime) leaves, finely shredded

2½ tablespoons lime juice

1½ tablespoons finely grated palm sugar (jaggery) or brown sugar

2 tablespoons fish sauce

¾ cup whole mint leaves, ¾ cup coriander (cilantro) leaves and steamed rice, to serve

1 Heat the oil in the insert pan of a 5 litre (175 fl oz/ 20 cup) slow cooker or a large frying pan over medium–low heat. Add the onion, ginger and lemongrass and cook, stirring occasionally, for 6 minutes, or until the mixture has softened.

2 Return the insert pan, if using, to the slow cooker, or transfer the onion mixture to the slow cooker.

3 Stir in the coconut cream and curry paste. Add the chicken, chilli sauce and half the lime leaves. Cover and cook on high for 2½ hours, or until the chicken is just cooked through and tender.

4 Transfer the chicken pieces to a large serving bowl. Stir the lime juice, palm sugar and fish sauce through the coconut cream sauce, then ladle over the chicken. Top with the remaining lime leaves, mint and coriander. Serve with steamed rice.

⚙ *Tip: Often a curry paste may give a hotter result than you might like. A good way to check how much to use is to place 125 ml (4 fl oz/ ½ cup) coconut cream in a small saucepan, add 1 teaspoon of your curry paste and bring to a simmer, stirring to combine. Taste and see what you think, then add more if desired. For this recipe the ratio is based on 2 teaspoons curry paste per 250 ml (9 fl oz/1 cup) coconut cream. Once you're happy you have the right curry strength, combine the remaining coconut cream and curry paste in the same ratio before adding the mixture to the slow cooker.*

Chicken korma

Serves **4–6**   Preparation time **20 minutes (+ 2 hours marinating)**   Cooking time **5 hours 15 minutes**

80 g (2¾ oz/½ cup) cashew nuts, lightly toasted
3 teaspoons chopped fresh ginger
3 garlic cloves, chopped
3 tablespoons purchased korma paste
130 g (4½ oz/½ cup) plain yoghurt
1 kg (2 lb 4 oz) skinless chicken thigh fillets, trimmed of fat and cut into 5 cm (2 inch) chunks
2 brown onions, chopped
40 g (1½ oz) ghee
½ teaspoon cayenne pepper
¼ teaspoon freshly ground black pepper
125 ml (4 fl oz/½ cup) coconut milk
1–2 tablespoons lemon juice
1 teaspoon garam masala
Coriander (cilantro) leaves, to garnish
Steamed basmati rice, to serve

1   Reserve half the cashews. Using a mortar and pestle or spice grinder, grind the remaining cashews to a paste and scrape into a bowl. Grind the ginger and garlic to a smooth paste, then add to the cashew paste. Add 1 tablespoon of the korma paste and the yoghurt and mix well. Add the chicken and mix until well coated. Cover and marinate in the refrigerator for 2 hours, or overnight.

2   Purée the onion in a food processor. Heat the ghee in the insert pan of a 5 litre (175 fl oz/20 cup) slow cooker or a frying pan over medium–high heat. Add the onion, cayenne pepper and black pepper. Cook for 10 minutes, stirring frequently, until most of the liquid has evaporated. Add the remaining korma paste and cook for 2 minutes.

3   Increase the heat to high. Add the chicken and marinade and cook for 2–3 minutes, or until the chicken begins to change colour. Return the insert pan, if using, to the slow cooker, or transfer the chicken mixture to the slow cooker.

4   Add the coconut milk and 2 tablespoons water. Stir to combine and season with sea salt. Cover and cook on low for 4 hours, or until the chicken is just tender.

5   Add the reserved whole cashews and cook for a further 1 hour, or until the sauce has thickened and the chicken is tender. Stir the lemon juice and garam masala through and season to taste.

6   Garnish with coriander and serve with steamed rice.

Sri Lankan chicken

Serves **4–6**   Preparation time **20 minutes (+ 2 hours marinating)**   Cooking time **5 hours 5 minutes**

5 garlic cloves, finely chopped
3 teaspoons finely grated fresh
   ginger
¼–½ teaspoon chilli powder
1 teaspoon ground turmeric
1 teaspoon ground coriander
½ teaspoon garam masala
¼ teaspoon ground cloves
150 ml (5 fl oz) coconut milk
1 kg (2 lb 4 oz) skinless chicken
   thigh fillets, trimmed of fat
40 g (1½ oz) ghee
2 brown onions, finely chopped
1 teaspoon sea salt
15 curry leaves
2 tablespoons desiccated coconut
4 cardamom pods, bruised
1 cinnamon stick
1 tablespoon lemon juice
Steamed rice, to serve

1 Combine the garlic, ginger and spices in a bowl. Stir in 2 tablespoons of the coconut milk and mix well. Add the chicken and mix until well coated. Cover and marinate in the refrigerator for 2 hours, or overnight.

2 Heat the ghee in the insert pan of a 5 litre (175 fl oz/ 20 cup) slow cooker or a frying pan over medium–high heat. Add the onion, salt and curry leaves and cook for 4–5 minutes, or until the onion has softened.

3 Return the insert pan, if using, to the slow cooker, or transfer the onion mixture to the slow cooker.

4 Add the desiccated coconut, remaining coconut milk, cardamom pods and cinnamon stick. Gently mix the chicken and marinade through. Cover and cook on low for 5 hours, or until the chicken is tender.

5 Stir the lemon juice through and adjust the seasoning. Serve with steamed rice.

Creamy chicken curry

Serves **4**   Preparation time **30 minutes (+ 2 hours marinating)**   Cooking time **4 hours**

2 cm (¾ inch) piece fresh ginger, peeled and coarsely chopped
3 garlic cloves, coarsely chopped
80 g (2¾ oz/½ cup) blanched almonds
150 g (5½ oz) Greek-style yoghurt
½ teaspoon chilli powder
¼ teaspoon ground cloves
¼ teaspoon ground cinnamon
1 teaspoon garam masala
4 cardamom pods, lightly crushed
1 teaspoon sea salt
400 g (14 oz) tin chopped tomatoes
1 kg (2 lb 4 oz) skinless chicken thigh fillets, trimmed of fat and cut into large chunks
1 large brown onion, thinly sliced
80 ml (2½ fl oz/⅓ cup) thick (double/heavy) cream
½ cup coriander (cilantro) leaves, finely chopped
Steamed rice, to serve

1 Using a mortar and pestle or a spice grinder, pound or grind the ginger and garlic together to form a paste; scrape into a large bowl. Alternatively, finely grate the ginger, crush the garlic and mix them together in a large bowl.

2 Grind the almonds using a mortar and pestle or a food processor, or finely chop them with a knife. Add to the ginger and garlic paste with the yoghurt, spices, salt and tomatoes. Blend together with a fork. Add the chicken and mix until well coated. Cover and marinate in the refrigerator for 2 hours, or overnight.

3 Transfer the chicken and marinade to a 4.5 litre (157 fl oz / 18 cup) slow cooker. Stir in the onion. Cover and cook on high for 3 hours.

4 Stir in the cream and half the coriander and cook for a further 1 hour, or until the chicken is tender. Season to taste with sea salt and freshly ground black pepper.

5 Garnish with the remaining coriander and serve with steamed rice.

Butter chicken

Serves **6**   Preparation time **20 minutes**   Cooking time **4 hours 10 minutes**

1 kg (2 lb 4 oz) skinless chicken
   thigh fillets
2 teaspoons garam masala
2 teaspoons sweet paprika
2 teaspoons ground coriander
1 tablespoon finely grated fresh
   ginger
¼ teaspoon chilli powder
1 cinnamon stick
6 cardamom pods, bruised
375 ml (13 fl oz/1½ cups) tomato
   passata (puréed tomatoes)
70 g (2½ oz/¼ cup) plain yoghurt
2 tablespoons cornflour (cornstarch)
1 tablespoon sugar
125 ml (4 fl oz/½ cup) pouring
   cream
1 tablespoon lemon juice
Coriander (cilantro) sprigs, to garnish
Steamed rice, to serve

1 Trim the chicken of any fat, then cut each thigh into
   quarters. Place in a 4.5 litre (157 fl oz/18 cup) slow
   cooker with the spices and passata.

2 Cover and cook on low for 4 hours, or until the chicken
   is tender and cooked through.

3 Combine the yoghurt with the cornflour, then mix in the
   sugar, cream and lemon juice. Stir the yoghurt mixture
   through the chicken.

4 Turn the slow cooker setting to high. Cover and cook
   for a further 10 minutes, or until the sauce has thickened
   slightly. Garnish with coriander sprigs and serve with
   steamed rice.

Penang chicken curry

Serves **4** Preparation time **10 minutes** Cooking time **3 hours**

800 g (1 lb 12 oz) skinless chicken
 breast fillets
400 ml (14 fl oz) tin coconut cream
Coriander (cilantro) leaves and sliced
 fresh red chilli, to garnish
Steamed jasmine rice, to serve

Curry paste
1 red onion, thickly sliced
10 g (¼ oz) fresh galangal, peeled
 and sliced
2 garlic cloves, chopped
1 teaspoon chilli powder
2 coriander (cilantro) roots,
 well rinsed
1 teaspoon shrimp paste
3 tablespoons peanuts, toasted

1 Place all the curry paste ingredients in a food processor and blend until smooth. Alternatively, pound all the curry paste ingredients using a mortar and pestle to form a smooth paste.

2 Trim the chicken of any fat, then chop into 2 cm (¾ inch) chunks and place in a large bowl. Add the curry paste and mix well to coat the chicken in the paste.

3 Transfer the chicken to a 4.5 litre (157 fl oz / 18 cup) slow cooker. Cover and cook on high for 2 hours.

4 Stir in the coconut cream, then cover and cook for a further 1 hour.

5 Garnish with coriander leaves and chilli and serve with steamed rice.

Mild chicken curry with sweet potato and split peas

Serves **4–6**   Preparation time **20 minutes**   Cooking time **4 hours 5 minutes**

1 tablespoon vegetable oil

1 red onion, chopped

2 garlic cloves, crushed

1 tablespoon finely grated fresh ginger

3 teaspoons purchased mild curry powder

220 g (7¾ oz/1 cup) dried yellow split peas, rinsed

2 skinless chicken breast fillets, cut into 2 cm (¾ inch) chunks

500 g (1 lb 2 oz) orange sweet potato, cut into 2 cm (¾ inch) chunks

100 g (3½ oz) green beans, trimmed and cut into 4 cm (1½ inch) lengths

400 g (14 oz) tin chopped tomatoes

250 ml (9 fl oz/1 cup) good-quality chicken stock

125 ml (4 fl oz/½ cup) pouring cream

½ cup coriander (cilantro) leaves, chopped

Steamed basmati rice, to serve

1 Spread the oil over the base and side of a 4.5 litre (157 fl oz/18 cup) slow cooker bowl. Add the onion, garlic and ginger and stir in the curry powder. Add the split peas, chicken, sweet potato and beans, then pour in the tomatoes and stock. Season with sea salt and freshly ground black pepper.

2 Cover and cook on high for 3–4 hours, or until the split peas and sweet potato are cooked, stirring occasionally.

3 Just before serving, stir in the cream and coriander and heat through for a few minutes. Serve with steamed rice.

Vietnamese chicken curry

Serves 6   Preparation time **15 minutes**   Cooking time **6 hours**

1 kg (2 lb 4 oz) skinless chicken
   thigh fillets
1 sweet potato, cut into 2.5 cm
   (1 inch) chunks
1 tablespoon purchased mild Indian
   curry powder
1 tablespoon caster (superfine) sugar
1 lemongrass stem, bruised
3 fresh bay leaves
400 ml (14 fl oz) tin coconut milk
250 ml (9 fl oz/1 cup) good-quality
   chicken stock
2 teaspoons fish sauce
Steamed jasmine rice and lime
   wedges, to serve

Cucumber and tomato salad
1 Lebanese (short) cucumber,
   seeded and sliced
12 cherry tomatoes, quartered
1 long fresh red chilli, thinly sliced
25 g (1 oz/¼ cup) bean sprouts,
   tails trimmed
½ cup coriander (cilantro) leaves
1 teaspoon lime juice
¼ teaspoon sesame oil

1   Trim the chicken of any fat, then cut each thigh into
    quarters. Place in a 5.5 litre (192 fl oz/22 cup) slow
    cooker with the sweet potato. Sprinkle with the curry
    powder and sugar and gently mix them through.

2   Add the lemongrass and bay leaves, then pour in the
    coconut milk and stock. Cover and cook on low for
    6 hours.

3   Near serving time, combine the cucumber and tomato
    salad ingredients in a bowl and toss to combine.

4   Stir the fish sauce through the curry. Season to taste
    with freshly ground black pepper.

5   Serve with the salad, steamed rice and lime wedges.

*Tip: For a hotter curry, add ½ teaspoon chilli powder and
some chopped red chilli to the curry. Serve garnished with
extra sliced chilli.*

Chicken tikka masala

Serves **6**   Preparation time **20 minutes (+ overnight marinating)**   Cooking time **8 hours**

1.5 kg (3 lb 5 oz) skinless chicken thigh fillets, trimmed of fat
2 x 400 g (14 oz) tins chopped tomatoes
1 large brown onion, finely diced
½ teaspoon chilli powder
½ teaspoon ground ginger
125 ml (4 fl oz/½ cup) thick (double/heavy) cream
Coriander (cilantro) leaves, to garnish
Steamed rice and mango chutney, to serve

Marinade
260 g (9¼ oz/1 cup) Greek yoghurt
2 tablespoons lemon juice
2 tablespoons tomato paste (concentrated purée)
5 garlic cloves, crushed
1 tablespoon finely grated fresh ginger
2 teaspoons ground cumin
2 teaspoons ground coriander
1 teaspoon garam masala
1 teaspoon ground turmeric
2 teaspoons sugar
1 teaspoon sea salt
½ teaspoon ground cardamom

1 In a large bowl, mix together all the marinade ingredients. Add the chicken and toss to coat. Cover and refrigerate overnight, or for at least 6 hours.

2 Place the tomatoes, onion, chilli powder and ginger in a 5.5 litre (192 fl oz/22 cup) slow cooker and mix together. Stir in the chicken and marinade.

3 Cover and cook on low for 8 hours.

4 Stir the cream through the curry. Garnish with coriander and serve with steamed rice, with mango chutney to the side.

⚙ *Tip: A mint and chilli raita is lovely with this dish. Place ⅓ cup emint, 2 crushed garlic cloves, 1 long seeded and finely chopped fresh green chilli, 1 teaspoon ground cumin and 1 tablespoon Greek-style yoghurt in a food processor and blend until smooth. Add another 200 g (7 oz/ ¾ cup) Greek-style yoghurt and process until just combined. Season to taste and refrigerate until required.*

Chicken and lentil curry

Serves **4**   Preparation time **25 minutes (+ 3 hours marinating)**   Cooking time **4 hours 10 minutes**

1 kg (2 lb 4 oz) skinless chicken thigh fillets

2 tablespoons purchased Indian curry paste (see Tip)

2 garlic cloves, finely chopped

2 teaspoons finely grated fresh ginger

1 long fresh red chilli, seeded and finely chopped

8 spring onions (scallions), sliced diagonally

1 green capsicum (pepper), sliced

350 g (12 oz) purple sweet potato, cut into 3 cm (1¼ inch) chunks

400 g (14 oz) tin chopped tomatoes

125 ml (4 fl oz/½ cup) good-quality chicken stock

400 g (14 oz) tin green or brown lentils, drained and rinsed

Coriander (cilantro) sprigs, to garnish

Lime cheeks, steamed basmati rice and Greek-style yoghurt, to serve

1 Trim the chicken of any fat, then cut each thigh into quarters.

2 In a large bowl, mix together the curry paste, garlic, ginger and chilli. Add the chicken and mix until well coated. Cover and marinate in the refrigerator for 3 hours.

3 Add the spring onion, capsicum, sweet potato, tomatoes and stock to the chicken mixture. Gently toss together, then transfer to a 5.5 litre (192 fl oz/22 cup) slow cooker. Cover and cook on high for 4 hours, or until the chicken and sweet potato are tender.

4 Stir the lentils through the chicken mixture. Cover and cook for a further 10 minutes, or until the lentils are warmed through.

5 Garnish with coriander sprigs. Serve with lime cheeks, steamed rice and a small bowl of yoghurt.

⚙ *Tip: Add a little more curry paste if you prefer a stronger flavour. You can use any flavoured curry paste for this dish such as Madras.*

Lamb vindaloo

Serves **4–6**   Preparation time **25 minutes (+ 20 minutes soaking + 2 hours marinating)**
Cooking time **6 hours 15 minutes**

3–4 long dried red chillies
2 teaspoons mustard seeds
6 garlic cloves, chopped
1 tablespoon chopped fresh ginger
4 fresh bay leaves, torn
80 ml (2½ fl oz/⅓ cup) apple
   cider vinegar
½ teaspoon freshly ground
   black pepper
1 kg (2 lb 4 oz) boneless lamb
   shoulder, trimmed of fat and
   cut into 4 cm (1½ inch) chunks
40 g (1½ oz) ghee
2 brown onions, thinly sliced
3 tablespoons purchased vindaloo
   paste
2 tomatoes, chopped
2 teaspoons brown sugar
2 teaspoons sea salt
Steamed basmati rice, to serve

Raita
200 g (7 oz/¾ cup) plain yoghurt
½ Lebanese (short) cucumber,
   peeled and grated
½ teaspoon sea salt
¼ teaspoon freshly ground
   black pepper
A pinch of cayenne pepper

1 Soak the chillies in hot water for 20 minutes, then drain.

2 Grind the mustard seeds to a fine powder using a mortar and pestle or spice grinder and set aside. Pound or grind the chillies, garlic, ginger, bay leaves and 60 ml (2 fl oz/ ¼ cup) of the vinegar to a smooth paste. Transfer to a large bowl, add the black pepper and ground mustard seeds and mix to combine. Add the lamb and mix until well coated. Cover and marinate in the refrigerator for 2 hours.

3 Drain the lamb, reserving the marinade. Heat the ghee in the insert pan of a 5 litre (175 fl oz/20 cup) slow cooker or a frying pan over high heat. Add the onion and cook for 7–8 minutes, or until golden. Add the vindaloo paste and cook for 2 minutes.

4 Add the lamb and cook for 2–3 minutes, or until the lamb starts to change colour. Add the tomatoes, sugar, salt, remaining vinegar, reserved marinade and 80 ml (2½ fl oz/⅓ cup) water. Stir well to combine.

5 Return the insert pan, if using, to the slow cooker, or transfer the lamb mixture to the slow cooker. Cover and cook on low for 6 hours, or until the lamb is tender.

6 Near serving time, combine all the raita ingredients in a bowl and mix well.

7 Serve the curry with the raita and steamed rice.

Lamb saag

Serves **4**   Preparation time **30 minutes (+ overnight marinating)**   Cooking time **5 hours**

1 kg (2 lb 4 oz) boneless lamb leg
   or shoulder
1 teaspoon fenugreek seeds
1 teaspoon cumin seeds
1 teaspoon mustard seeds
2 brown onions, diced
2 garlic cloves, finely chopped
2 teaspoons finely grated fresh
   ginger
2 small fresh red chillies, seeded and
   finely diced
2 cinnamon sticks
4 curry leaves
250 ml (9 fl oz/1 cup) good-quality
   beef stock
400 g (14 oz) baby English spinach
   leaves
Steamed basmati rice, to serve

Coriander yoghurt
130 g (4½ oz/½ cup) Greek-style
   yoghurt
1 tablespoon lemon juice
¼ cup coriander (cilantro) leaves,
   chopped

1 Trim the lamb of excess fat, then cut into 3 cm
   (1¼ inch) chunks. Place in a large bowl.

2 Using a mortar and pestle or spice grinder, pound
   or grind the fenugreek, cumin and mustard seeds.
   Combine in a small bowl with the onion, garlic, ginger
   and chilli. Stir the spice mixture through the lamb
   and mix until well coated. Cover and marinate in the
   refrigerator overnight.

3 Transfer the lamb and marinade to a 4.5 litre
   (157 fl oz/18 cup) slow cooker. Add the cinnamon
   sticks and curry leaves, then pour in the stock.
   Cover and cook on high for 4 hours.

4 Stir in the spinach, then cover and cook for a further
   1 hour, or until the lamb is tender.

5 Near serving time, combine the coriander yoghurt
   ingredients in a small bowl.

6 Serve the curry with the coriander yoghurt and
   steamed rice.

Lamb madras

Serves **4**   Preparation time **25 minutes (+ 2 hours marinating)**   Cooking time **4 hours**

1 kg (2 lb 4 oz) boneless lamb leg or shoulder
3 tablespoons purchased madras curry paste
1 brown onion, finely chopped
6 cardamom pods
4 whole cloves
2 dried bay leaves
1 cinnamon stick
200 g (7 oz/¾ cup) Greek-style yoghurt
¼ teaspoon garam masala
2 long fresh red chillies, chopped (optional)
Steamed rice, to serve

1 Trim the lamb of excess fat, then cut into 3 cm (1¼ inch) chunks. Place in a large bowl. Stir the curry paste through the lamb and mix until well coated. Cover and marinate in the refrigerator for 2 hours, or overnight.

2 Put the lamb in a 4.5 litre (157 fl oz/18 cup) slow cooker with the onion, cardamom pods, cloves, bay leaves, cinnamon stick and yoghurt. Gently mix together.

3 Cover and cook on high for 4 hours, or until the lamb is tender and cooked through.

4 Season to taste with sea salt and sprinkle with the garam masala. Garnish with chilli, if desired, and serve with steamed rice.

Rogan josh

Serves **6**   Preparation time **20 minutes (+ 2 hours marinating)**   Cooking time **6 hours**

1 kg (2 lb 4 oz) boneless lamb leg
   or shoulder
3 garlic cloves, crushed
6 cm (2½ inch) piece fresh ginger,
   peeled and finely grated
2 teaspoons ground cumin
1 teaspoon chilli powder
2 teaspoons paprika
2 teaspoons ground coriander
1 onion, finely chopped
6 cardamom pods, crushed
4 whole cloves
2 dried bay leaves
1 cinnamon stick
200 g (7 oz/¾ cup) plain yoghurt
4 saffron threads
2 tablespoons milk
½ teaspoon garam masala
Steamed rice, to serve
Coriander (cilantro) sprigs, to garnish

1 Trim the lamb of excess fat, then cut into 4 cm (1½ inch) chunks.

2 In a large bowl, mix together the garlic, ginger, cumin, chilli powder, paprika and ground coriander. Add the lamb and mix until well coated. Cover and marinate in the refrigerator for at least 2 hours, or overnight.

3 Transfer the lamb mixture to a 4.5 litre (157 fl oz/ 18 cup) slow cooker. Stir in the onion, cardamom, cloves, bay leaves, cinnamon stick, yoghurt and 60 ml (2 fl oz/¼ cup) water. Cover and cook on low for 6 hours, or until the lamb is tender.

4 Near serving time, combine the saffron with the milk and set aside to soak for 10 minutes.

5 Just before serving, stir the saffron milk and garam masala through the curry. Season to taste with sea salt and freshly ground black pepper.

6 Garnish with coriander and serve with steamed rice.

Lamb korma

Serves **4–6** Preparation time **20 minutes** Cooking time **3 hours 10 minutes**

1 kg (2 lb 4 oz) boneless lamb leg
  or shoulder
2 tablespoons Greek-style yoghurt
3 tablespoons purchased korma
  paste
2 brown onions
2 tablespoons desiccated coconut
3 long fresh green chillies, roughly
  chopped
4 garlic cloves, crushed
5 cm (2 inch) piece fresh ginger,
  peeled and finely grated
50 g (1¾ oz/⅓ cup) cashew nuts
6 whole cloves
¼ teaspoon ground cinnamon
125 ml (4 fl oz/½ cup) good-quality
  chicken stock
6 cardamom pods, crushed
2 tablespoons pouring cream
Coriander (cilantro) leaves,
  to garnish
Steamed rice, to serve

1 Trim the lamb of excess fat, then cut into 2.5 cm (1 inch) chunks. Place in a large bowl. Add the yoghurt and korma paste and mix until well coated.

2 Coarsely chop one onion and thinly slice the other. Put the chopped onion in a food processor with the coconut, chilli, garlic, ginger, cashews, cloves and cinnamon. Pour in the stock and process to form a smooth paste. Alternatively, finely chop the ingredients with a knife before adding the stock.

3 Mix the spice mixture through the lamb with the sliced onion, cardamom and a pinch of sea salt.

4 Transfer the mixture to a 4.5 litre (157 fl oz/18 cup) slow cooker. Cover and cook on high for 3 hours, or until the lamb is tender.

5 Stir the cream through the curry, then cover and cook for a further 10 minutes. Season to taste with sea salt and freshly ground black pepper.

6 Garnish with coriander and serve with steamed rice.

Jamaican lamb with sweet potato mash

Serves **4** Preparation time **20 minutes** Cooking time **6 hours**

1 kg (2 lb 4 oz) boneless lamb leg
   or shoulder
Finely grated zest of 1 lime
60 ml (2 fl oz/¼ cup) lime juice
60 ml (2 fl oz/¼ cup) olive oil
3 garlic cloves, crushed
2 teaspoons ground cumin
1½ teaspoons cayenne pepper,
   or to taste
1 teaspoon ground allspice
1 teaspoon ground white pepper
1 teaspoon ground cinnamon
1 tablespoon thyme leaves
Lime cheeks, to serve

Sweet potato mash
900 g (2 lb) sweet potato, peeled and
   cut into 3 cm (1¼ inch) chunks
1 teaspoon ground cinnamon
40 g (1½ oz) butter

Mango and red chilli salsa
1 mango, finely diced
2 spring onions (scallions), finely
   chopped
1 small fresh red chilli, finely
   chopped

1 Trim the lamb of excess fat, then cut into 4 cm (1½ inch) chunks. Place in a 5.5 litre (192 fl oz/22 cup) slow cooker with the lime zest, lime juice, olive oil, garlic, ground spices and thyme. Gently mix to coat the lamb.

2 Cover and cook on low for 5–6 hours, or until the lamb is tender, aromatic and has a little browning on top.

3 Near serving time, make the sweet potato mash. Bring a saucepan of water to the boil, then place the sweet potato in a steamer basket and set it over the saucepan. Steam the sweet potato for 10–15 minutes, or until tender. Place in a bowl, mash using a potato masher, then stir the cinnamon and butter through.

4 Put the mango and red chilli salsa ingredients in a small bowl and gently mix together.

5 Spoon the sweet potato mash into wide shallow bowls. Ladle the lamb mixture over the top. Serve with the salsa, with lime cheeks for squeezing over.

⚙ *Tip: To get the most juice from limes or other citrus fruit, heat them in a microwave for 20 seconds before juicing. If you're in a hurry you can cook the lamb on high, reducing the cooking time to 3½ hours. You can also serve the finished dish drizzled with a little coconut milk.*

Tamarind lamb

Serves **4**   Preparation time **20 minutes**   Cooking time **8 hours 15 minutes**

60 ml (2 fl oz/¼ cup) tamarind pulp
2 garlic cloves, crushed
1 tablespoon garam masala
1 teaspoon chilli flakes
1 teaspoon shrimp paste
1 teaspoon sugar
1 teaspoon freshly ground black
   pepper
½ teaspoon ground turmeric
2 tablespoons vegetable oil
1 kg (2 lb 4 oz) boneless lamb leg
   or shoulder, trimmed of excess
   fat and cut into 2 cm (¾ inch)
   chunks
2 large brown onions, coarsely
   chopped
500 ml (17 fl oz/2 cups) good-quality
   chicken stock
Coriander (cilantro) sprigs, to garnish
Lime wedges, to serve

Lemon couscous
375 ml (13 fl oz/1½ cups) good-
   quality chicken stock
40 g (1½ oz) butter
280 g (10 oz/1½ cups) instant
   couscous
1 teaspoon finely grated lemon zest
1½ tablespoons lemon juice

1 Put the tamarind pulp in a small bowl. Pour in 125 ml (4 fl oz/½ cup) hot water and mix well. Leave to soak for 5 minutes, then strain the mixture through a fine sieve into another small bowl, pressing on the solids with a spoon to extract all the pulp. Discard the solids.

2 Stir the garlic, garam masala, chilli flakes, shrimp paste, sugar, pepper and turmeric into the tamarind water and set aside.

3 Heat the oil in the insert pan of a 5.5 litre (192 fl oz/ 22 cup) slow cooker or a frying pan over medium–high heat. Add the lamb in batches and fry for 2–3 minutes, or until brown on all sides, removing each batch to a plate.

4 Return the insert pan, if using, to the slow cooker. Place all the lamb in the slow cooker. Scatter the onion over the lamb, then pour in the tamarind mixture and stock. Cover and cook on low for 8 hours.

5 Near serving time, prepare the lemon couscous. Bring the stock to the boil in a saucepan. Remove from the heat, add the butter and stir until melted. Place the couscous in a heatproof bowl with the lemon zest and lemon juice. Season well with sea salt and freshly ground black pepper and pour the hot stock over. Cover with a tea towel (dish towel) and leave to stand for 5 minutes, or until the liquid has been absorbed. Fluff up the grains with a fork.

6 Spoon the couscous into wide shallow bowls. Ladle the lamb mixture over the top. Garnish with coriander and serve with lime wedges.

Beef rendang

Serves **4–6**   Preparation time **25 minutes**   Cooking time **6 hours 20 minutes**

30 g (1 oz/⅓ cup) desiccated coconut
2 lemongrass stems, white part only, chopped
2 tablespoons chopped fresh ginger
3 cm (1¼ inch) piece fresh galangal, peeled and chopped
5 garlic cloves, chopped
4 long fresh red chillies
1 brown onion, chopped
60 ml (2 fl oz/¼ cup) peanut oil
1 kg (2 lb 4 oz) chuck steak or gravy beef, trimmed of excess fat and cut into 4 cm (1½ inch) chunks
2 teaspoons ground coriander
1 teaspoon ground cumin
2 teaspoons grated palm sugar (jaggery) or brown sugar
2 teaspoons tamarind purée
1 cinnamon stick
1 teaspoon sea salt
270 ml (9½ fl oz) tin coconut milk
Steamed rice, to serve

1 Toast the coconut in a small dry frying pan over medium heat until golden, tossing often so it doesn't burn. Remove from the pan and set aside.

2 Put the lemongrass, ginger, galangal and garlic in a small food processor and blend to a smooth paste. Cut two of the chillies in half lengthways, then scrape out and discard the seeds. Roughly chop all four chillies and add to the food processor with the onion. Blend until smooth.

3 Heat the peanut oil in the insert pan of a 5 litre (175 fl oz/20 cup) slow cooker or a frying pan over medium–high heat. Cook the spice paste for 7–8 minutes, or until aromatic. Increase the heat to high, add the beef and cook for 4–5 minutes, or until browned all over. Add the coriander, cumin and toasted coconut and cook for a further 1 minute.

4 Return the insert pan, if using, to the slow cooker, or transfer the mixture to the slow cooker. Add the palm sugar, tamarind purée, cinnamon stick, salt and coconut milk, then stir to combine.

5 Cover and cook on low for 6 hours, or until the oil has separated from the sauce and the beef is tender.

6 Season to taste with sea salt and freshly ground black pepper and serve with steamed rice.

Massaman beef curry with chunky potatoes and peanuts

Serves **8**   Preparation time **25 minutes**   Cooking time **8 hours 30 minutes**

2 tablespoons vegetable or
   peanut oil
1.5 kg (3 lb 5 oz) beef, such as
   beef brisket or chuck steak,
   trimmed of excess fat and cut
   into 4 cm (1½ inch) chunks
400 ml (14 fl oz) tin coconut cream
130 g (4½ oz/½ cup) purchased
   massaman or yellow curry paste
2 cinnamon sticks
2 star anise
2 cardamom pods, bruised
1 fresh bay leaf
4 waxy potatoes, about 180 g
   (6 oz) each, peeled and cut
   into large chunks
2 brown onions, coarsely chopped
2 x 400 ml (14 fl oz) tins coconut
   milk
2 tablespoons fish sauce
2 tablespoons brown sugar
2 tablespoons tamarind concentrate
1 tablespoon lime juice, or to taste
80 g (2¾ oz/½ cup) toasted peanuts,
   plus extra, to serve
Coriander (cilantro) sprigs and sliced
   fresh red chilli, to garnish
Steamed rice, to serve

1 Heat the oil in the insert pan of a 7 litre (245 fl oz/ 28 cup) slow cooker or a large frying pan over high heat. Add the beef in batches and cook for 3–5 minutes, or until browned all over. Remove and set aside.

2 Reduce the heat to medium–low. Add the coconut cream and cook for 5–6 minutes, or until it splits. Stir in the curry paste, spices and bay leaf and cook for 1–2 minutes, or until aromatic. Stir in the potato and onion and cook, stirring occasionally, for 3–4 minutes, or until the vegetables begin to soften.

3 Return the insert pan, if using, to the slow cooker, or transfer the mixture to the slow cooker. Add the coconut milk and all the beef. Cover and cook on low for 8 hours, or until the beef is very tender.

4 Stir in the fish sauce, sugar, tamarind concentrate and lime juice, to taste. Adjust the seasonings — the curry should be sweet, salty and sour. Stir the peanuts through.

5 Garnish with coriander and chilli, scatter some extra peanuts over the top and serve with steamed rice.

Chilli con carne

Serves **6**   Preparation time **20 minutes**   Cooking time **8 hours 15 minutes**

1 tablespoon olive oil
1 large brown onion, finely chopped
750 g (1 lb 10 oz) minced (ground) beef
250 g (9 oz) bacon slices, trimmed and chopped
2 garlic cloves, chopped
1 long fresh red chilli, thinly sliced
1 teaspoon ground cumin
½ teaspoon chilli flakes
¼ teaspoon chilli powder
1 red capsicum (pepper), finely diced
2 x 400 g (14 oz) tins chopped tomatoes
2 x 400 g (14 oz) tins red kidney beans, drained and rinsed
1 teaspoon sea salt
Warmed tortillas or corn chips, sour cream, grated cheddar cheese and chopped coriander (cilantro) leaves, to serve

1 Heat the olive oil in the insert pan of a 5 litre (175 fl oz/ 20 cup) slow cooker or a large frying pan over medium–high heat. Add the onion and cook for 3 minutes, or until softened. Add the beef and cook for 3 minutes, using a wooden spoon to break up any lumps.

2 Add the bacon and cook for a further 3 minutes, or until browned. Stir in the garlic, chilli, cumin, chilli flakes and chilli powder and cook, stirring, for 1–2 minutes.

3 Return the insert pan, if using, to the slow cooker, or transfer the beef mixture to the slow cooker. Add the capsicum, tomatoes, kidney beans and salt, stirring to combine. Cover and cook on low for 8 hours or until well cooked.

4 Season to taste with sea salt and freshly ground black pepper. Serve with warmed tortillas or corn chips, and small bowls of sour cream, grated cheddar and coriander for adding to the dish.

Pork vindaloo

Serves **4**   Preparation time **25 minutes (+ 3 hours marinating)**   Cooking time **3 hours 30 minutes**

6 cardamom pods
1 teaspoon black peppercorns
4 small dried red chillies
1 teaspoon whole cloves
10 cm (4 inch) cinnamon stick, coarsely broken
1 teaspoon cumin seeds
½ teaspoon coriander seeds
¼ teaspoon fenugreek seeds
½ teaspoon ground turmeric
80 ml (2½ fl oz/⅓ cup) white wine vinegar
1 tablespoon balsamic vinegar
800 g (1 lb 12 oz) boneless pork leg
2 brown onions, thinly sliced
10 garlic cloves, thinly sliced
5 cm (2 inch) piece fresh ginger, peeled and cut into matchsticks
250 ml (9 fl oz/1 cup) tomato passata (puréed tomatoes)
4 long fresh green chillies, seeded and chopped
1 teaspoon grated palm sugar (jaggery) or brown sugar
Steamed rice, to serve

1 Split open the cardamom pods and remove the seeds; discard the empty pods. Using a mortar and pestle or a spice grinder, finely pound or grind the cardamom seeds, peppercorns, dried chillies, cloves, cinnamonstick, cumin seeds, coriander seeds, fenugreek seeds and turmeric.

2 Tip the ground spices into a large bowl. Stir in the white wine vinegar and balsamic vinegar.

3 Trim the pork leg of any excess fat, then cut into 2.5 cm (1 inch) chunks. Add to the spice mixture and mix until well coated. Cover and marinate in the refrigerator for 3 hours.

4 Transfer the pork mixture to a 4.5 litre (157 fl oz/18 cup) slow cooker and add the onion, garlic, ginger, passata, fresh chilli and palm sugar. Gently mix together.

5 Cover and cook on high for 3½ hours, or until the pork is very tender. Serve with steamed rice.

Vietnamese beef brisket

Serves **4**   Preparation time **20 minutes**   Cooking time **7 hours**

1.5 kg (3 lb 5 oz) beef brisket
2 carrots, thinly sliced
2 lemongrass stems, white part only, chopped
2 long fresh red chillies, seeded and sliced diagonally
10 cm (4 inch) piece fresh ginger, peeled and cut into matchsticks
60 ml (2 fl oz/¼ cup) soy sauce
2 tablespoons fish sauce
2 tablespoons lime juice
100 g (3½ oz) bean sprouts, tails trimmed
Quartered cherry tomatoes, Vietnamese mint and small basil leaves, to garnish
Steamed jasmine rice, to serve

1 Trim the beef of excess fat, then cut into 3 cm (1¼ inch) chunks. Place in a 5.5 litre (192 fl oz/22 cup) slow cooker with the carrot, lemongrass, chilli, ginger, soy sauce and fish sauce. Gently mix together.

2 Cover and cook for 6 hours on low. Skim any fat from the surface of the sauce, then stir in the lime juice.

3 Turn the slow cooker setting to high, then cover and cook for a further 1 hour.

4 Scatter the bean sprouts over the top. Garnish with the cherry tomatoes, Vietnamese mint and basil and serve with steamed rice.

Tip: This dish may also be served with rice noodles. Simply cover 300 g (10½ oz) rice noodles with boiling water and allow to soak for 5 minutes, or until softened, then drain and rinse. Before serving with the beef brisket, stir some chopped coriander (cilantro) leaves through the noodles if desired.

Caramelised pork curry

Serves 6   Preparation time **20 minutes**   Cooking time **6 hours 25 minutes**

2 tablespoons caster (superfine) sugar
60 ml (2 fl oz/¼ cup) fish sauce
3 teaspoons tamarind purée
3 garlic cloves, crushed
1 lemongrass stem, white part only, finely chopped
½ teaspoon freshly ground black pepper
2 teaspoons finely grated palm sugar (jaggery) or brown sugar
1 kg (2 lb 4 oz) pork shoulder, trimmed of excess fat and cut into 4 cm (1½ inch) chunks
450 g (1 lb) pumpkin (winter squash), peeled, seeded and cut into 3 cm (1¼ inch) chunks
150 g (5½ oz) green beans, trimmed and cut into 5 cm (2 inch) lengths
3 teaspoons finely shredded fresh ginger
2 tablespoons coriander (cilantro) leaves, chopped
Steamed rice, to serve

1 Put the caster sugar and 1 tablespoon water in the insert pan of a 5 litre (175 fl oz/20 cup) slow cooker or a frying pan over medium–high heat. Cook for 7–8 minutes, or until the caramel is lightly golden.

2 Add the fish sauce, tamarind purée, garlic, lemongrass, black pepper, palm sugar, pork and 185 ml (6 fl oz/¾ cup) water. Stir to combine.

3 Return the insert pan, if using, to the slow cooker, or transfer the pork mixture to the slow cooker. Cover and cook on low for 4 hours.

4 Stir in the pumpkin, then cover and cook for a further 2 hours, or until the pork is very tender and the pumpkin is just cooked.

5 Add the beans and ginger and stir to combine. Cover and cook for 15 minutes, or until the beans are tender.

6 Stir the coriander through the curry and season to taste with sea salt and freshly ground black pepper. Serve with steamed rice.

Pork and lemongrass curry

Serves **4**   Preparation time **15 minutes**   Cooking time **6 hours 20 minutes**

1 tablespoon peanut oil

1 kg (2 lb 4 oz) pork shoulder, trimmed of excess fat and cut into 2 cm (¾ inch) chunks

270 ml (9½ fl oz) tin coconut cream

40 g (1½ oz/¼ cup) toasted peanuts, chopped

Chopped mint and thinly sliced fresh red chilli, to garnish

Lime wedges and steamed jasmine rice, to serve

Lemongrass curry paste

1 brown onion, chopped

2 garlic cloves, chopped

2 fresh red bird's eye chillies, chopped

2 red Asian shallots, peeled and chopped (see Tip)

3 tablespoons chopped lemongrass, white part only

½ cup coriander (cilantro) leaves, chopped

2 tablespoons green curry paste

1 Put the lemongrass curry paste ingredients in a food processor with 2 tablespoons water. Blend to a smooth paste and set aside.

2 Heat the peanut oil in the insert pan of a 5.5 litre (192 fl oz/22 cup) slow cooker or a large frying pan over medium heat. Add the pork in batches and fry for 5 minutes, turning to brown all over, and transferring each batch to a bowl.

3 Return the insert pan, if using. to the slow cooker. Transfer all the pork to the slow cooker, along with any pan juices from the pork. Add the lemongrass curry paste, pour in the coconut cream and gently mix together. Cover and cook on low for 6 hours.

4 Sprinkle with the peanuts, mint and chilli. Serve with lime wedges and steamed rice.

⚙ *Tip: Red Asian shallots are small purplish-red onions that resemble French shallots (eschalots). If unavailable, use ½ small chopped red or brown onion in the lemongrass curry paste.*

Mojo pork

Serves **6**   Preparation time **20 minutes**   Cooking time **8 hours**

1.5 kg (3 lb 5 oz) boneless pork loin
2 teaspoons dried oregano
1 teaspoon chilli flakes
½ teaspoon freshly ground black
   pepper
2 tablespoons olive oil
1 large red onion, thinly sliced
2 x 400 g (14 oz) tins chopped
   tomatoes
60 ml (2 fl oz/¼ cup) lime juice
60 ml (2 fl oz/¼ cup) orange juice
250 ml (9 fl oz/1 cup) good-quality
   chicken stock
Coriander (cilantro) leaves,
   to garnish

Bean and orange salad

2 oranges, peel and white pith
   removed, cut into segments
300 g (10½ oz) tin butterbeans
   (lima beans), drained and rinsed
300 g (10½ oz) tin chickpeas,
   drained and rinsed
1 red onion, halved and thinly sliced
¼ cup coriander (cilantro) leaves,
   chopped
2 tablespoons olive oil
2 tablespoons red wine vinegar
A pinch of caster (superfine) sugar

1 Remove the rind and fat from the pork loin, then cut the meat into 2 cm (¾ inch) chunks. Place in a 5.5 litre (192 fl oz/22 cup) slow cooker and sprinkle with the oregano, chilli flakes and pepper. Drizzle with the olive oil and gently mix to coat.

2 Add the onion and tomatoes, then pour in the lime juice, orange juice and stock. Cover and cook on low for 6–8 hours, or until the pork is tender.

3 Near serving time, make the bean and orange salad. In a salad bowl, toss together the orange segments, beans, chickpeas, onion and coriander. Whisk together the oil, vinegar and sugar until the sugar has dissolved. Season to taste with sea salt and freshly ground black pepper, drizzle over the salad and gently toss.

4 Sprinkle the pork mixture with coriander and serve with the bean and orange salad.

⚙ *Tip: 'Mojo' refers to a sauce that contains spices and citrus juice (generally lime and/or orange juice). It is used in Cuban cooking.*

Spicy fish curry

Serves **4**   Preparation time **20 minutes**   Cooking time **2 hours 30 minutes**

400 ml (14 fl oz) tin coconut milk
5 long fresh green chillies, seeded
  and chopped
2 small dried red chillies, chopped
½ cinnamon stick
2 teaspoons finely grated fresh
  ginger
2 garlic cloves, finely chopped
4 curry leaves (optional)
1 teaspoon ground turmeric
¼ teaspoon chilli powder
1 teaspoon purchased curry powder
2 tomatoes, finely chopped
250 ml (9 fl oz/1 cup) good-quality
  fish or chicken stock
800 g (1 lb 12 oz) snapper or other
  firm white fish fillets, diced
2 spring onions (scallions), sliced
  diagonally
Juice of 2 limes, or to taste
Steamed rice, to serve

1 Pour the coconut milk into a 4.5 litre (157 fl oz/18 cup) slow cooker. Add the fresh green chilli, dried red chilli, cinnamon stick, ginger, garlic, curry leaves if using, turmeric, chilli powder, curry powder, tomato and stock. Stir to combine, then cover and cook on low for 2 hours, or until the flavours have developed.

2 Add the fish and gently mix to coat. Cover and cook for a further 30 minutes, or until the fish is cooked through and flakes when tested with a fork.

3 Stir half the spring onion and most of the lime juice through, then taste to see if more lime juice is needed.

4 Garnish with the remaining spring onion and serve with steamed rice.

Sri Lankan fish curry

Serves **6**   Preparation time **15 minutes**   Cooking time **3 hours**

1 brown onion, cut into wedges
2 long fresh green chillies, halved
    lengthways, seeded and
    chopped
2 garlic cloves, finely chopped
1 tablespoon purchased Indian curry
    powder
2 cm (¾ inch) piece fresh ginger,
    peeled and cut into matchsticks
1 cinnamon stick
1 small handful curry leaves
2 teaspoons tamarind purée
400 ml (14 fl oz) tin coconut milk
125 ml (4 fl oz/½ cup) good-quality
    chicken or fish stock
900 g (2 lb) firm white fish fillets,
    such as ling
2 tablespoons lime juice
2 tomatoes, seeded and finely
    chopped, to garnish
Coriander (cilantro) leaves,
    to garnish
Steamed rice and lime wedges,
    to serve

1 Put the onion, chilli, garlic, curry powder, ginger, cinnamon stick and curry leaves in a 5.5 litre (192 fl oz/ 22 cup) slow cooker. Drizzle the tamarind purée over the top. Pour in the coconut milk and stock and mix together. Add the fish and gently mix to coat. Cover and cook on low for 3 hours.

2 Stir the lime juice through the curry and season well with sea salt and freshly ground black pepper.

3 Garnish with chopped tomato and coriander. Serve with steamed rice, with lime wedges on the side for squeezing over.

Braises

Spring chicken pot-au-feu

Serves **4** Preparation time **25 minutes** Cooking time **2 hours 45 minutes**

1.8 kg (4 lb) whole chicken, briefly
rinsed

1.5 litres (52 fl oz/6 cups) good-
quality chicken stock

8 small new potatoes, peeled
and halved

12 baby carrots, trimmed

2 thyme sprigs

1 fresh bay leaf

8 baby leeks, trimmed

Chopped flat-leaf (Italian) parsley,
to garnish

Extra virgin olive oil, for drizzling

1 Tie the legs of the chicken together securely with kitchen
string and tuck under the wings. Put the chicken breast
side up in a 5 litre (175 fl oz/20 cup) slow cooker. Add the
stock, potatoes, carrots, thyme sprigs and bay leaf. Cover
and cook on low for 1½–2 hours, or until the chicken is
almost cooked through.

2 Add the leeks, then cover and cook for 30–45 minutes,
or until the chicken is tender and the juices run clear
when the thigh is pierced with a skewer.

3 Remove and discard the thyme sprigs and bay leaf.
Carefully take out the chicken, remove the string
and leave to rest for 5 minutes before carving.

4 Stir the broth, then season to taste with sea salt and
freshly ground black pepper.

5 Serve the chicken with the vegetables and broth,
garnished with parsley and drizzled with olive oil.

⚙ *Tip: Tarragon would also be a lovely herb to add to this dish,
being a classic match with chicken.*

Chicken with 40 cloves of garlic

Serves **4**   Preparation time **20 minutes**   Cooking time **2 hours 35 minutes**

1.8 kg (4 lb) whole chicken
1 lemon, halved
2 tablespoons olive oil
40 unpeeled cloves garlic (from about 3 whole garlic bulbs)
150 ml (5 fl oz) dry white wine
1 fresh bay leaf
½ bunch thyme sprigs
1 leek, white part only, coarsely chopped
Green salad, to serve

1 Briefly rinse the chicken inside and out and pat dry with paper towels. Place the lemon halves in the cavity of the chicken, then season the bird with sea salt and freshly ground black pepper. Tie the legs together securely with kitchen string and tuck under the wings.

2 Heat the olive oil in the insert pan of a 5 litre (175 fl oz/ 20 cup) slow cooker or a frying pan over medium–high heat. Add the chicken, breast side down. Cook, turning once, for 3–4 minutes, or until golden.

3 Return the insert pan, if using, to the slow cooker, or transfer the chicken, breast side up, to the slow cooker. Add the remaining ingredients except the green salad.

4 Cover and cook on high for 2–2½ hours, or until the chicken is tender and the juices run clear when the thigh is pierced with a skewer. Remove the string.

5 Allow the chicken to rest for 5 minutes before carving. Serve with the garlic cloves, juices and a green salad to the side.

⚙ *Tip: A bitter green leaf salad with a tangy mustard dressing would pair well with the chicken.*

Braised chicken with potatoes, lemon and olives

Serves **4** Preparation time **20 minutes** Cooking time **2 hours 10 minutes**

2 tablespoons olive oil

4 chicken drumsticks, plus 4 chicken thigh fillets, with the skin and bones

400 g (14 oz) small potatoes, peeled and halved

2 red onions, cut into wedges

4 garlic cloves, crushed

400 g (14 oz) tin chopped or cherry tomatoes

1 lemon, quartered

8 thyme sprigs

2 teaspoons smoked paprika

90 g (3¼ oz/½ cup) unpitted black olives

2 tablespoons sherry vinegar

Coarsely chopped flat-leaf (Italian) parsley, to serve

1 Heat the olive oil in the insert pan of a 7 litre (245 fl oz/ 28 cup) slow cooker or a large frying pan over medium– high heat. Add the chicken pieces, skin side down. Cook, turning once, for 3–4 minutes, or until golden, then transfer to a plate. Add the potato, onion and garlic and cook, stirring occasionally, for 3–4 minutes, or until the mixture is golden.

2 Add the chicken and return the insert pan, if using, to the slow cooker, or transfer all the chicken and vegetables to the slow cooker. Add the tomatoes, lemon quarters, thyme sprigs, paprika, olives and half the vinegar. Season with sea salt and freshly ground black pepper.

3 Cover and cook on high for 2 hours, or until the chicken is tender and cooked through.

4 Season well and stir in the remaining vinegar, to taste. Scatter with parsley and serve.

Chicken cooked in white wine

Serves **4**   Preparation time **20 minutes**   Cooking time **6 hours**

30 g (1 oz/½ cup, lightly packed)
   fresh breadcrumbs
4 garlic cloves, crushed
3 rosemary sprigs, leaves removed
   and chopped
1 teaspoon finely grated lemon zest
1.5 kg (3 lb 5 oz) whole chicken
200 ml (7 fl oz) good-quality
   chicken stock
200 ml (7 fl oz) white wine

1 Combine the breadcrumbs, garlic, rosemary and lemon zest in a small bowl to make a stuffing.

2 Rinse the chicken inside and out and pat dry with paper towels. Loosely push the stuffing into the cavity of the chicken, then tie or skewer the legs together to secure the stuffing inside the chicken. Put the chicken, breast side down, in a 4.5 litre (157 fl oz/18 cup) slow cooker.

3 Pour the stock and wine into a small saucepan and bring to the boil. Pour the hot stock mixture over the chicken.

4 Cover and cook on low for 6 hours, or until the chicken is tender and the juices run clear when the thigh is pierced with a skewer.

5 Allow the chicken to rest for 5 minutes before carving.

✿ *Tip: This chicken dish is delicious with steamed buttered potatoes and green vegetables.*

Chicken with tarragon and fennel

Serves **6**   Preparation time **25 minutes**   Cooking time **6 hours 15 minutes**

300 g (10½ oz) kipfler (fingerling)
    potatoes
1 large fennel bulb
1 red onion, peeled
1.8 kg (4 lb) whole chicken
1 lemon, halved
2–3 tablespoons olive oil
4 garlic cloves, finely chopped
3 tarragon sprigs
125 ml (4 fl oz/½ cup) good-quality
    chicken stock
125 ml (4 fl oz/½ cup) verjuice
250 g (9 oz) cherry tomatoes
2 tablespoons chopped flat-leaf
    (Italian) parsley

1 Peel the potatoes and cut into 2 cm (¾ inch) chunks; cover with water and set aside. Remove the tough outer shell of the fennel. Slice the bulb into 8–10 wedges, leaving the root section attached so each wedge doesn't fall apart. Cut the onion into 8–10 wedges, again leaving the root attached.

2 Rinse the chicken inside and out and pat dry with paper towels. Place the lemon halves in the cavity of the chicken. Sprinkle the bird with sea salt and set aside.

3 Heat the olive oil in the insert pan of a 4.5 litre (157 fl oz/ 18 cup) slow cooker or a large frying pan over medium heat. Add the fennel and onion and cook, in batches if necessary, for 5 minutes, or until golden all over. Add the garlic, reduce the heat to low and cook for 2 minutes, or until lightly browned. Remove and set aside.

4 Return the pan to medium heat. Brown the chicken for about 3 minutes on each side, then remove to a plate.

5 Return the insert pan, if using to the slow cooker Transfer the fennel mixture to the slow cooker. Drain the potatoes and spread over the top. Add the tarragon sprigs, then place the chicken on top of the vegetables.

6 Pour in the stock and verjuice and add the tomatoes. Cover and cook on low for 6 hours, or until the chicken is tender and the juices run clear when the thigh is pierced with a skewer.

7 Allow the chicken to rest for 5 minutes before carving. Season with sea salt and freshly ground black pepper and serve with the tomatoes and sprinkled with the parsley.

Chicken braised with ginger and star anise

Serves **4**   Preparation time **15 minutes**   Cooking time **2 hours**

1 kg (2 lb 4 oz) skinless chicken
   thigh fillets
1 teaspoon sichuan peppercorns
3 x 2 cm (1¼ x ¾ inch) piece fresh
   ginger, peeled and shredded
2 garlic cloves, chopped
80 ml (2½ fl oz/⅓ cup) Chinese
   rice wine
60 ml (2 fl oz/¼ cup) light soy sauce
1 tablespoon honey
1 star anise
3 spring onions (scallions), thinly
   sliced diagonally
Steamed rice, to serve

1 Trim the chicken of any fat, then cut each thigh in half. Place in a 4.5 litre (157 fl oz/18 cup) slow cooker with the peppercorns, ginger, garlic, Chinese rice wine, soy sauce, honey and star anise. Gently mix together.

2 Cover and cook on high for 2 hours, or until the chicken is tender and cooked through.

3 Season to taste with sea salt and freshly ground black pepper. Garnish with the spring onion and serve with steamed rice.

Braised duck legs with prunes and caramelised brussels sprouts

Serves **6**   Preparation time **30 minutes**   Cooking time **3 hours 20 minutes**

6 duck legs, about 250 g (9 oz) each
10 small French shallots (eschalots),
    peeled and diced
150 g (5½ oz) speck or pancetta,
    diced
3 garlic cloves, crushed
1 fresh bay leaf
2 rosemary sprigs
250 ml (9 fl oz/1 cup) red wine
100 ml (3½ fl oz) good-quality
    chicken stock
12 pitted prunes
1½ tablespoons red wine vinegar
Coarsely chopped flat-leaf (Italian)
    parsley, to garnish

Caramelised brussels sprouts
1 kg (2 lb 4 oz) brussels sprouts
2 tablespoons olive oil
30 g (1 oz) butter, diced

1   Place the duck legs, skin side down, in the insert pan of a 5 litre (175 fl oz/20 cup) slow cooker or a large frying pan. Cook over medium heat for 5–7 minutes, or until the fat begins to render. Remove and set aside.

2   Heat 2 tablespoons of the duck fat (reserve the rest for another use) over medium heat. Add the shallot and speck and cook for 7–10 minutes, or until the shallot is starting to soften. Stir in the garlic, bay leaf and rosemary sprigs, then add the wine, stock and duck legs and bring to a simmer.

3   Return the insert pan, if using, to the slow cooker, or transfer the duck legs and sauce to the slow cooker. Cover and cook on high for 2 hours.

4   Stir the prunes through, then cover and cook for a further 1 hour, or until the duck is tender.

5   Near serving time, prepare the brussels sprouts. Blanch them in a saucepan of boiling salted water for 2 minutes, until bright green. Drain and refresh in iced water. Drain, cut in half and pat dry with paper towels. Heat the olive oil in a large frying pan over medium heat, add the sprouts, cut side down, and cook for 3 minutes, or until turning golden. Add the butter and stir for 2–3 minutes, or until the sprouts are golden and cooked through. Season to taste.

6   Stir the vinegar through the duck braise and season with sea salt and freshly ground black pepper. Garnish with chopped parsley and serve with the brussels sprouts.

⚙ *Tip: A bowl of braised French-style lentils makes a perfect side dish.*

Confit duck legs with braised red cabbage and hazelnuts

Serves **6**   Preparation time **35 minutes (+ 12 hours curing)**   Cooking time **5 hours**

6 duck legs, about 250 g (9 oz) each
160 g (5¾ oz/½ cup) rock sea salt
5 thyme sprigs
5 juniper berries, coarsely crushed
4 orange zest strips, white pith removed
1 fresh bay leaf
1 kg (2 lb 4 oz) warm duck fat (see Tip)

Braised cabbage
60 ml (2 fl oz/¼ cup) olive oil
500 g (1 lb 2 oz) red cabbage, thinly sliced or shredded
200 ml (7 fl oz) red wine
100 ml (3½ fl oz) red wine vinegar
2 tablespoons brown sugar
3 tablespoons coarsely chopped flat-leaf (Italian) parsley
2 tablespoons toasted hazelnuts, coarsely chopped

1 Place the duck legs in a single layer in a glass or ceramic container. Add the salt, thyme sprigs, juniper berries, orange zest strips and bay leaf and rub the mixture all over the duck legs. Cover and leave to cure in the refrigerator for 12 hours, or overnight.

2 Rinse the duck legs under cold running water, then pat dry with paper towels. Place in a 7 litre (245 fl oz/28 cup) slow cooker. Pour the duck fat over until the legs are completely covered. Cover and cook on low for 4–5 hours, or until the duck is tender.

3 About 30 minutes before the duck is ready, prepare the braised cabbage. Heat the olive oil in a large saucepan over medium heat. Add the cabbage, wine, vinegar and sugar and stir to combine. Cover and cook for 20–25 minutes, stirring occasionally, until the cabbage is tender. Season to taste with sea salt and freshly ground black pepper and stir the parsley through. Scatter the hazelnuts over the top.

4 Carefully remove the duck legs from the slow cooker and drain on paper towels (to remove excess fat). Serve the duck legs with the warm braised cabbage.

⚙ *Tip: Duck fat is sometimes available from the meat section of the supermarket or from good local butchers. You'll also have leftover duck fat from the recipe opposite; the duck fat can be refrigerated in a clean airtight container for several months and used in this recipe.*

Braised duck with buttered polenta

Serves **4**   Preparation time **40 minutes (+ overnight marinating)**   Cooking time **4 hours 30 minutes**

1 whole duck, about 2 kg (4 lb 8 oz)
750 ml (26 fl oz/3 cups) red wine
2 tablespoons olive oil
1 brown onion, finely diced
3 garlic cloves, thinly sliced
2 carrots, diced
2 x 400 g (14 oz) tins chopped
  or cherry tomatoes
5 thyme sprigs
2 fresh bay leaves

Buttered polenta
1 litre (35 fl oz/4 cups) milk
190 g (6¾ oz/1 cup) instant polenta
40 g (1½ oz) butter, chopped
95 g (3¼ oz/⅔ cup) finely grated
  parmesan

1 Rinse the duck and pat dry with paper towels. Place in a glass or ceramic container and pour the wine over. Cover and marinate overnight in the refrigerator.

2 Drain the duck, reserving the red wine marinade. Heat the oil in the insert pan of a 5 litre (175 fl oz/20 cup) slow cooker or a frying pan over medium heat. Add the onion, garlic and carrot and cook for 6–8 minutes, or until softened. Add the reserved red wine and bring to a simmer. Cook for 15–20 minutes, or until reduced by half.

3 Return the insert pan, if using, to the slow cooker, or transfer the vegetable mixture to the slow cooker. Stir in the tomatoes, thyme sprigs and bay leaves. Season to taste with sea salt and freshly ground black pepper, then add the duck.

4 Cover and cook on high for 3–4 hours, or until the duck is very tender and the meat is starting to fall off the bone. Carefully remove the duck and set aside until cool enough to handle. Remove the thyme sprigs and bay leaves.

5 Near serving time, prepare the buttered polenta. Bring the milk to a simmer in a saucepan over medium heat. Whisking continuously, add the polenta and stir over low heat for 10–12 minutes, or until tender. Stir in the butter and parmesan and season to taste. Keep warm.

6 Roughly shred the duck meat, discarding the skin and bones. Stir the duck meat through the sauce and gently reheat if needed. Serve with the buttered polenta.

Braised duck legs with soy, ginger and garlic

Serves **4**   Preparation time **20 minutes**   Cooking time **3 hours 20 minutes**

150 ml (5 fl oz) soy sauce

125 ml (4 fl oz/½ cup) kecap manis

125 ml (4 fl oz/½ cup) good-quality
chicken stock

100 ml (3½ fl oz) Chinese rice wine
or dry sherry

60 ml (2 fl oz/¼ cup) orange juice

3 thin orange zest strips, white
pith removed

4 cm (1½ inch) piece fresh ginger,
peeled and thinly sliced

3 garlic cloves, crushed

2 star anise

1 cinnamon stick

1½ tablespoons brown sugar

4 duck legs, about 250 g (9 oz) each

Thinly sliced spring onion (scallion)
and sliced fresh red chilli, to
garnish

Steamed Asian greens and steamed
rice, to serve

1 Pour the soy sauce, kecap manis, stock, Chinese rice
wine and orange juice into the insert pan of a 5 litre
(175 fl oz/20 cup) slow cooker or a saucepan. Add the
orange zest strips, ginger, garlic, star anise, cinnamon
stick and sugar. Place over medium heat, bring to a
simmer and stir until the sugar has dissolved.

2 Return the insert pan, if using, to the slow cooker,
or transfer the mixture to the slow cooker. Add the
duck legs.

3 Cover and cook on high for 2½–3 hours, or until the
duck is tender. Using a slotted spoon, transfer the duck
legs to a warm platter, cover with foil and keep warm.

4 Simmer the braising liquid over medium heat in the insert
pan or in a saucepan for 10–15 minutes, or until it has
reduced to a sauce consistency.

5 Drizzle the braising sauce over the duck legs and garnish
with spring onion and chilli. Serve with steamed Asian
greens and steamed rice.

Chicken, pumpkin and honey braise

Serves **4–6**   Preparation time **20 minutes**   Cooking time **3 hours**

750 g (1 lb 10 oz) butternut
  pumpkin (squash), peeled,
  seeded and chopped into
  2.5 cm (1 inch) chunks
1 large brown onion, chopped
1 kg (2 lb 4 oz) skinless chicken
  thigh fillets, trimmed of fat
2 tablespoons honey
2 tablespoons honey mustard
  (see Tip)
250 ml (9 fl oz/1 cup) good-quality
  chicken stock
2 tablespoons chopped flat-leaf
  (Italian) parsley
Steamed basmati rice, to serve

1 Place the pumpkin and onion in a 5.5 litre (192 fl oz/
22 cup) slow cooker, then arrange the chicken on top.

2 In a bowl, mix together the honey, honey mustard and
stock, then pour over the chicken.

3 Cover and cook on high for 3 hours, or until the chicken
is tender and cooked through.

4 Stir half the parsley through the chicken mixture.
Sprinkle with the remaining parsley and serve with
steamed rice.

⚙ *Tip: Honey mustard, as its name suggests, is a ready-made condiment
containing honey and mustard. The mustard used in it is generally
mild, but can vary in tang and spiciness, with the honey contributing
a mellow sweetness. Honey mustard can be used in salad dressings,
glazes, meat marinades or as a dipping sauce, but if you don't have
any, you can just use wholegrain mustard in this recipe.*

Chicken with satay sauce

Serves **4** Preparation time **15 minutes (+ overnight marinating)** Cooking time **6 hours**

1 kg (2 lb 4 oz) skinless chicken
 thigh fillets, trimmed of fat
290 ml (10 fl oz) tin satay sauce
125 ml (4 fl oz/½ cup) coconut milk
1 tablespoon toasted peanuts,
 chopped
100 g (3½ oz) bean sprouts,
 tails trimmed (see Tip)
Coriander (cilantro) sprigs, to garnish
Steamed jasmine rice, to serve

Soy and lemongrass marinade
2 teaspoons purchased red curry
 paste
4 garlic cloves, crushed
2 lemongrass stems, white part only,
 chopped
125 ml (4 fl oz/½ cup) soy sauce
1 tablespoon brown sugar

1 Combine the soy and lemongrass marinade ingredients in a food processor and blend until smooth. Place the chicken in a bowl, pour the marinade over and mix until well coated. Cover and marinate in the refrigerator overnight.

2 Transfer the chicken and marinade to a 5.5 litre (192 fl oz/22 cup) slow cooker. Pour the satay sauce and coconut milk over and gently mix to combine. Cover and cook on low for 6 hours. (Don't be tempted to cook this dish on high as the coconut milk will split.)

3 Check the satay sauce for taste and season with sea salt if required. Remove the chicken to a chopping board using tongs or a slotted spoon. Thickly slice each chicken thigh and arrange on a platter.

4 Drizzle the chicken with the satay sauce. Scatter the peanuts and bean sprouts over the top, garnish with coriander sprigs and serve with steamed rice.

⚙ *Tip: Bean sprouts are the shoots of the mung bean. They're very nutritious and add a pleasing texture and crunch to Asian-style dishes — just trim off any scraggly tail ends before using.*

Mexican chilli chicken

Serves **4**   Preparation time **20 minutes**   Cooking time **6 hours 20 minutes**

1 tablespoon chilli flakes
2 teaspoons ground cumin
¼ teaspoon ground cinnamon
60 ml (2 fl oz/¼ cup) olive oil
1.25 kg (2 lb 12 oz) chicken pieces,
   skin on
1 red onion, finely chopped
2 green jalapeño chillies, finely
   chopped
4 garlic cloves, finely chopped
200 ml (7 fl oz) hot taco sauce
125 ml (4 fl oz/½ cup) good-quality
   chicken stock
1 red capsicum (pepper), chopped
   into 2 cm (¾ inch) chunks
1 green capsicum (pepper), chopped
   into 2 cm (¾ inch) chunks
2 corn cobs, silks and husks removed,
   each cut into thick rounds
100 g (3½ oz) whole black olives
Coriander (cilantro) leaves, to garnish
80 g (2¾ oz/⅓ cup) sour cream,
   steamed basmati rice and
   warmed flour tortillas, to serve
   (optional)

1 In a small bowl, mix together the chilli flakes, cumin, cinnamon and 2 tablespoons of the olive oil.

2 Place the chicken pieces in a large bowl, add the spice and oil mixture and toss to coat. Rub the spice mixture into the chicken skin with your fingers, making sure the chicken is entirely covered. Season with sea salt.

3 Heat the remaining oil in a large frying pan over medium heat. Add the chicken pieces in batches and cook for 10 minutes, turning occasionally, or until the skin has browned, transferring each batch to a 5.5 litre (192 fl oz/22 cup) slow cooker.

4 Add the onion, jalapeño, garlic, taco sauce, stock, capsicum and corn to the slow cooker. Mix well to ensure all the ingredients are evenly distributed. Cover and cook on low for 6 hours.

5 Stir the olives through the chicken mixture and garnish with the coriander. Serve with the sour cream and steamed rice, and warmed flour tortillas, if desired.

Vietnamese caramel chicken

Serves **4–6**   Preparation time **15 minutes**   Cooking time **5 hours 10 minutes**

1 kg (2 lb 4 oz) skinless chicken
   thigh fillets, with the bones,
   flesh scored
2 lemongrass stems, bruised
2 small carrots, peeled and cut
   into thin slivers, to garnish
3 spring onions (scallions), sliced
   diagonally
Toasted peanuts and baby basil
   leaves, to garnish
Steamed jasmine rice, to serve

Caramel sauce
1 tablespoon peanut oil
2 teaspoons finely grated fresh
   ginger
2 garlic cloves, crushed
80 ml (2½ fl oz/⅓ cup) soy sauce
125 g (4½ oz/⅔ cup, lightly packed)
   dark brown sugar
60 ml (2 fl oz/¼ cup) fish sauce
60 ml (2 fl oz/¼ cup) Chinese
   rice wine

1   To make the caramel sauce, heat the peanut oil in a small
saucepan over medium heat. Add the ginger and garlic
and cook for 1 minute. Add the soy sauce and sugar
and cook, stirring, for 3 minutes, or until the sugar has
dissolved. Stir in the fish sauce and Chinese rice wine and
reduce the heat to low. Simmer for 5 minutes, or until the
sauce has thickened to a syrup consistency.

2   Place the chicken in a 5.5 litre (192 fl oz/22 cup) slow
cooker. Pour the caramel sauce over and mix until well
coated. Add the lemongrass.

3   Cover and cook on low for 5 hours, or until the chicken
is tender and cooked through.

4   Garnish with the carrot slivers, spring onion, peanuts
and basil and serve with steamed rice.

⚙ *Tip: Bruising the lemongrass stems helps to release their flavours.
To do this, hit the stems with the back of a cleaver or heavy knife.
If you're in a hurry you can cook the chicken on high, reducing the
slow cooking time to 3½ hours.*

Red cooked chicken

Serves **6–8**   Preparation time **20 minutes**   Cooking time **6 hours**

2 x 1.2 kg (2 lb 10 oz) whole
  chickens, jointed
4 cm (1½ inch) piece fresh
  ginger, peeled and sliced
110 g (3¾ oz/½ cup, firmly packed)
  brown sugar
1½ teaspoons fennel seeds
125 ml (4 fl oz/½ cup) hoisin sauce
250 ml (9 fl oz/1 cup) Chinese rice
  wine or medium–sweet sherry
250 ml (9 fl oz/1 cup) soy sauce
1 cinnamon stick
2 star anise
3 orange zest strips, each about
  2 cm (¾ inch) wide, white pith
  removed, plus thin orange zest
  strips, to garnish
500 ml (17 fl oz/2 cups) good-quality
  chicken stock
2 spring onions (scallions), cut into
  long thin slivers
Steamed Jasmine rice and steamed
  bok choy (pak choy), to serve

1 Put the chicken pieces in a 5.5 litre (192 fl oz/22 cup) slow cooker. In a small bowl, combine the ginger, sugar, fennel seeds, hoisin sauce, Chinese rice wine and soy sauce. Mix well to dissolve the sugar, then pour over the chicken pieces.

2 Add the cinnamon stick, star anise and thick orange zest strips, then pour in the stock. Cover and cook on low for 5–6 hours, or until the chicken is tender and cooked through.

3 Remove the chicken to a warm plate, cover with foil and keep warm. Skim as much excess fat from the surface of the cooking liquid as possible. Discard the cinnamon stick, star anise and orange zest strips.

4 Divide the chicken among wide shallow bowls, then ladle the broth over the top. Garnish with the thin orange zest strips and spring onion slivers and serve with steamed rice and bok choy.

Chicken with harissa

Serves **4–6**   Preparation time **25 minutes**   Cooking time **7 hours 20 minutes**

2 kg (4 lb 8 oz) whole chicken
1 brown onion, peeled and halved
2 lemon zest strips, white pith
 removed
2 dried bay leaves
400 g (14 oz) tin chopped tomatoes
Steamed couscous, to serve

Harissa
1 red capsicum (pepper), seeded
 and cut into quarters
1 teaspoon chilli flakes, or to taste
1 tablespoon ground cumin
3 garlic cloves, crushed
1 tablespoon extra virgin olive oil

1 Start by making the harissa. Preheat the grill (broiler) to high. Place the capsicum on the grill tray, skin side up. Grill for 10 minutes, or until the skin blisters and blackens. Place in a bowl, cover with plastic wrap and leave for 10 minutes, or until cool enough to handle. Peel the capsicum, discard the skin, then chop the flesh.

2 Put the capsicum in a small food processor with the chilli flakes, cumin and garlic. Blend until finely chopped. Add the olive oil and process until almost smooth. Season to taste with sea salt and freshly ground black pepper.

3 Rinse the chicken inside and out and pat dry with paper towels. Place half the onion in the cavity of the chicken with the lemon zest strips and bay leaves. Tie the legs together with kitchen string, then rub half the harissa over the chicken.

4 Finely chop the remaining onion half and place in a 5.5 litre (192 fl oz/22 cup) with the tomatoes and remaining harissa. Gently mix together, then rest the chicken on top.

5 Cover and cook on low for 7 hours, or until the chicken is tender and the juices run clear when the thigh is pierced with a skewer. Remove the chicken to a warm platter and cover with foil to keep warm.

6 Transfer the sauce from the slow cooker to a small saucepan. Simmer over medium heat for 10 minutes, or until slightly reduced. Season to taste.

7 Carve the chicken and serve on a bed of couscous, generously drizzled with the reduced sauce.

Chicken quarters with lemon and green olives

Serves **4**   Preparation time **25 minutes**   Cooking time **7 hours 15 minutes**

2 desiree potatoes, about 500 g
(1 lb 2 oz), peeled and cut
into 2 cm (¾ inch) wedges
8 pickling onions or French shallots,
(eschalots) peeled
8 chicken leg quarters
1 tablespoon olive oil
125 ml (4 fl oz/½ cup) white wine
2 tablespoons lemon juice
200 g (7 oz) green beans, trimmed
90 g (3¼ oz/½ cup) green olives,
pitted
1 cup flat-leaf (Italian) parsley,
coarsely chopped, plus extra,
to garnish
Lemon wedges, to serve

Herb butter
60 g (2¼ oz) butter, softened
3 garlic cloves, crushed
1 tablespoon chopped lemon thyme
1 teaspoon chopped tarragon
60 ml (2 fl oz/¼ cup) lemon juice

1 Place the potato and onions in a 5.5 litre (192 fl oz/ 22 cup) slow cooker.

2 In a small bowl, mix together the herb butter ingredients until well combined. Use your fingers to gently loosen the skin away from the flesh of each chicken leg, working as far down into the drumstick as you can. Ease the herb butter under the skin. Season the skin with sea salt and freshly ground black pepper.

3 Heat the olive oil in a large frying pan over medium heat. Add the chicken in batches, skin side down, and fry for 3 minutes, or until golden. Transfer each batch to the slow cooker.

4 Drain the fat from the frying pan. Add the wine to the pan and bring to the boil, using a wooden spoon to scrape up any stuck-on bits from the base of the pan. Add the lemon juice and cook for another 1–2 minutes, or until the liquid has reduced by half.

5 Pour the pan juices over the chicken in the slow cooker. Cover and cook on low for 6 hours.

6 Turn the slow cooker heat to high. Add the beans, then cover and cook for a further 1 hour, or until the chicken is tender and cooked through.

7 Stir the olives and parsley through. Scatter with extra parsley and serve with lemon wedges.

Lamb dolmades with avgolemono sauce

Serves **6–8**   Preparation time **40 minutes (+ cooling time)**   Cooking time **1 hour 30 minutes**

2 tablespoons olive oil
2 brown onions, finely diced
2 garlic cloves, finely chopped
450 g (1 lb) minced (ground) lamb
200 g (7 oz/1 cup) long-grain white
    rice
2 tablespoons mint, finely chopped
2 tablespoons dill, finely chopped
1½ teaspoons ground cumin
Finely grated zest and juice of
    1 lemon
30 large vine leaves, in brine, rinsed

Avgolemono sauce
3 egg yolks
80 ml (2½ fl oz/⅓ cup) lemon juice
250 ml (9 fl oz/1 cup) good-quality
    chicken stock
1 tablespoon finely chopped flat-leaf
    (Italian) parsley

1 Heat half the olive oil in a large frying pan over medium heat. Add the onion and garlic and cook for 6–8 minutes, or until the onion has softened. Transfer to a large bowl.

2 Wipe the pan clean with paper towels. Increase the heat to high, heat the remaining oil and cook the lamb for 3–5 minutes, or until golden, stirring occasionally.

3 Add the lamb to the onion mixture. Stir in the rice, herbs, cumin, lemon zest and lemon juice. Season with sea salt and freshly ground black pepper and set aside to cool.

4 Line the base of a 5 litre (175 fl oz/20 cup) slow cooker with about six vine leaves, overlapping them slightly.

5 Place the remaining leaves on a work surface. Fill each vine leaf with 2 tablespoons of the lamb mixture, fold the sides over to form a cylinder, then roll them up to enclose.

6 Place the rolls in the slow cooker. Pour in just enough cold water to cover them. Cover and cook on low for 1–1¼ hours, or until the rice is just tender. Remove the lid and cool to room temperature.

7 To make the avgolemono sauce, whisk the egg yolks in a bowl until pale and frothy. Add the lemon juice and whisk to combine. Bring the stock to a simmer in a saucepan over medium heat. Whisking all the time, add half the stock to the egg yolks in a thin continuous stream, then whisk the mixture into the remaining stock. Reduce the heat to low and cook, stirring, for 3–5 minutes, or until the mixture thickly coats a wooden spoon. Stir through the parsley, season to taste and serve with the dolmades.

Lamb shanks with tomato, chilli and honey

Serves 4   Preparation time **15 minutes**   Cooking time **8 hours**

2 garlic cloves, thinly sliced
1 large brown onion, sliced
250 ml (9 fl oz/1 cup) red wine
2 teaspoons dried oregano
½ teaspoon chilli flakes
500 ml (17 fl oz/2 cups) tomato passata (puréed tomatoes)
250 ml (9 fl oz/1 cup) chicken stock
90 g (3¼ oz/¼ cup) honey
8 small French-trimmed lamb shanks
1 tablespoon chopped flat-leaf (Italian) parsley
Steamed rice, to serve

1 Put the garlic, onion, wine, oregano, chilli flakes, passata, stock and honey in a 4.5 litre (157 fl oz/18 cup) slow cooker. Mix until combined, then add the lamb shanks and turn to coat.

2 Cover and cook on low for 8 hours, or until the shanks are tender and falling off the bone.

3 Stir the parsley through and season with sea salt and freshly ground black pepper. Serve with steamed rice.

Tip: French-trimmed lamb shanks have a lovely neat presentation as some of the meat has been scraped away from the bone towards the end of the shank. They will also fit more easily in the slow cooker.

Rosemary, garlic and anchovy lamb

Serves **4**   Preparation time **30 minutes**   Cooking time **6 hours 20 minutes**

2 tablespoons olive oil
1.2 kg (2 lb 10 oz) lamb shoulder, bone in, trimmed of excess fat
2 tablespoons dijon mustard
8 anchovy fillets, in oil, drained, halved
6 rosemary sprigs, broken into 3 cm (1¼ inch) lengths
4 garlic cloves, sliced into thin wedges
125 ml (4 fl oz/½ cup) white wine
125 ml (4 fl oz/½ cup) good-quality chicken stock
1 tablespoon lemon juice

1 Heat the olive oil in the insert pan of a 5 litre (175 fl oz/ 20 cup) slow cooker or a large frying pan over medium heat. Add the lamb and cook for 2–3 minutes on each side, or until golden all over. Transfer the lamb to a plate and set aside until cool enough to handle.

2 Return the insert pan, if using, to the slow cooker.

3 Using a small sharp knife, pierce about eight 2 cm (¾ inch) holes in the lamb. Brush the lamb with the mustard, then push the anchovies, rosemary and garlic into the holes.

4 Place the lamb in the slow cooker, then pour in the wine and stock. Cover and cook on low for 5–6 hours, or until the lamb is tender.

5 Remove the lamb to a warm platter and cover loosely with foil while finishing the sauce.

6 Transfer the pan juices to a saucepan and simmer over medium heat for 5–10 minutes, or until reduced to a sauce consistency (don't over-reduce or the sauce will become too salty). Stir in the lemon juice.

7 Carve the lamb and serve drizzled with the sauce.

Tip: This lamb shoulder would be perfect with a classic potato mash and crisp steamed baby green beans.

Lamb ragu

Serves **4**   Preparation time **20 minutes**   Cooking time **5 hours 30 minutes**

1 kg (2 lb 4 oz) boneless lamb
  shoulder or leg
2 tablespoons olive oil
2 garlic cloves, crushed
1 brown onion, finely chopped
3 anchovy fillets, chopped
1 carrot, finely chopped
1 celery stalk, finely chopped
2 tablespoons rosemary leaves,
  chopped
½ teaspoon chilli flakes
2 tablespoons tomato paste
  (concentrated purée)
250 ml (9 fl oz/1 cup) white wine
2 teaspoons fennel seeds
250 ml (9 fl oz/1 cup) good-quality
  chicken stock
3 tablespoons chopped flat-leaf
  (Italian) parsley
Hot cooked short pasta, such as
  ditali or tubetti and
  shaved parmesan, to serve

1 Trim the lamb of excess fat, then cut into seven or eight large pieces. Season with sea salt and freshly ground black pepper.

2 Heat the olive oil in the insert pan of a 5 litre (175 fl oz/20 cup) slow cooker or a large frying pan over medium–high heat. Brown the lamb in two batches for 3–5 minutes, or until golden on all sides. Remove to a plate.

3 Reduce the heat to medium. Add the garlic, onion, anchovy, carrot, celery, rosemary and chilli flakes and cook for 7–8 minutes, or until the vegetables begin to soften. Increase the heat to high, stir in the tomato paste and cook for 1 minute. Stir in the wine and cook until the liquid has reduced by two-thirds.

4 Return the insert pan, if using, to the slow cooker, or transfer the vegetable mixture to the slow cooker. Stir in the fennel seeds and stock, then add the lamb. Season lightly with salt and pepper.

5 Cover and cook on low for 5 hours, or until the lamb is falling apart.

6 Remove the meat and, using two forks, shred finely. Return the meat to the sauce, stir in the parsley and season to taste. Spoon over hot pasta and serve scattered with shaved parmesan.

Lamb shoulder cooked with rosemary

Serves **6**   Preparation time **20 minutes**   Cooking time **5 hours 15 minutes**

1.8 kg (4 lb) lamb shoulder, bone in
1 tablespoon olive oil
170 ml (5½ fl oz/⅔ cup) red wine
185 ml (6 fl oz/¾ cup) good-quality
    chicken stock
6 garlic cloves, unpeeled
5 rosemary sprigs
Lemon wedges, soft polenta and
    green salad, to serve

1 Trim the lamb of excess fat, then season generously with sea salt and freshly ground black pepper.

2 Heat the olive oil in the insert pan of a 5 litre (175 fl oz/ 20 cup) slow cooker or a large frying pan over medium– high heat. Brown the lamb for 3 minutes on one side. Carefully turn the lamb over, being careful of the hot fat, and cook for a further 3 minutes. Remove the lamb to a plate.

3 Drain any excess fat from the pan, then return to the heat. Add the wine and boil for 4–5 minutes, or until the liquid has reduced by one-third.

4 Return the insert pan, if using, to the slow cooker, or transfer the wine mixture to the slow cooker. Mix in the stock, garlic and rosemary sprigs, then add the lamb. Cover and cook on high for 5 hours, or until the lamb is tender and flakes easily when tested with a fork.

5 Transfer the lamb to a warm platter and sprinkle with sea salt.

6 Skim any fat from the surface of the sauce. Take out the rosemary sprigs. Remove the garlic cloves with a slotted spoon, then discard the skins. Crush the garlic flesh, stir into the cooking liquid and season to taste.

7 Drizzle a little sauce over the lamb. Serve with lemon wedges, soft polenta and a green salad.

Slow-cooked lamb leg with burghul and herb salad

Serves 6   Preparation time **35 minutes (+ 1 hour soaking)**   Cooking time **8 hours 20 minutes**

2 tablespoons olive oil
2.5 kg (5 lb 8 oz) lamb leg, bone in
4 garlic cloves, coarsely chopped
Finely grated zest of 1 lemon
2 tablespoons thyme leaves
200 ml (7 fl oz) good-quality
   chicken stock
150 ml (5 fl oz) white wine

Burghul and herb salad
265 g (9½ oz/1½ cups) burghul
   (bulgur)
2 tablespoons currants
1 cup coarsely torn mint
1 cup coarsely torn flat-leaf
   (Italian) parsley
100 g (3½ oz/⅔ cup) crumbled feta
   cheese
60 ml (2 fl oz/¼ cup) extra virgin
   olive oil
2 tablespoons red wine vinegar
2 tablespoons lemon juice

1 Heat half the olive oil in the insert pan of a 7 litre (245 fl oz/28 cup) slow cooker or a large frying pan over high heat. Add the lamb and cook, turning occasionally, for 6–7 minutes, or until golden. Remove from the heat.

2 Using a mortar and pestle or spice grinder, pound or grind the garlic, lemon zest and thyme together. Mix in the remaining oil. Season with sea salt and freshly ground black pepper and spread the mixture over the lamb.

3 Return the insert pan, if using, to the slow cooker, or transfer the lamb to the slow cooker. Pour in the stock and wine. Cover and cook on low for 7–8 hours, or until the lamb is tender and cooked through.

4 About an hour before the lamb is ready, make the burghul and herb salad. Combine the burghul and 500 ml (17 fl oz/ 2 cups) hot water in a large bowl and leave to soak for 1 hour, or until softened. Drain well, then combine in a bowl with the remaining salad ingredients. Toss gently to combine and season to taste.

5 Remove the lamb to a warm platter and cover loosely with foil while finishing the sauce.

6 Cook the pan juices over medium–high heat in the insert pan or in a saucepan for 5 minutes or until reduced to a sauce consistency.

7 Carve the lamb and serve with the sauce and the burghul and herb salad.

Braised lamb with capsicum and fennel

Serves **4**   Preparation time **15 minutes**   Cooking time **4 hours 10 minutes**

1 kg (2 lb 4 oz) boneless lamb
   shoulder or leg
1 large brown onion, chopped
1 red capsicum (pepper), sliced
   into strips
1 yellow capsicum (pepper), sliced
   into strips
2 fennel bulbs, trimmed and cut
   lengthways into thick slices
4 garlic cloves, chopped
250 ml (9 fl oz/1 cup) tomato
   passata (puréed tomatoes)
60 ml (2 fl oz/¼ cup) good-quality
   beef stock
1 tablespoon tomato paste
   (concentrated purée)
1 teaspoon worcestershire sauce
1 tablespoon cornflour (cornstarch)
Fennel fronds, to garnish

1 Trim the lamb of excess fat, then cut into 4 cm (1½ inch) chunks. Place in a 4.5 litre (157 fl oz/18 cup) slow cooker with the onion, capsicum, fennel, garlic, passata, stock, tomato paste and worcestershire sauce. Season with sea salt and freshly ground black pepper and gently mix together.

2 Cover and cook on high for 4 hours, or until the lamb is tender and cooked through.

3 Combine the cornflour with a little water to make a smooth paste, then stir it through the lamb mixture. Cook for a further 5–10 minutes to thicken the juices a little.

4 Divide the lamb braise among bowls and serve garnished with fennel fronds.

Greek leg of lamb with oregano

Serves **6**   Preparation time **15 minutes**   Cooking time **10 hours**

1.8 kg (4 lb) lamb leg, bone in
1 tablespoon dried oregano
8 small all-purpose potatoes, such
   as desiree, peeled and halved
400 g (14 oz) tin chopped tomatoes
80 ml (2½ fl oz/⅓ cup) red wine
250 ml (9 fl oz/1 cup) good-quality
   chicken stock
1 lemon zest strip, white pith
   removed
2 dried bay leaves
1 tablespoon lemon juice
2 tablespoons chopped fresh
   oregano

1 Place the lamb in a 4.5 litre (157 fl oz/18 cup) slow cooker. Sprinkle with the dried oregano and arrange the potatoes around the lamb. Add the tomatoes, wine, stock and 250 ml (9 fl oz/1 cup) water.

2 Season with freshly ground black pepper and add the lemon zest strip and bay leaves. Cover and cook on low for 10 hours, or until the lamb is cooked through.

3 Transfer the lamb and potatoes to a warm platter.

4 Skim the fat from the surface of the sauce and stir in the lemon juice and fresh oregano. Season with sea salt and freshly ground black pepper.

5 Carve the lamb and serve with the potatoes and sauce.

Chutney chops with potatoes and peas

Serves **6**   Preparation time **25 minutes**   Cooking time **4 hours 30 minutes**

600 g (1 lb 5 oz) all-purpose
   potatoes, peeled and thickly
   sliced
3 carrots, thickly sliced
1 brown onion, cut into 16 wedges
1 small leek, white part only,
   thickly sliced
150 g (5½ oz) savoy cabbage,
   thinly sliced
4 bacon slices, cut into strips
8 lamb neck chops
375 ml (13 fl oz/1½ cups) good-
   quality beef stock
2 tablespoons finely chopped
   flat-leaf (Italian) parsley
Crusty bread, to serve

1 Layer half the potato, carrot, onion, leek, cabbage and
bacon in a 4.5 litre (157 fl oz/18 cup) slow cooker.
Arrange the lamb chops in a single layer over the top,
then cover with layers of the remaining vegetables and
bacon. Pour in the stock.

2 Cover and cook on low for 4½ hours, or until the lamb
chops are very tender and the sauce is slightly reduced.
Season to taste with salt and freshly ground black pepper.

3 Divide among shallow bowls and sprinkle with the
parsley. Serve with crusty bread to mop up the juices.

Slow-cooked lamb in red wine

Serves **6** Preparation time **20 minutes (+ 24 hours marinating)** Cooking time **10 hours 15 minutes**

2 kg (4 lb 8 oz) lamb leg, bone in
50 g (1¾ oz) butter, softened
2½ tablespoons plain (all-purpose)
    flour

Marinade
750 ml (26 fl oz/3 cups) red wine
60 ml (2 fl oz/¼ cup) brandy
10 garlic cloves, bruised
1 tablespoon chopped rosemary
2 teaspoons chopped thyme
2 dried bay leaves, torn into
    small pieces
1 large carrot, diced
1 large celery stalk, diced
1 brown onion, finely chopped
60 ml (2 fl oz/¼ cup) olive oil

1 Trim any really thick pieces of fat from the lamb, but leave it with a decent covering all over if possible.

2 Combine the marinade ingredients in a glass or ceramic baking dish, then add the lamb and turn to coat in the marinade. Cover and marinate in the refrigerator for 24–48 hours, turning occasionally so the marinade is evenly distributed. Wrap and rewrap the dish tightly with plastic wrap each time to ensure the strong odours from the marinade do not permeate other foods in the refrigerator.

3 Transfer the lamb and marinade to a 4.5 litre (157 fl oz/18 cup) slow cooker. Cover and cook on low for 10 hours, or until the lamb is tender.

4 Carefully remove the lamb to a warm platter using two strong wide spatulas. Cover the lamb with foil and a tea towel (dish towel) to keep warm while finishing the sauce.

5 Skim the fat from the surface of the sauce. Transfer the contents of the slow cooker to a food processor and purée. Strain the liquid back into the slow cooker and turn the slow cooker setting to high. Mix together the butter and flour and gradually whisk the mixture into the sauce. Cook for a further 10–15 minutes, or until the sauce has thickened slightly.

6 Carve the lamb and serve with the sauce.

⌘ Tip: This dish is delicious with potato gratin and green vegetables.

Indian spiced leg of lamb

Serves **4–6**   Preparation time **30 minutes (+ 24 hours marinating)**   Cooking time **7 hours 40 minutes**

1.2 kg (2 lb 10 oz) lamb leg, bone in
100 g (3½ oz) plain yoghurt
2 egg yolks, lightly beaten
Steamed rice, to serve

Marinade
1 onion, coarsely chopped
4 garlic cloves, peeled
4 cm (1½ inch) piece fresh ginger,
   peeled and diced
2 tablespoons chopped coriander
   (cilantro) leaves
½ teaspoon ground cinnamon
½ teaspoon cardamom seeds
2 teaspoons ground cumin
½ teaspoon chilli powder
1 teaspoon ground turmeric
½ teaspoon garam masala
2 teaspoons purchased curry powder
200 g (7 oz/¾ cup) plain yoghurt
Juice of ½ lemon

1 To make the marinade, put the onion, garlic, ginger and coriander in a food processor and process until smooth. Add the spices and a pinch of sea salt and process until combined. Stir in the yoghurt and lemon juice.

2 Rinse the lamb and pat dry with paper towels. Cut slits in the side of the lamb, then coat the lamb in the yoghurt mixture, filling the slits. Cover with plastic wrap and marinate in the refrigerator for 24 hours.

3 Transfer the lamb and marinade to a 4.5 litre (157 fl oz/18 cup) slow cooker. Cover and cook on low for 7 hours, or until the lamb is tender.

4 Remove the lamb to a warm platter and cover loosely with foil while finishing the sauce.

5 Combine the yoghurt and egg yolks. Stir into the liquid in the slow cooker and cook for 20–30 minutes, stirring occasionally, until the sauce has thickened slightly.

6 Return the lamb to the slow cooker and cook for a further 10 minutes. Carve the lamb and serve with the sauce and steamed rice.

Lamb with white beans

Serves **4**   Preparation time **15 minutes**   Cooking time **4 hours 15 minutes**

1 kg (2 lb 4 oz) boneless lamb
  shoulder
2 carrots, diced
2 large brown onions, chopped
2 garlic cloves, unpeeled
1 bouquet garni
125 ml (4 fl oz/½ cup) dry red wine
125 ml (4 fl oz/½ cup) good-quality
  chicken stock
400 g (14 oz) tin cannellini beans,
  drained and rinsed

1 Tie the lamb with kitchen string to keep its shape. Rub the lamb all over with sea salt and freshly ground black pepper.

2 Place the lamb in a 4.5 litre (157 fl oz/18 cup) slow cooker with the carrot, onion, garlic, bouquet garni, wine and stock. Cover and cook on high for 4 hours, or until the lamb is tender.

3 Remove the lamb to a warm platter and cover loosely with foil while finishing the sauce.

4 Discard the bouquet garni and garlic cloves. Skim the fat from the surface of the sauce, then stir in the beans. Cook, uncovered, for 10–15 minutes, or until the beans are heated through and the sauce has thickened slightly. Season to taste.

5 Carve the lamb and arrange on a platter. Spoon the beans around the lamb and drizzle with the sauce. Serve any remaining sauce separately.

Lamb shanks with barley and root vegetables

Serves **4**   Preparation time **30 minutes**   Cooking time **10 hours**

150 g (5½ oz/¾ cup) pearl barley
   rinsed under cold running water
1 brown onion, chopped
3 garlic cloves, crushed
1 large carrot, cut into 4 cm
   (1½ inch) chunks
1 large parsnip, cut into 4 cm
   (1½ inch) chunks
1 swede (rutabaga) or turnip, cut
   into 4 cm (1½ inch) chunks
4 French-trimmed lamb shanks,
   about 1.2 kg (2 lb 10 oz)
1 teaspoon dried oregano
2 x 400 g (14 oz) tins chopped
   tomatoes
2 tablespoons tomato paste
   (concentrated purée)
125 ml (4 fl oz/½ cup) white wine
   or water
1 rosemary sprig, plus small extra
   sprigs, to garnish

1 Place the barley in a 4.5 litre (157 fl oz/18 cup) slow cooker. Spread the onion, garlic, carrot, parsnip and swede over the barley. Top with the lamb shanks, arranged in a single layer. Sprinkle with the oregano.

2 Combine the tomatoes, tomato paste and wine and pour over the shanks. Tuck the rosemary sprig in and season well with sea salt and freshly ground black pepper.

3 Cover and cook on low for 8–10 hours, or until the lamb and barley are tender. Remove the rosemary sprig, then remove the lamb shanks to a plate.

4 Skim any fat from the surface of the sauce. Spoon the barley and vegetable mixture into wide bowls, top each with a shank and serve garnished with a rosemary sprig.

Spanish lamb, mint and almond meatballs

Serves **6 (makes 24 balls)** Preparation time **25 minutes** Cooking time **6 hours 20 minutes**

2 tablespoons olive oil
1 brown onion, finely chopped
2 garlic cloves, finely chopped
1–2 tablespoons dry sherry
500 ml (17 fl oz/2 cups) tomato
  passata (puréed tomatoes)
Chopped mint, to garnish
Steamed rice, to serve

Meatballs
45 g (1½ oz/⅓ cup) slivered
  almonds, toasted
750 g (1 lb 10 oz) minced
  (ground) lamb
4 garlic cloves, finely chopped
½ cup mint leaves, chopped,
2 eggs, lightly beaten
20 g (¾ oz/⅓ cup, lightly packed)
  fresh white breadcrumbs
80 ml (2½ fl oz/⅓ cup) dry sherry
Finely grated zest of 1 lemon
1 teaspoon sweet paprika
2 teaspoons sea salt
½ teaspoon freshly ground black
  pepper

1 To make the meatballs, roughly chop 2 tablespoons of the almonds and reserve the rest. Place the chopped almonds in a bowl with the remaining meatball ingredients and mix together well. Using wet hands, roll the mixture, about 2 tablespoons at a time, into 5 cm (2 inch) balls.

2 Heat the olive oil in the insert pan of a 7 litre (245 fl oz/ 28 cup) slow cooker or a large frying pan over medium– high heat. Fry the meatballs in batches for 3–4 minutes, or until well browned on all sides. Remove using a slotted spoon and set aside.

3 Add the onion and garlic to the pan and cook, stirring, for 3–4 minutes, or until the onion has softened. Stir in the sherry and cook for 30 seconds, scraping the pan.

4 Return the insert pan, if using, to the slow cooker, or transfer the onion mixture to the slow cooker. Add the passata, season with sea salt and freshly ground black pepper and stir to combine.

5 Add the meatballs and turn to coat them in the sauce. Cover and cook on low for 6 hours, or until the meatballs are cooked through.

6 Remove the meatballs from the cooker with a slotted spoon and place in bowls of steamed rice. Stir the sauce to recombine and season to taste. Pour the sauce over the meatballs and serve garnished with mint and the reserved almonds.

Rosemary and redcurrant lamb roast

Serves **6**   Preparation time **20 minutes**   Cooking time **8 hours**

2.25 kg (5 lb) lamb leg, bone in
1 garlic clove, halved lengthways
3 rosemary sprigs, cut in half
160 g (5¾ oz/½ cup) redcurrant
   jelly, melted
½ small pumpkin (winter squash),
   about 650 g (1 lb 7 oz)
1 brown onion
12 new potatoes, about 900 g (2 lb),
   peeled
1 dried bay leaf
1 tablespoon olive oil
Steamed peas, to serve

1 Trim the lamb of excess fat. Cut six large incisions into the lamb, then rub the lamb all over with the cut garlic. Insert the rosemary sprigs into the incisions. Brush the lamb well with half the redcurrant jelly and season generously with sea salt and freshly ground black pepper.

2 Leaving the skin on, remove the seeds from the pumpkin and cut the flesh into 5 cm (2 inch) wedges. Peel the onion and cut it into rounds, but don't separate the rings. Cut any larger potatoes in half.

3 Place the potatoes, pumpkin, onion and bay leaf in a 5.5 litre (192 fl oz/22 cup) slow cooker, then rest the lamb on top. Cover and cook on low for 8 hours.

4 Remove the lamb from the slow cooker and place on a warm platter. Cover with foil and leave to rest in a warm place for 10 minutes before carving.

5 Drizzle the vegetables in the slow cooker with the olive oil and season to taste.

6 Carve the lamb and serve with the remaining redcurrant jelly, the braised vegetables and steamed peas.

Tip: Instead of the pumpkin (winter squash), you can use 600 g (1 lb 5 oz) chopped sweet potato in this recipe. You can leave the skin on if you wish, but wash the sweet potato well before using.

Lamb meatballs with spicy saffron sauce

Serves **4**   Preparation time **30 minutes (+ 30 minutes chilling)**   Cooking time **8 hours 15 minutes**

2 tablespoons olive oil
400 g (14 oz) fresh pappardelle
   pasta
Grated parmesan cheese, to serve
Basil leaves, to garnish

Meatballs
650 g (1 lb 7 oz) minced (ground)
   lamb
110 g (3¾ oz/1 cup) dry breadcrumbs
1 egg, lightly beaten
1 garlic clove, crushed
2 teaspoons dried oregano
½ teaspoon sea salt
½ teaspoon freshly ground black
   pepper
2 tablespoons olive oil

1   Combine all the meatball ingredients in a large bowl and mix together well using your hands.

2   Using wet hands, form the mixture into 24 meatballs, using about 1 heaped tablespoon of mixture per ball. Place the meatballs on a tray, then cover and refrigerate for 30 minutes.

3   Meanwhile, make the spicy saffron sauce. In a small bowl, soak the saffron threads in 2 tablespoons hot water for 5 minutes to infuse.

4   Place the almonds and garlic in a food processor and pulse until a smooth paste forms. Add the ground hazelnuts, passata, vinegar, capsicum and one tin of chopped tomatoes and process to a smooth consistency. Add the saffron water, paprika, cayenne pepper, chilli flakes and sugar and pulse until thoroughly mixed. Pour the sauce into a 5.5 litre (192 fl oz/22 cup) slow cooker with the remaining tin of tomatoes.

5   Heat the oil in a frying pan over medium heat. Add the meatballs in batches and fry for 3–4 minutes each time, or until evenly browned, turning often and transferring each batch to the slow cooker.

6   Turn the meatballs to coat them in the sauce. Cover and cook on low for 8 hours.

continued ➤

Spicy saffron sauce

1 teaspoon saffron threads

115 g (4 oz/¾ cup) blanched
   almonds, toasted

1 garlic clove, crushed

55 g (2 oz/½ cup) ground hazelnuts

2 tablespoons tomato passata
   (puréed tomatoes)

2 tablespoons red wine vinegar

340 g (12 oz) jar roasted red
   capsicum (pepper) strips,
   drained

2 x 400 g (14 oz) tins chopped
   tomatoes

2 teaspoons sweet paprika

1 teaspoon cayenne pepper

1 teaspoon chilli flakes

2 teaspoons brown sugar

7 When the meatballs are nearly ready, add the pasta to a large pot of rapidly boiling salted water and cook according to the packet instructions until al dente. Drain well.

8 Divide the pasta among bowls. Season the meatball mixture to taste with sea salt and freshly ground black pepper, then spoon the meatballs and sauce over the pasta. Sprinkle with parmesan and serve garnished with basil.

⚙ *Tip: For a richer sauce, stir 185 ml (6 fl oz/¾ cup) pouring cream through the finished meatball mixture just before serving it over the pasta.*

Lamb with garlic and spices

Serves **6**   Preparation time **25 minutes (+ 8 hours marinating)**   Cooking time **8 hours 40 minutes**

2.5 kg (5 lb 8 oz) lamb leg,
  bone in
2 brown onions, quartered
1 cinnamon stick
1 litre (35 fl oz/4 cups) good-quality
  chicken stock
2 tablespoons cornflour (cornstarch)
2½ tablespoons chopped mint
Naan bread amd lemon cheeks,
  to serve

Yoghurt marinade
2½ teaspoons cumin seeds
10 green cardamom pods, seeds
  extracted
5 garlic cloves, chopped
Finely grated zest of 1 lemon
2½ tablespoons lemon juice
1 teaspoon ground turmeric
½ teaspoon chilli flakes, or to taste
500 g (1 lb 2 oz) Greek-style
  yoghurt
2 teaspoons freshly ground black
  pepper

1 Start by making the yoghurt marinade. Heat a small, heavy-based frying pan over low heat, add the cumin seeds and toast them without any oil, shaking the pan often, for 3–4 minutes, or until aromatic. Use a mortar and pestle or electric spice grinder to coarsely crush together the cumin and cardamom seeds. Tip the spice mixture into a small food processor. Add the garlic, lemon zest, lemon juice, turmeric and chilli flakes and process until the garlic is very finely chopped and the mixture is well combined. Scrape the mixture into a glass or ceramic container large enough to fit the lamb. Add the yoghurt and pepper and mix together.

2 Trim the lamb of excess fat. Using a small sharp knife, make deep incisions all over the lamb. Place the lamb in the container and turn to coat well in the yoghurt mixture. Cover with plastic wrap and marinate in the refrigerator for at least 8 hours, or overnight.

3 Scrape as much of the yoghurt mixture from the lamb as possible, reserving the yoghurt mixture in the refrigerator for finishing off the sauce.

4 Place the onion quarters in a 5.5 litre (192 fl oz/22 cup) slow cooker with the cinnamon stick. Place the lamb on top and pour in the stock. Season the lamb well with sea salt, then cover and cook on low for 6–8 hours, turning the lamb over halfway during cooking.

continued ➤

5 About an hour before the lamb is ready, bring the reserved yoghurt mixture to room temperature.

6 Remove the lamb to a warm platter, cover loosely with foil and keep warm while finishing the sauce.

7 Remove the onion from the sauce mixture using a slotted spoon and discard. Turn the slow cooker setting to high. Combine the cornflour with enough of the yoghurt mixture to make a smooth paste, then stir it back into the remaining yoghurt mixture. Whisk the yoghurt mixture into the sauce in the slow cooker. Cover and cook for 30–40 minutes, or until the sauce has thickened, whisking often to prevent lumps forming. Stir in the mint.

8 Tear the lamb into chunks. Serve drizzled with the yoghurt sauce, naan bread and lemon cheeks.

⬡ *Tip: Serve the lamb with a tomato and mint salad, made by simply tossing together 200 g (7 oz) halved grape tomatoes, 1 small handful mint leaves, 1 small handful coriander (cilantro) leaves and 1 thinly sliced small red onion.*

Chilli and anchovy lamb neck

Serves **4**   Preparation time **25 minutes**   Cooking time **6 hours**

1 brown onion, finely chopped
1 celery stalk, finely chopped
1 carrot, finely chopped
4 anchovy fillets, finely chopped
2 garlic cloves, finely chopped
1 long fresh red chilli, chopped
2 kg (4 lb 8 oz) lamb neck chops,
    trimmed of excess fat and sinew
    (see Tip)
400 g (14 oz) tin chopped tomatoes
250 ml (9 fl oz/1 cup) good-quality
    chicken stock
125 ml (4 fl oz/½ cup) red wine
Steamed green beans, to serve

Mashed potato
800 g (1 lb 12 oz) spunta, sebago or
    coliban potatoes, peeled
40 g (1½ oz) butter, chopped
80 ml (2½ fl oz/⅓ cup) hot milk

Gremolata
1 cup flat-leaf (Italian) parsley,
    finely chopped
Finely grated zest of 1 orange
1 small fresh red chilli, seeded and
    finely chopped

1 Put half the onion, celery and carrot in a 5.5 litre (192 fl oz/22 cup) slow cooker.

2 In a small bowl, mix together the anchovy, garlic and chilli. Spread the mixture over both sides of the lamb chops. Season well with freshly ground black pepper.

3 Arrange the lamb in the slow cooker in a single layer. Scatter the remaining vegetables over the top, then pour in the tomatoes, stock and wine. Cover and cook on high for 6 hours, or until the lamb is tender.

4 Near serving time, make the mashed potato. Cook the potatoes in a large saucepan of boiling salted water for 20 minutes, or until very tender but not falling apart. Drain well, then return to the saucepan over low heat. Shake the pan gently until any remaining water evaporates. Using a potato masher, roughly mash the potatoes. Add the butter and hot milk and beat with a wooden spoon until fluffy. Season with sea salt and freshly ground black pepper.

5 Mix together the gremolata ingredients and set aside.

6 Use tongs to remove the bones from the lamb chops if desired. Divide the lamb among plates and drizzle with the sauce from the slow cooker. Sprinkle with the gremolata and serve with the mashed potato and steamed green beans.

⚙ *Tip: You can use 4 trimmed lamb shoulder chops instead of neck chops.*

Korean braised beef ribs (galbi jim)

Serves **6**   Preparation time **30 minutes**   Cooking time **7 hours 10 minutes**

6 beef short ribs, about 350 g (12 oz) each
1 brown onion, coarsely chopped
1 carrot, coarsely chopped
4 spring onions (scallions), thinly sliced, plus extra, to serve
2 all-purpose potatoes, peeled and coarsely chopped
250 ml (9 fl oz/1 cup) good-quality beef stock
1 tablespoon sesame oil
Toasted sesame seeds and steamed rice, to serve

Soy and ginger marinade
125 ml (4 fl oz/½ cup) soy sauce
3 tablespoons brown sugar
5 cm (2 inch) piece fresh ginger, peeled and finely grated
2 garlic cloves, grated
2 tablespoons mirin

1 Trim the fat off the ribs and cut some slashes into the meat using a sharp knife. Place the ribs in the insert pan of a 5 litre (175 fl oz/20 cup) slow cooker or a saucepan. Cover with cold water and bring to the boil over high heat. Reduce the heat to low and simmer for 5 minutes. Drain, then rinse under cold running water.

2 Combine the soy and ginger marinade ingredients in a large bowl and mix together well. Add the ribs and massage the marinade into the meat.

3 Return the ribs to the slow cooker pan, if using, or transfer to the slow cooker. Add the onion, carrot, spring onion, potato and stock. Cover and cook on low for 6 hours, or until the meat is very tender, stirring occasionally.

4 Remove the lid and cook on high for a further 1 hour, or until the sauce has reduced. Stir the sesame oil through the mixture and season to taste with sea salt and freshly ground black pepper.

5 Sprinkle with sesame seeds and extra spring onion and serve with steamed rice.

Tip: As an added garnish and to cut through the richness, serve the ribs sprinkled with some peeled and finely julienned nashi pear.

Braised beef short ribs

Serves **6**   Preparation time **15 minutes**   Cooking time **4–5 hours**

2 kg (4 lb 8 oz) beef short ribs, chopped into 4 cm (1½ inch) lengths
180 g (6½ oz) bacon slices, rind and fat removed, finely diced
2 brown onions, chopped
1 garlic clove, crushed
1 small fresh red chilli, seeded and thinly sliced
500 ml (17 fl oz/2 cups) good-quality beef stock
400 g (14 oz) tin chopped tomatoes
8 bulb spring onions (scallions), trimmed, leaves removed
2 lemon zest strips, white pith removed
1 teaspoon mild paprika
1 teaspoon chopped rosemary
1 dried bay leaf
1 tablespoon brown sugar
1 teaspoon worcestershire sauce
2 tablespoons chopped basil
2 tablespoons chopped flat-leaf (Italian) parsley

1 Put the ribs in a 4.5 litre (157 fl oz/18 cup) slow cooker. Add the bacon, onion, garlic, chilli, stock, tomatoes, spring onions, lemon zest strips, paprika, rosemary, bay leaf, sugar and worcestershire sauce. Gently mix together.

2 Cover and cook on high for 4–5 hours, or until the meat is tender.

3 Skim off as much fat as you can from the surface of the sauce. Stir the basil and parsley through the mixture just before serving.

Tip: These ribs go well with mashed potato and soft polenta.

Corned beef with cabbage and potatoes

Serves **4–6**   Preparation time **20 minutes**   Cooking time **10 hours 15 minutes**

1.5 kg (3 lb 5 oz) piece of corned beef
1 small brown onion, peeled
8 whole cloves
500 g (1 lb 2 oz) small new potatoes, peeled
8 black peppercorns
2 dried bay leaves
1 tablespoon brown sugar
1 tablespoon malt vinegar
500 g (1 lb 2 oz) savoy cabbage, core left attached, cut into 4–6 wedges

Mustard and parsley sauce
1 egg
2 tablespoons caster (superfine) sugar
1 tablespoon plain (all-purpose) flour
1 teaspoon mustard powder
60 ml (2 fl oz/¼ cup) malt vinegar
2 tablespoons finely chopped flat-leaf (Italian) parsley

1 Rinse the corned beef and pat dry with paper towels. Trim off any excess fat. Stud the onion with the cloves.

2 Put the potatoes in a 4.5 litre (157 fl oz/18 cup) slow cooker in a single layer and rest the corned beef on top. Pour in just enough cold water to barely cover the beef. Add the onion, peppercorns and bay leaves. Combine the sugar and vinegar and add to the slow cooker. Cover and cook on low for 8–10 hours, or until the beef is tender.

3 About 45 minutes before the beef is ready, arrange the cabbage wedges around the meat and continue cooking.

4 When the beef is cooked, remove it to a warm platter and cover loosely with foil while preparing the sauce.

5 To make the mustard and parsley sauce, remove 250 ml (9 fl oz/1 cup) of the liquid from the slow cooker and set aside. Whisk together the egg and sugar in a small bowl, then whisk in the flour and mustard powder. Gradually add the reserved cooking liquid and vinegar, mixing until smooth. Pour into a small saucepan and stir over medium heat until thickened. Stir the parsley through.

6 Carve the corned beef into thick slices. Use a slotted spoon to lift the potatoes and cabbage out of the slow cooker onto serving plates, and discard the onion. Serve with the mustard and parsley sauce.

⚙ *The beef is delicious with steamed carrots and green beans. Store any leftover corned beef in a bowl with the remaining cooking liquid; cover with plastic wrap and refrigerate.*

Beef short ribs with molasses, bourbon and thyme

Serves **4**   Preparation time **20 minutes (+ 24 hours marinating)**   Cooking time **6 hours 15 minutes**

8 beef short ribs, about 2 kg
   (4 lb 8 oz), separated
1 tablespoon olive oil
2 brown onions, chopped
2 carrots, cut in half lengthways
   and sliced
4 garlic cloves, chopped
125 ml (4 fl oz/½ cup) red wine
690 ml (24 fl oz) tomato passata
   (puréed tomatoes)
115 g (4 oz/⅓ cup) molasses
60 ml (2 fl oz/¼ cup) bourbon
1 tablespoon dijon mustard
3 thyme sprigs, plus extra, to garnish
1 dried bay leaf
1 teaspoon freshly ground black
   pepper

Molasses marinade
375 ml (13 fl oz/1½ cups) beer
60 g (¼ oz) molasses
5 thyme sprigs
1 teaspoon sea salt
1 teaspoon chilli flakes
1 teaspoon mustard powder
60 ml (2 fl oz/¼ cup) worcestershire
   sauce

1 Place the molasses marinade ingredients in a small bowl and whisk to combine.

2 Arrange the ribs in a 30 x 25 cm (12 x 10 inch) rectangular dish in one layer. Pour the marinade over the ribs and toss to coat. Cover and marinate in the refrigerator for 24 hours, turning the ribs over after about 12 hours.

3 Drain the ribs from the marinade and discard the marinade.

4 Heat the olive oil in the insert pan of a 5.5 litre (192 fl oz/22 cup) slow cooker or a frying pan over medium–high heat. Add the ribs in batches and fry for 2–3 minutes on each side, or until browned on all sides, removing each batch to a plate.

5 Return the insert pan, if using to the slow cooker. Place all the ribs in the slow cooker. Add the remaining ingredients and gently mix to combine. Cover and cook on low for 6 hours.

6 Skim the fat from the surface of the sauce. Serve the ribs drizzled generously with the sauce and garnished with extra thyme.

Prosciutto-wrapped beef with broad beans

Serves 4   Preparation time **25 minutes (+ 15 minutes resting)**   Cooking time **2 hours 30 minutes**

500 g (1 lb 2 oz) thick beef fillet
3 garlic cloves, thinly sliced
2 tablespoons chopped rosemary
8–10 thin slices prosciutto, pancetta
  or smoked bacon
20 g (¾ oz) dried wild mushrooms,
  such as porcini
2 tablespoons olive oil
1 brown onion, halved and sliced
170 ml (5½ fl oz/⅔ cup) red wine
400 g (14 oz) tin chopped tomatoes
400 g (14 oz) peeled broad (fava)
  beans
Mashed potato or soft polenta,
  to serve

1 Trim the beef of excess fat and make several small incisions around the meat. Push a slice of garlic into each incision, using up one of the garlic cloves. Sprinkle 1 tablespoon of the rosemary over the beef and season with sea salt and freshly ground black pepper.

2 Lay the prosciutto slices on a board in a line next to each other, creating a sheet of prosciutto to wrap the beef in. Place the beef fillet across them and fold the prosciutto over to enclose the beef. Tie several times with kitchen string to keep the beef and prosciutto together. Leave in the refrigerator to rest for at least 15 minutes.

3 Meanwhile, put the dried mushrooms in a bowl with 185 ml (6 fl oz/¾ cup) hot water and soak for 10 minutes.

4 Heat the olive oil in the insert pan of a 4.5 litre (157 fl oz/18 cup) slow cooker or a frying pan over high heat. Add the beef and sear on all sides until the prosciutto is golden brown, but not burnt. Some of the prosciutto might fall off, but this won't matter: just make sure the beef is well sealed.

5 Return the insert pan, if using, to the slow cooker, or transfer the beef to the slow cooker. Add the remaining garlic and rosemary, the mushrooms and their soaking liquid, as well as the onion, wine and tomatoes. Cover and cook on low for 2 hours, or until the beef is tender.

6 Add the broad beans and cook for a further 20 minutes. Season with sea salt and freshly ground black pepper and serve with mashed potato or soft polenta.

Marmalade-glazed corned beef

Serves **4–6**   Preparation time **15 minutes**   Cooking time **8 hours 5 minutes**

3 all-purpose potatoes, about
     500 g (1 lb 2 oz)
85 g (3 oz/¼ cup) orange
     marmalade
2 tablespoons dijon mustard
1 tablespoon brown sugar
1.5 kg (3 lb 5 oz) corned beef,
     trimmed of excess fat
350 g (12 oz/1 bunch) baby carrots,
     trimmed and peeled
½ small red onion, very thinly sliced,
     to garnish (optional)
30 g (1 oz/¼ cup) walnut halves,
     to garnish (optional)

1 Peel the potatoes, cut into large chunks and place in a 5.5 litre (192 fl oz/22 cup) slow cooker.

2 In a small bowl, mix together 2 tablespoons of the marmalade, the mustard and sugar.

3 Rub the marmalade mixture all over the beef, rubbing it in well. Rest the beef in the slow cooker, on top of the potatoes, and drizzle with any marmalade mixture remaining in the bowl. Cover and cook for 6 hours on low.

4 Add the carrots to the slow cooker, then cover and cook for a further 2 hours.

5 Remove the corned beef from the slow cooker and place on a warm platter. Cover with foil and set aside to rest in a warm place for 10 minutes before carving.

6 Meanwhile, melt the remaining marmalade. To do this, either warm it in the microwave, in a microwave-safe bowl for about 20 seconds, or place it in a small saucepan over low heat and cook, stirring, for 1–2 minutes. Brush the marmalade over the hot beef to glaze it.

7 Carve the beef into thick slices. Serve with the potatoes and baby carrots, garnished with red onion slices and walnut halves if desired.

⚙ *Tip: Many of us think of corned beef as a hearty winter meal, but in summer it is equally delicious cold — try serving it with coleslaw, or enjoy it sliced on sandwiches.*

Braised beef cheeks with pappardelle and gremolata

Serves **6–8**   Preparation time **20 minutes (+ overnight marinating)**
Cooking time **6 hours 35 minutes**

750 ml (26 fl oz/3 cups) red wine
3 garlic cloves, crushed
1 fresh bay leaf
1 teaspoon whole black peppercorns
10 thyme sprigs
6 trimmed beef cheeks, about
   250 g (9 oz) each
2 tablespoons olive oil
2 brown onions, finely chopped
1 carrot, diced
3 garlic cloves, finely chopped
1 tablespoon tomato paste
   (concentrated purée)
400 g (14 oz) tin chopped tomatoes
100 ml (3½ fl oz) good-quality
   beef stock
600 g (1 lb 5 oz) fresh pappardelle
   pasta

Gremolata
3 tablespoons finely chopped
   flat-leaf (Italian) parsley
Finely grated zest and juice of
   1 lemon
½ garlic clove, finely chopped
60 ml (2 fl oz/¼ cup) extra virgin
   olive oil

1   Combine the wine, garlic, bay leaf, peppercorns and half the thyme in a glass or ceramic container. Add the beef and mix until well coated. Cover and marinate in the refrigerator overnight. Strain the beef, reserving the red wine marinade, but discarding the herbs and garlic.

2   Heat half the oil in the insert pan of a 7 litre (245 fl oz/ 28 cup) slow cooker or a deep frying pan over medium heat. Pat the beef dry with paper towels. Brown in batches for 2–3 minutes, or until golden, turning once. Remove and set aside.

3   Heat the remaining oil in the pan. Cook the onion, carrot and garlic for 5–7 minutes, or until softened. Add the tomato paste and cook, stirring, for 1 minute, or until the paste darkens. Stir in half the reserved marinade and cook for 8–10 minutes, or until reduced by half.

4   Add the beef, tomatoes and stock and bring to a simmer. Add remaining thyme and season with sea salt and freshly ground black pepper. Return the insert pan, if using to the slow cooker, or transfer the mixture to the slow cooker. Cover and cook on low for 6 hours, or until the beef is very tender.

5   Remove the beef and set aside until cool enough to handle. Remove the thyme sprigs. Coarsely shred the meat, stir through the sauce and keep warm.

6   Near serving time, mix together the gremolata ingredients and set aside. Cook the pasta according to the packet instructions or until al dente, then drain well.

7   Toss the pasta through beef mixture and serve scattered with the gremolata.

Beef cheeks with red wine, port and Guinness

Serves 6   Preparation time **30 minutes**   Cooking time **8 hours**

6 untrimmed beef cheeks, about
  2.5 kg (5 lb 8 oz)
Plain (all-purpose) flour, for dusting
3 tablespoons olive oil
2 large brown onions, coarsely
  chopped
3 celery stalks, cut into 8 cm
  (3¼ inch) lengths
3 large carrots, cut in quarters
  lengthways
6 garlic cloves, peeled
400 ml (14 fl oz) red wine
100 ml (3½ fl oz) red wine vinegar
60 ml (2 fl oz/¼ cup) port
125 ml (4 fl oz/½ cup) Guinness
500 ml (17 fl oz/2 cups) good-quality
  chicken stock
4 thyme sprigs
2 dried bay leaves
8 peppercorns
1½ tablespoons chopped flat-leaf
  (Italian) parsley
Mashed potato, to serve

1 Trim the beef cheeks of any fat and sinew — they should weigh about 1.5 kg (3 lb 5 oz) once trimmed. Season the beef with sea salt and freshly ground black pepper, then lightly dust with flour.

2 Heat half the olive oil in the insert pan of a 7 litre (245 fl oz/28 cup) slow cooker or deep frying pan over medium–high heat. Brown half the beef for 2 minutes on each side, or until deep golden. Remove and set aside. Add the remaining oil and brown the remaining beef cheeks. Set aside.

3 Reduce the heat to medium–low. Add the onion, celery, carrot and garlic to the pan (there should be enough oil still in the pan) and cook for 5 minutes, stirring occasionally. Remove with a slotted spoon.

4 Add the wine, vinegar and port to the pan, stirring with a wooden spoon to dislodge any cooked-on bits. Increase the heat to high and boil for 8–10 minutes, or until the liquid has reduced by half.

5 Pour in the Guinness and bring back to the boil. Return the insert pan, if using, to the slow cooker, or transfer the sauce mixture to the slow cooker.

6 Add the beef, vegetables, stock, thyme, bay leaves and peppercorns. Cover and cook on low for 7½ hours, or until the beef is very tender.

7 Stir the parsley through and serve with mashed potato.

Italian meatballs with tomato sauce

Serves **4–6**   Preparation time **25 minutes (+ 20 minutes chilling)**   Cooking time **4 hours**

700 ml (24 fl oz) tomato passata
   (puréed tomatoes)
125 ml (4 fl oz/½ cup) red wine
2 tablespoons chopped basil

Meatballs
500 g (1 lb 2 oz) minced (ground)
   pork or beef
1 brown onion, finely chopped
80 g (2¾ oz/½ cup) pine nuts,
   coarsely chopped
2 garlic cloves, crushed
1 cup flat-leaf (Italian) parsley
   leaves, coarsely chopped
1 teaspoon chopped rosemary
2 teaspoons fennel seeds, ground
40 g (1½ oz/⅔ cup, lightly packed)
   fresh breadcrumbs (made from
   day old bread)
30 g (1 oz/¼ cup) coarsely grated
   parmesan cheese
Finely grated zest of 1 large lemon
1 egg, lightly beaten

1 Combine all the meatball ingredients in a bowl and mix together well. Using wet hands, roll the mixture into walnut-sized balls and place on a tray. Refrigerate the meatballs for 20 minutes.

2 Put the passata and wine in a 4.5 litre (157 fl oz/18 cup) slow cooker and stir together. Add the meatballs and turn them in the sauce to coat. Season with sea salt and freshly ground black pepper.

3 Cover and cook on high for 4 hours, or until the meatballs are tender and cooked through. Stir the basil through and serve.

⚙ *Tip: Serve the meatballs and tomato sauce with hot spaghetti, steamed rice or mashed potato, and a lovely crisp side salad.*

Veal rolls with prosciutto and sage

Serves 6   Preparation time **30 minutes**   Cooking time **8 hours**

6 x 150 g (5½ oz) veal leg steaks
   (schnitzels)
6 prosciutto slices, trimmed of fat
50 g (1¾ oz/½ cup) finely grated
   parmesan cheese
Finely grated zest of 1 lemon
12 sage leaves, plus extra, to garnish
1 tablespoon olive oil
20 g (¾ oz) butter
1 tablespoon cornflour (cornstarch)
   (optional)

Tomato and olive sauce
400 g (14 oz) tin chopped tomatoes
2 semi-dried (sun-blushed) tomatoes,
   finely chopped
2 spring onions (scallions), chopped
2 garlic cloves, crushed
10 black olives, pitted and chopped
1 teaspoon caster (superfine) sugar

1 Combine the tomato and olive sauce ingredients in a bowl and season with sea salt and freshly ground black pepper. Pour half the sauce into a 4.5 litre (157 fl oz/18 cup) slow cooker and set the remainder aside.

2 Place each veal steak between two sheets of plastic wrap. Use the flat side of a meat mallet to pound them to 5 mm (¼ inch) thick and about 25 x 10 cm (10 x 4 inches) in size.

3 Lay the prosciutto slices along the top of each veal steak. Divide the parmesan, lemon zest and sage leaves along each piece of veal, then season with black pepper. Roll up each veal steak and secure with a toothpick.

4 Heat the olive oil and butter in a large frying pan over medium heat. Add the veal rolls and cook for 5 minutes, turning frequently, until browned. Pack the veal rolls in the slow cooker, side by side. Pour the reserved tomato sauce over.

5 Cover and cook on low for 6–8 hours, or until the veal is tender. Remove the veal rolls to a warm plate and remove the toothpicks. Cover loosely with foil and keep warm while finishing the sauce.

6 If the sauce needs thickening, mix the cornflour in a bowl with 1 tablespoon water until smooth, then stir into the sauce. Stir over high heat until the sauce has thickened.

7 Thickly slice each veal roll on the diagonal. Serve drizzled with the sauce and garnished with extra sage.

Tip: Serve with mashed potato or soft polenta, and vegetables or salad.

Veal braised with lemon thyme

Serves **4**   Preparation time **15 minutes**   Cooking time **3 hours 35 minutes**

2 tablespoons olive oil
1.5 kg (3 lb 5 oz) rack of veal
(6 cutlets), trimmed to a
neat shape
2 leeks, white part only, thinly
sliced
30 g (1 oz) butter
1 tablespoon plain (all-purpose)
flour
1 tablespoon finely grated lemon
zest
125 ml (4 fl oz/½ cup) good-quality
chicken stock
125 ml (4 fl oz/½ cup) white wine
2 tablespoons lemon thyme
125 ml (4 fl oz/½ cup) pouring
cream
Boiled baby potatoes, to serve

1 Heat the olive oil in a deep heavy-based frying pan over medium heat. Add the veal rack and brown well on all sides. Place in a 4.5 litre (157 fl oz/18 cup) slow cooker.

2 Add the leek and butter to the frying pan, reduce the heat and cook, stirring occasionally, for 10 minutes, or until the leek is soft. Add the flour and cook for 2 minutes, stirring continuously. Add the lemon zest and season with freshly ground black pepper. Stir in the stock and wine and bring to the boil, stirring continuously.

3 Transfer the leek mixture to the slow cooker. Cover and cook on low for 3 hours, or until the veal is tender and cooked through.

4 Remove the veal to a warm platter and cover loosely with foil while finishing the sauce.

5 Turn the slow cooker setting to high. Add the lemon thyme and cream to the slow cooker and cook, uncovered, for a further 10 minutes. Season to taste with sea salt and freshly ground black pepper.

6 Serve the veal with the sauce and boiled baby potatoes.

Braised veal shanks

Serves **4–6**   Preparation time **30 minutes**   Cooking time **4 hours 5 minutes**

4–6 veal shanks, about 2 kg
   (4 lb 8 oz)
Plain (all-purpose) flour, for dusting
1 leek, white part only, finely diced
1 brown onion, finely diced
1 carrot, finely diced
1 celery stalk, finely diced
2 garlic cloves, finely chopped
1 dried bay leaf
1 rosemary sprig, leaves chopped
125 ml (4 fl oz/½ cup) red wine
500 ml (17 fl oz/2 cups)
   good-quality veal stock
200 g (7 oz) tinned or bottled
   artichoke halves, drained
75 g (2½ oz/½ cup) frozen peas
Mashed potato or creamy polenta,
   to serve

Orange gremolata
1 garlic clove, finely chopped
Finely grated zest of 1 orange
3 tablespoons flat-leaf (Italian)
   parsley, finely chopped

1 Coat the veal shanks in the flour and shake off the excess.

2 Place the shanks in a 4.5 litre (157 fl oz/18 cup) slow cooker. Add the leek, onion, carrot, celery, garlic, bay leaf, rosemary, wine and stock. Cover and cook on high for 3 hours.

3 Add the artichokes to the slow cooker. Continue to cook on high, uncovered, for 1 hour.

4 Stir in the peas and cook for a further 5 minutes, or until the peas are cooked through. Season to taste with sea salt and freshly ground black pepper.

5 Meanwhile, combine the orange gremolata ingredients in a bowl.

6 Serve the veal shanks on a bed of mashed potato or creamy polenta, sprinkled with the gremolata.

Veal with Jerusalem artichokes and mustard cream

Serves **4–6**   Preparation time **20 minutes**   Cooking time **7 hours 30 minutes**

50 g (1¾ oz/⅓ cup) plain
  (all-purpose) flour
1.5 kg (3 lb 5 oz) veal osso bucco
60 ml (2 fl oz/¼ cup) olive oil
400 g (14 oz) Jerusalem artichokes,
  peeled and quartered
1 brown onion, thinly sliced
2 garlic cloves, crushed
60 ml (2 fl oz/¼ cup) verjuice or
  white wine
375 ml (13 fl oz/1½ cups) good-
  quality chicken stock
2 tablespoons chopped rosemary,
  plus extra, to garnish
2 tablespoons pouring cream
1 tablespoon wholegrain mustard
Soft polenta and lemon cheeks,
  to serve

1 Place half the flour in a bowl and season with sea salt and freshly ground black pepper. Toss the veal in the seasoned flour to coat well, shaking off the excess.

2 Heat half the olive oil in a large frying pan over medium–high heat. Add half the veal and cook for 5 minutes, or until golden, turning halfway through. Transfer the veal to a 5.5 litre (192 fl oz/22 cup) slow cooker. Brown the remaining veal and place in the slow cooker, then scatter the Jerusalem artichokes over the top.

3 Heat the remaining oil in the pan over medium heat. Add the onion and cook, stirring, for 5 minutes, or until golden. Add the garlic and cook for 1 minute. Add the remaining flour and cook, stirring, for 2 minutes. Gradually stir in the verjuice and stock, then add the rosemary. Simmer for 3 minutes, or until slightly thickened.

4 Pour the sauce over the veal. Cover and cook on low for 7 hours, or until the veal is very tender.

5 Remove the veal to a large warm bowl and cover loosely with foil while finishing the sauce.

6 Skim any fat from the surface of the sauce. Transfer the sauce to a small saucepan, then stir in the cream and mustard. Simmer over medium heat for 5 minutes, or until slightly thickened.

7 Serve the veal on a bed of polenta, drizzled with the sauce and sprinkled with extra rosemary. Serve with lemon cheeks for squeezing over.

Braised Mexican pork shoulder

Serves 4–6   Preparation time **25 minutes**   Cooking time **6 hours 25 minutes**

2 tablespoons olive oil
2 teaspoons ground cumin
¼ teaspoon ground allspice
¼ teaspoon ground cloves
1.2 kg (2 lb 10 oz) boneless pork
    shoulder, trimmed of excess fat
    and cut into 8 pieces
200 g (7 oz) tinned chopped
    tomatoes
1 tablespoon cider vinegar
1 small cinnamon stick
⅓ cup chopped coriander (cilantro)
    leaves
Warmed corn tortillas, guacamole,
    lime wedges and Tabasco sauce,
    to serve

Spice paste
1 brown onion, coarsely chopped
4 garlic cloves, chopped
1½ tablespoons raisins
2 fresh jalapeño or long green
    chillies, chopped
1 teaspoon dried oregano
½ teaspoon dried thyme
1 teaspoon sea salt

Green chilli salsa
1 fresh jalapeño or long green
    chilli, seeded and finely chopped
½ white onion, finely chopped
¼ cup chopped coriander (cilantro)
    leaves

1 To make the spice paste, put the onion, garlic, raisins and chilli in a food processor and blend until smooth. Stir in the oregano, thyme and salt.

2 Heat the olive oil in the insert pan of a 5 litre (175 fl oz/ 20 cup) slow cooker or a large frying pan over medium– high heat. Fry the spice paste for 7–8 minutes, or until the mixture starts to darken and the onion loses its rawness.

3 Add the cumin, allspice and cloves and cook for 1 minute. Increase the heat to high. Add the pork and cook for 5–7 minutes, in batches if necessary, until browned all over, turning occasionally.

4 Return the insert pan, if using, to the slow cooker, or transfer the pork mixture to the slow cooker. Stir in the tomatoes, vinegar, cinnamon stick and 60 ml (2 fl oz/¼ cup) water.

5 Cover and cook on low for 6 hours, or until the pork is falling apart.

6 Remove the pork to a board. Using two forks, shred the meat into small chunks and return it to the slow cooker. Stir in the coriander and cover with the lid to keep warm.

7 Combine the green chilli salsa ingredients in a small bowl.

8 To assemble, place a small amount of the pork mixture on a warm tortilla with some guacamole. Top with some green chilli salsa, add a squeeze of lime juice and Tabasco, before rolling up the tortilla.

Pork with cider and apples

Serves **4**   Preparation time **25 minutes**   Cooking time **5 hours 50 minutes**

1.3 kg (3 lb) piece of pork belly,
    cut into long slices about 3 cm
    (1¼ inches) thick (see Tip)
2 teaspoons olive oil
300 g (10½ oz) bacon, chopped
2 brown onions, cut into wedges
2 garlic cloves, crushed
6 juniper berries, lightly crushed
2 teaspoons thyme leaves
1½ tablespoons wholegrain mustard
170 ml (5½ fl oz/⅔ cup) apple cider
2 pink lady apples, skin on, cut into
    wedges 3 cm (1¼ inches) wide
600 g (1 lb 5 oz) waxy or boiling
    potatoes, skin on, sliced 1.5 cm
    (⅝ inch) thick

1 Season the pork belly generously with sea salt. Heat the olive oil in the insert pan of a 5 litre (175 fl oz/ 20 cup) slow cooker or a large frying pan. Brown the pork in batches for 2–3 minutes on each side, or until golden brown. Remove to a plate.

2 Add the bacon to the pan and cook for 2 minutes, or until golden. Return the insert pan, if using, to the slow cooker, or transfer the bacon to the slow cooker.

3 Add the pork to the slow cooker, along with the onion, garlic, juniper berries, thyme, mustard, cider and apple. Layer the potato slices over the top.

4 Cover and cook on high for 5½ hours, or until the pork and potato are tender. Season to taste with sea salt and freshly ground black pepper and serve.

Tip: If possible, ask your butcher for the thicker end of the pork belly, which will be the meatiest. (Pork belly is essentially just layers of meat and fat.)

Pork neck with Marsala and pears

Serves **8–10**   Preparation time **25 minutes**   Cooking time **4 hours 20 minutes**

60 ml (2 fl oz/¼ cup) olive oil
1 pork neck, about 2 kg (4 lb 8 oz)
4 brown onions, thinly sliced
200 ml (7 fl oz) dry white wine
125 ml (4 fl oz/½ cup) Marsala
2 pears, cored and quartered
3 tablespoons thyme leaves
2 tablespoons red wine vinegar
Creamy mashed potato, to serve

1 Heat half the olive oil in the insert pan of a 7 litre (245 fl oz/28 cup) slow cooker or a frying pan over medium heat. Add the pork neck and cook, turning occasionally, for 4–5 minutes, or until sealed all over. Remove and set aside.

2 Heat the remaining oil in the pan. Add the onion and cook, stirring occasionally, for 8–10 minutes, or until it starts to caramelise. Stir in the wine and Marsala and bring to a simmer.

3 Return the insert pan, if using, to the slow cooker, or transfer the mixture to the slow cooker. Add the pork, then scatter the pear and thyme around the pork.

4 Cover and cook on high for 3½–4 hours, or until the pork is tender.

5 Stir the vinegar through, then season to taste with sea salt and freshly ground black pepper. Serve with creamy mashed potato.

⚙ *Tip: This cut of pork is wonderfully flavoursome and tender and makes a great budget meal when served with creamy mashed potato.*

Pulled pork with coleslaw and pickled chilli

Serves **8–10**   Preparation time **35 minutes**   Cooking time **7 hours 25 minutes**

250 ml (9 fl oz/1 cup) tomato sauce (ketchup)

250 g (9 oz/1 cup) chopped tinned tomatoes

185 ml (6 fl oz/¾ cup) cider vinegar

60 g (2¼ oz/¼ cup) hot American mustard

1 brown onion, finely diced

100 g (3½ oz/½ cup, lightly packed) brown sugar

60 ml (2 fl oz/¼ cup) worcestershire sauce

1.5 kg (3 lb 5 oz) boneless pork shoulder, cut in half

60 ml (2 fl oz/¼ cup) Tabasco chipotle chilli sauce, or other smoky chilli sauce, to taste

Soft white bread rolls and pickled chilli, to serve

Coleslaw

60 ml (2 fl oz/¼ cup) white wine vinegar

2 tablespoons caster (superfine) sugar

250 g (9 oz) white cabbage, shredded

2 tablespoons extra virgin olive oil

1 Combine the tomato sauce, tomatoes, vinegar, mustard, onion, sugar and worcestershire sauce in a 7 litre (245 fl oz/28 cup) slow cooker. Season with sea salt and freshly ground black pepper and stir to combine.

2 Add the pork pieces, turning to coat them completely. Cover and cook on low for 6–7 hours, or until the pork is very tender, turning occasionally.

3 To make the coleslaw, combine the vinegar and sugar in a saucepan over medium heat. Bring to a simmer, season to taste, then cool slightly. Place the cabbage in a bowl, pour the vinegar mixture over and set aside to cool. Drain, toss the olive oil through and season to taste.

4 When the pork is tender, remove it to a board and leave until cool enough to handle.

5 Meanwhile, place the insert pan of the slow cooker over medium–high heat, or transfer the sauce to a saucepan. Allow the sauce to reduce over medium–high heat for 20–25 minutes, or until thick and rich. Season to taste and add the Tabasco.

6 When the pork is cool enough to handle, shred the meat, discarding the fat and skin. Stir the pork through the sauce and keep warm.

7 To assemble, fill the bread rolls with the pork mixture, top with some coleslaw and pickled chilli, if desired, and season to taste. Serve immediately so the rolls don't become soggy.

Asian braised pork belly with chilli caramel

Serves **6**   Preparation time **40 minutes**   Cooking time **6 hours 15 minutes**

1.6 kg (3 lb 8 oz) piece of pork belly
Sea salt, to sprinkle
Steamed rice and Asian greens,
   to serve

Braising liquid
375 ml (13 fl oz/1½ cups) soy sauce
2 tablespoons kecap manis
60 ml (2 fl oz/¼ cup) Chinese rice
   wine or dry sherry
5 cm (2 inch) piece fresh ginger,
   peeled and thinly sliced
5 garlic cloves, crushed
5 spring onions (scallions), coarsely
   chopped
2 tablespoons brown sugar
2 long fresh red chillies, split
   lengthways
2 star anise

Chilli caramel
150 g (5½ oz/1 cup) grated
   palm sugar (jaggery), or 185 g
   (6½ oz/1 cup, lightly packed)
   brown sugar
1 long fresh red chilli, thinly sliced
2 teaspoons finely grated fresh
   ginger
60 ml (2 fl oz/¼ cup) fish sauce
60 ml (2 fl oz/¼ cup) lime juice

1 Combine the braising liquid ingredients in the insert pan of a 5 litre (175 fl oz/20 cup) slow cooker or a large saucepan. Pour in 1.5 litres (52 fl oz/6 cups) water and bring to the boil over medium heat, stirring to dissolve the sugar.

2 Return the insert pan, if using, to the slow cooker, or transfer the braising liquid to the slow cooker. Add the pork belly and turn to coat in the liquid. Cover and cook for 5–6 hours, or until the pork is very tender.

3 Near serving time, make the chilli caramel. Put the palm sugar in a saucepan with 60 ml (2 fl oz/¼ cup) water. Simmer over medium heat for 5–6 minutes, or until the sugar caramelises. Add the chilli, ginger and another 60 ml (2 fl oz/¼ cup) water and stir to combine. Stir in the fish sauce and lime juice and bring to a simmer. Allow to simmer for another 2–3 minutes, or until the liquid becomes syrupy. Set aside and keep warm.

4 Preheat the grill (broiler) to high. Remove the pork from the braising liquid and place on a foil-lined baking tray, skin side up. Sprinkle sea salt all over the pork, then grill for 4–5 minutes, or until the skin is crisp.

5 Thickly slice the pork and serve with the chilli caramel, steamed rice and Asian greens.

Spare ribs with beer and barbecue sauce

Serves **4–6**   Preparation time **20 minutes**   Cooking time **4–5 hours**

1.5 kg (3 lb 5 oz) pork spare ribs
185 ml (6 fl oz/¾ cup) beer
185 ml (6 fl oz/¾ cup) barbecue
    sauce
2 tablespoons sweet chilli sauce
1 tablespoon worcestershire sauce
1 tablespoon honey
2 spring onions (scallions), thinly
    sliced
2 garlic cloves, crushed
1 tablespoon cornflour (cornstarch)
Coriander (cilantro) leaves, to garnish

1 Cut the pork ribs into individual ribs, or into sets of two or three if preferred. Trim away any excess fat.

2 In a large bowl, combine the beer, barbecue sauce, sweet chilli sauce, worcestershire sauce, honey, spring onion and garlic. Season with sea salt and freshly ground black pepper. Add the ribs and turn them around to thoroughly coat them in the sauce.

3 Transfer the ribs and marinade to a 4.5 litre (157 fl oz/ 18 cup) slow cooker. Cover and cook on high for 4 hours.

4 After 4 hours, check to see if the ribs are tender — however, the meat should not be falling off the bone. If necessary, continue to cook the ribs for a further 1 hour.

5 Using tongs, remove the ribs to a warm platter and cover loosely with foil while finishing the sauce.

6 Mix the cornflour with 1 tablespoon water until smooth, then stir into the sauce in the slow cooker. Cook, stirring, on high heat for 5–10 minutes, or until the sauce has thickened.

7 Serve the ribs drizzled with the sauce and sprinkled with coriander. Supply lots of paper napkins for sticky fingers.

Braised pork neck with orange and star anise

Serves **6**   Preparation time **30 minutes**   Cooking time **4 hours 20 minutes**

1 cup flat-leaf (Italian) parsley leaves
1 tablespoon ground cinnamon
1 tablespoon finely grated fresh
    ginger
2 garlic cloves, crushed
1.6 kg (3 lb 8 oz) pork neck
1 orange, peeled and segmented
80 ml (2½ fl oz/⅓ cup) olive oil
4 star anise
Mashed sweet potato, to serve

1 Put the parsley in a heatproof bowl and pour over enough boiling water to cover. Strain, then transfer the blanched parsley to a small food processor. Add the cinnamon, ginger and garlic and process to a paste.

2 Slice the pork lengthways along the middle and open it out flat on a clean work surface. Brush with the parsley and cinnamon paste, then lay the orange segments along the centre. Roll the pork tightly to form a cylinder, enclosing the orange, and tie at intervals with kitchen string. Brush the pork with the olive oil and generously season with sea salt and freshly ground black pepper.

3 Heat the remaining oil in the insert pan of a 4.5 litre (157 fl oz/18 cup) slow cooker or a frying pan over high heat. Seal the pork for 4 minutes on each side, or until golden all over.

4 Return the insert pan, if using, to the slow cooker, or transfer the pork to the slow cooker. Add the star anise.

5 Cover and cook on high for 4 hours, or until the pork is tender and cooked through. Season to taste and serve with mashed sweet potato.

Pork loin rack with pancetta and sweet potato

Serves **4**   Preparation time **20 minutes**   Cooking time **5 hours 10 minutes**

1.2 kg (2 lb 10 oz) pork loin rack, with 4 chops
90 g (3¼ oz) piece of pancetta, about 1 cm (½ inch) thick, diced
6 bulb spring onions (scallions), trimmed leaving about 3 cm (1¼ inches) of stem attached, then halved lengthways
2 garlic cloves, chopped
350 g (12 oz) purple sweet potato, cut into 5 cm (2 inch) chunks
250 ml (9 fl oz/1 cup) sparkling apple juice (cider)
1 cinnamon stick
1 tablespoon cornflour (cornstarch)
2 tablespoons chopped flat-leaf (Italian) parsley

1 Trim the pork of skin and fat. Press some sea salt and freshly ground black pepper all over the pork, then place in a 4.5 litre (157 fl oz/18 cup) slow cooker.

2 Add the pancetta, spring onion, garlic, sweet potato, apple juice and cinnamon stick. Cover and cook on high for 4–5 hours, or until the pork is tender.

3 Transfer the pork and vegetables to a warm serving platter, discarding the cinnamon stick. Cover loosely with foil while finishing the sauce.

4 Mix the cornflour with a little water to make a smooth paste, then stir into the juices in the slow cooker. Cook, stirring, for a further 5–10 minutes, or until the sauce has thickened a little.

5 Cut through the pork rack to serve one chop per person. Serve the pork topped with the vegetables and sauce spooned over and scattered with parsley.

Pork belly with vegetables and lentils

Serves **6**   Preparation time **20 minutes**   Cooking time **5 hours**

1 kg (2 lb 4 oz) piece of pork belly
1 brown onion, peeled
4 whole cloves
1 large carrot, cut into chunks
200 g (7 oz) swede (rutabaga) or
  turnips, cut into chunks
100 g (3½ oz) leek, white part only,
  thickly sliced
1 parsnip, cut into chunks
1 garlic clove
1 bouquet garni
2 dried bay leaves
6 juniper berries, slightly crushed
350 g (12 oz/1⅔ cups) puy lentils
  or tiny blue-green lentils
2 tablespoons chopped flat-leaf
  (Italian) parsley

1 Slice the pork belly into thick strips and place in a 4.5 litre (157 fl oz/18 cup) slow cooker. Stud the onion with the cloves and add to the slow cooker, along with all the remaining ingredients except the lentils and parsley.

2 Stir thoroughly, then add just enough water to half-cover the ingredients. Cover and cook on high for 4 hours.

3 Put the lentils in a sieve and rinse under cold running water. Add to the slow cooker, stirring them in a bit. Cover and cook for a further 1 hour, or until the pork and lentils are tender.

4 Drain the mixture into a colander, discarding the liquid. Return the contents of the colander to the slow cooker, except for the onion, which can be discarded.

5 Season the mixture with plenty of freshly ground black pepper and taste to see if you need any salt.

6 Just before serving, stir the parsley through.

Pork with a spicy barbecue sauce

Serves **4–6**   Preparation time **20 minutes**   Cooking time **7 hours**

1 brown onion, thinly sliced
1.6 kg (3 lb 8 oz) boneless rolled
    pork loin
1 tablespoon coriander (cilantro)
    leaves, chopped
Fresh bread rolls and side salad,
    to serve (optional)

Spicy barbecue sauce
250 ml (9 fl oz/1 cup) barbecue
    sauce
1½ tablespoons coarsely chopped
    jalapeño chilli
½ teaspoon ground cumin
¼ teaspoon ground cinnamon
1 teaspoon sweet paprika
45 g (1½ oz/¼ cup, lightly packed)
    brown sugar
2 garlic cloves, chopped
1 teaspoon dijon mustard
2 tablepoons red wine vinegar
2 teaspoons worcestershire sauce

1 Combine the spicy barbecue sauce ingredients in a bowl. Add 250 ml (9 fl oz/1 cup) water and mix well to dissolve the sugar.

2 Scatter the onion into a 4.5 litre (157 fl oz/18 cup) slow cooker. Add the pork and pour the sauce over the top. Cover and cook on high for 7 hours, or until the pork is tender.

3 Remove the pork to a board and leave until cool enough to handle. Shred the meat using two forks or your fingers.

4 Stir the coriander through the sauce in the slow cooker.

5 Serve the pork on fresh bread rolls, topped with the spicy barbecue sauce, with a side salad, if desired.

Japanese slow-cooked pork belly

Serves **4–6** Preparation time **20 minutes** Cooking time **5 hours**

1 kg (2 lb 4 oz) piece of pork belly
100 g (3½ oz) piece of fresh ginger,
    peeled and thickly sliced
500 ml (17 fl oz/2 cups) dashi
    (made up according to the
    packet instructions)
170 ml (5½ fl oz/⅔ cup) sake
60 ml (2 fl oz/¼ cup) mirin
80 g (2¾ oz/⅓ cup, firmly packed)
    dark brown sugar
125 ml (4 fl oz/½ cup) Japanese
    soy sauce
Steamed rice and Japanese mustard,
    to serve (optional)

1 Cut the pork belly into 5 cm (2 inch) dice. Place in a 4.5 litre (157 fl oz/18 cup) slow cooker with the ginger, dashi, sake, mirin, sugar and soy sauce.

2 Pour in 375 ml (13 fl oz/1½ cups) water and gently mix together. Cover and cook on low for 4½ hours, or until the pork is tender.

3 Remove the lid and turn the slow cooker setting to high. Cook, uncovered, for a further 30 minutes, or until the sauce has reduced slightly.

4 Serve the pork with steamed rice, with Japanese mustard on the side, if desired.

Pork and veal meatballs with herbs and parmesan

Serves **6**   Preparation time **35 minutes (+ 10 minutes soaking)**   Cooking time **3 hours 40 minutes**

2 tablespoons olive oil
1 brown onion, finely chopped
4 garlic cloves, thinly sliced
1.2 litres (42 fl oz) tomato passata
   (puréed tomatoes)
1 cup basil leaves
100 g (3½ oz) sourdough bread,
   coarsely torn
200 ml (7 fl oz) milk
1½ teaspoons fennel seeds
500 g (1 lb 2 oz) minced (ground)
   pork
500 g (1 lb 2 oz) minced (ground)
   veal
70 g (2½ oz/½ cup) finely grated
   parmesan cheese, plus extra, to
   serve
1½ tablespoons finely chopped
   rosemary leaves
600 g (1 lb 5 oz) spaghetti

1 Heat the olive oil in the insert pan of a 5 litre (175 fl oz/ 20 cup) slow cooker or a frying pan over medium heat. Add the onion and garlic and cook for 5–7 minutes, or until softened. Add the passata and basil and season with sea salt and freshly ground black pepper.

2 Return the insert pan, if using, to the slow cooker, or transfer the sauce to the slow cooker. Cover and cook on high for 1½–2 hours, stirring occasionally, until slightly reduced.

3 Meanwhile, put the bread and milk in a bowl. Set aside for 5–10 minutes, or until the bread has soaked up the milk.

4 Toast the fennel seeds in a small frying pan over medium heat for 30–60 seconds, or until aromatic. Grind the seeds using a mortar and pestle or an electric spice grinder.

5 Combine the pork, veal, parmsesan, rosemary, bread and fennel seeds in a large bowl. Season with salt and pepper and mix to combine. Roll into walnut-sized balls.

6 Add the meatballs to the passata sauce, turning them to coat in the sauce. Cover and cook on high for 1 hour, or until the meatballs are tender and cooked through. Remove the lid and cook for a further 30 minutes, or until the sauce has reduced slightly.

7 Meanwhile, add the spaghetti to a large saucepan of boiling salted water and cook according to packet instructions or until al dente. Drain well.

8 Toss the spaghetti through the meatballs and passata sauce. Serve sprinkled with extra parmesan.

Adobe pork

Serves **6**   Preparation time **20 minutes**   Cooking time **4 hours 30 minutes**

1 kg (2 lb 4 oz) pork neck
1 red onion, sliced
2 garlic cloves, chopped
125 ml (4 fl oz/½ cup) light soy
   sauce
1½ tablespoons apple cider vinegar
250 ml (9 fl oz/1 cup) good-quality
   beef stock
2 tablespoons brown sugar
1 tablespoon shredded fresh ginger
2 dried bay leaves
2 tablespoons plain (all-purpose)
   flour
1½ tablespoons lime juice
Steamed rice, to serve

1 Cut the pork into 4 cm (1½ inch) chunks and place in a 4.5 litre (157 fl oz/18 cup) slow cooker.

2 Add the onion, garlic, soy sauce, vinegar, stock, sugar, ginger, bay leaves and flour, then gently mix together. Cover and cook on high for 4 hours, or until the pork is tender.

3 Remove the lid and cook for a further 30 minutes, or until the sauce has thickened slightly.

4 Stir the lime juice through and season to taste with sea salt and freshly ground black pepper.

5 Serve with steamed rice.

Red-cooked pork belly

Serves **6**   Preparation time **15 minutes**   Cooking time **7 hours**

1 kg (2 lb 4 oz) piece of pork belly
500 ml (17 fl oz/2 cups) good-
    quality chicken stock
60 ml (2 fl oz/¼ cup) dark soy sauce
60 ml (2 fl oz/¼ cup) Chinese rice
    wine
6 dried shiitake mushrooms
4 garlic cloves, bruised
5 x 5 cm (2 x 2 inch) piece fresh
    ginger, peeled and sliced
1 piece of dried mandarin or
    tangerine zest
2 teaspoons sichuan peppercorns
2 star anise
1 cinnamon stick
2 tablespoons Chinese rock sugar
    (see Tip)
1 teaspoon sesame oil
3 spring onions (scallions), thinly
    sliced diagonally
Steamed rice, to serve

1 Put the pork belly in a 4.5 litre (157 fl oz/18 cup) slow cooker. Add the stock, soy sauce, rice wine, mushrooms, garlic, ginger, mandarin zest, peppercorns, star anise, cinnamon stick, rock sugar and sesame oil. Gently mix together. Cover and cook on low for 6 hours, or until the pork is very tender.

2 Remove the pork from the stock and set aside.

3 Strain the liquid into a bowl, set the mushrooms aside, then return the strained liquid to the slow cooker.

4 Turn the slow cooker setting to high. Cook, uncovered, for a further 1 hour, or until the liquid has reduced and thickened. About 15 minutes before the end of the cooking time, return the pork and mushrooms to the slow cooker to heat through.

5 Remove the pork from the stock and cut into 1 cm (½ inch) thick slices. Transfer to a warm platter with the mushrooms and spoon over some of the cooking liquid. Sprinkle with the spring onions and serve with rice.

Tip: Chinese rock sugar is a crystallised form of pure sugar and is named for its irregular rock-shaped pieces. It imparts a rich flavour, especially to braised or 'red-cooked' foods, and gives them a translucent glaze. Rock sugar is sold in Asian grocery stores.

Mapo dofu

Serves **4**   Preparation time **15 minutes (+ 20 minutes soaking)**   Cooking time **3 hours 5 minutes**

8 small dried shiitake mushrooms
(about 30 g/1 oz)
500 g (1 lb 2 oz) minced (ground)
pork
1 tablespoon Chinese rice wine or
dry sherry
60 ml (2 fl oz/¼ cup) peanut oil
1 tablespoon finely shredded
fresh ginger
2 garlic cloves, crushed
1–2 tablespoons crushed chilli
(from a jar)
310 ml (10¾ fl oz/1¼ cups) good-
quality chicken stock
1½ tablespoons black bean sauce
1½ teaspoons white miso paste
1 teaspoon sugar
3 small dried red chillies, or
½ teaspoon chilli flakes
3 spring onions (scallions), finely
sliced, white and green parts
separated
300 g (10½ oz) silken firm tofu,
cut into 8 cubes
½ teaspoon sichuan peppercorns,
ground
Steamed rice and steamed Asian
greens, to serve

1 Place the mushrooms in a bowl and pour in enough hot water to cover. Leave to soak for 20 minutes, then drain. Thickly slice the mushrooms and set aside.

2 Combine the pork and rice wine in a bowl and mix thoroughly.

3 Heat the peanut oil in the insert pan of a 5 litre (175 fl oz/20 cup) slow cooker or a frying pan over high heat. Cook the pork for 2–3 minutes, or until it starts to brown, breaking up any lumps with the back of a wooden spoon. Add the ginger, garlic and crushed chilli and cook for 2 minutes, or until aromatic.

4 Return the insert pan, if using, to the slow cooker, or transfer the pork mixture to the slow cooker.

5 In a bowl, mix together the stock, black bean sauce, miso paste and sugar. Add to the slow cooker with the reserved shiitake mushrooms, dried chillies, and the white part of the spring onion. Stir well, then cover and cook on low for 2 hours.

6 Add the tofu and gently stir to coat it in the sauce. Cover and cook for a further 1 hour.

7 Sprinkle with the sichuan pepper and the reserved spring onion. Serve with steamed rice and steamed Asian greens.

Sweet and sour braised pork

Serves **4**   Preparation time **10 minutes (+ overnight marinating)**   Cooking time **8 hours**

1.25 kg (2 lb 12 oz) piece of pork
  belly, cut into 8 thick strips
½ small pineapple, about 500 g
  (1 lb 2 oz), peeled and cored, then
  cut into 2 cm (¾ inch) chunks
1 carrot, thickly sliced
1 red onion, coarsely chopped
Steamed jasmine rice, to serve
2 spring onions (scallions), sliced
  diagonally and 1 long fresh
  red chilli, sliced to garnish

Soy marinade
2 teaspoons cornflour (cornstarch)
1 teaspoon sea salt
60 ml (2 fl oz/¼ cup) Chinese
  rice wine
2 tablespoons tomato sauce
  (ketchup)
2 tablespoons soy sauce
1 tablespoon grated palm sugar
  (jaggery), or brown sugar

1 Combine the soy marinade ingredients in a large glass or ceramic bowl. Mix well to dissolve the palm sugar, then add the pork and turn to coat. Cover and marinate in the refrigerator overnight.

2 Transfer the pork and marinade to a 5.5 litre (192 fl oz/22 cup) slow cooker. Add the pineapple, carrot and onion and gently mix together. Cover and cook on low for 8 hours.

3 Serve the pork and sauce with steamed rice, garnished with spring onion and chilli.

⚙ *Tip: If you have time, refrigerate the cooked braised pork mixture overnight. The fat will set in a layer on top of the stew, making it easy to skim off. Gently reheat the stew, adding a little water to loosen the mixture if needed. The flavour will also intensify if refrigerated overnight.*

Pork with apple sauce

Serves **4**   Preparation time **25 minutes**   Cooking time **5 hours 15 minutes**

1 kg (2 lb 4 oz) boneless pork leg, trimmed of excess fat and cut into 4 cm (1½ inch) chunks
1 tablespoon rosemary
1 leek, white part only, finely chopped
500 g (1 lb 2 oz) sweet potatoes, peeled and cut into 3 cm (1¼ inch) chunks
1 small fennel bulb, trimmed and thickly sliced
100 g (3½ oz) button mushrooms, halved
1 granny smith apple, peeled, cored and chopped
2 garlic cloves, chopped
375 ml (13 fl oz/1½ cups) sparkling apple cider
1 tablespoon cornflour (cornstarch)
2 tablespoons chopped flat-leaf (Italian) parsley
Steamed English spinach, to serve

1 Place the pork in a 5.5 litre (192 fl oz/22 cup) slow cooker. Sprinkle with the rosemary, then season well with sea salt and freshly ground black pepper. Gently toss to coat the pork.

2 Add the leek, sweet potato, fennel, mushrooms, apple and garlic and gently mix together. Pour in the cider. Cover and cook on high for 5 hours, or until the pork is tender.

3 Blend the cornflour with 1 tablespoon water until smooth, then stir through the pork mixture.

4 Cook, uncovered, for a further 15 minutes, or until the sauce has thickened slightly.

5 Sprinkle with the parsley and serve with steamed spinach.

Sticky pork ribs

Serves **4–6**   Preparation time **20 minutes**   Cooking time **4 hours**

Olive oil, for brushing

1.25 kg (2 lb 12 oz) pork barbecue
ribs (not spare ribs)

1 red onion, finely chopped

1 green capsicum (pepper), finely
chopped

1 long fresh green chilli, seeded
and finely chopped

2 garlic cloves, finely chopped

185 ml (6 fl oz/¾ cup) barbecue
sauce

2 tablespoons white wine vinegar

2 tablespoons soft brown sugar

1 tablespoon sweet chilli sauce

2 teaspoons worcestershire sauce

A dash of Tabasco sauce

Coriander (cilantro) leaves, to garnish

Trussed cherry tomatoes, to serve

Corn salsa

350 g (12 oz/2⅓ cups) frozen corn
kernels

2 spring onions (scallions), finely
chopped

1 tablespoon finely chopped
coriander (cilantro) leaves

1 tablespoon extra virgin olive oil

2 tablespoons lime juice

1 Lightly brush the bowl of a 5.5 litre (192 fl oz/22 cup)
slow cooker with olive oil.

2 Cut the ribs into sets of two or three, then trim off any
excess fat. Place the ribs in the slow cooker. Scatter the
onion, capsicum, chilli and garlic over the top and season
well with sea salt and freshly ground black pepper.

3 In a small bowl, combine the barbecue sauce, vinegar,
sugar, chilli sauce, worcestershire sauce and Tabasco.
Add 60 ml (2 fl oz/¼ cup) water, mix well to dissolve
the sugar, then pour over the ribs.

4 Cover and cook on high for 3½ hours, or until the ribs
are tender. During cooking, stir the mixture once or
twice to keep the ribs covered with the sauce.

5 After 3½ hours, check the ribs — the meat should be
tender, but not falling off the bone. If the meat isn't
yet tender, put the lid back on and continue to cook for
another 30 minutes.

6 Near serving time, prepare the corn salsa. Bring a
saucepan of water to the boil over high heat. Add the
corn and cook for 2–3 minutes, or until just tender.
Drain well, then place in a bowl. Add the spring onion,
coriander, oil and lime juice and gently toss to combine.

7 Using tongs, remove the ribs to a large serving plate.
Skim off any fat from the surface of the sauce, then spoon
the sauce over the ribs. Garnish with coriander and serve
with the corn salsa and cherry tomatoes.

Bacon-wrapped pork cooked with maple syrup

Serves **6**   Preparation time **25 minutes**   Cooking time **8 hours 40 minutes**

1.25 kg (2 lb 12 oz) pork neck, trimmed of any visible fat
400 g (14 oz) bacon slices, rind removed
Olive oil, for brushing
2 rosemary sprigs
125 ml (4 fl oz/½ cup) maple syrup
1 tablespoon cornflour (cornstarch)
Steamed asparagus, to serve

Creamy celeriac and potato mash
1 celeriac, peeled and cut into 2.5 cm (1 inch) chunks
1 large roasting potato, such as russet or king idaho, peeled and cut into 2.5 cm (1 inch) chunks
250 ml (9 fl oz/1 cup) milk
20 g (¾ oz) unsalted butter, softened

1 Season the pork with sea salt and freshly ground black pepper. Cut six lengths of kitchen string, each about 80 cm (31½ inches) long. Lay them on a clean work surface, evenly spaced to the width of the pork. Lay the bacon slices so they just overlap on top of the string, and run the same way as the string. Place the pork in the centre crossways to the bacon. Roll up firmly and tie the strings to secure the pork into a roll — the bacon should cover the pork.

2 Heat a large non-stick frying pan over high heat. Add the pork and brown for 10 minutes, turning regularly.

3 Lightly brush the bowl of a 5.5 litre (192 fl oz/22 cup) slow cooker with oil. Place the rosemary sprigs in the slow cooker and rest the pork on top. Season again with black pepper, then pour the maple syrup over. Cover and cook on low heat for 8 hours, or until pork is very tender.

4 Transfer the pork to a warm platter and cover with foil. Leave to rest in a warm place while finishing the sauce.

5 Turn the slow cooker setting to high. Blend the cornflour with 1 tablespoon water until smooth, then stir into the sauce. Cover and cook for a further 30 minutes, or until the sauce has thickened slightly.

6 Near serving time, make the creamy celeriac and potato mash. Bring the celeriac, potato and milk to the boil in a saucepan over high heat. Cover and cook for 15 minutes, or until tender. Mash well, season to taste and mix in the butter.

7 Carve the pork and drizzle with the sauce. Serve with the celeriac and potato mash and steamed asparagus.

Thai chilli basil pork ribs

Serves 4   Preparation time **10 minutes (+ overnight marinating)**   Cooking time **10 hours**

250 ml (9 fl oz/1 cup) Thai sweet
 chilli sauce
2 tablespoons tomato sauce
 (ketchup)
2 tablespoons dry sherry
2 tablespoons fish sauce
2 garlic cloves, crushed
2 teaspoons finely grated fresh
 ginger
1.5–2 kg (3 lb 5 oz–4 lb 8 oz)
 American-style pork spare ribs
Steamed rice and lime wedges,
 to serve

Apple salad
1 granny smith apple, cored and cut
 into thick matchsticks
1 small handful coriander (cilantro)
 leaves
1 long fresh green chilli, seeded
 and sliced
2 teaspoons lime juice

1 In a dish large enough to hold all the ribs, mix together the sweet chilli sauce, tomato sauce, sherry, fish sauce, garlic and ginger.

2 Cut the ribs into segments of two or three ribs per piece. Add them to the sweet chilli mixture and turn until well coated. Cover with plastic wrap and marinate in the refrigerator overnight.

3 Transfer the ribs to a 5.5 litre (192 fl oz/22 cup) slow cooker. Pour the marinade over the top.

4 Cover and cook on low for 8–10 hours, or until the meat is tender, turning the ribs occasionally during cooking and basting them with the sauce.

5 Near serving time, place the apple salad ingredients in a small salad bowl and gently mix together.

6 Divide the ribs among plates and drizzle with the sauce from the slow cooker. Serve with the apple salad, steamed rice and lime wedges.

Tip: If you're in a hurry you can cook the ribs on high, reducing the cooking time to 4–5 hours.

Five-spice caramel pork

Serves **6** Preparation time **20 minutes** Cooking time **6 hours 15 minutes**

1.3 kg (3 lb) piece of pork belly
1 tablespoon vegetable oil
55 g (2 oz/¼ cup) caster (superfine) sugar
1 teaspoon five-spice
1 star anise
250 ml (9 fl oz/1 cup) good-quality chicken stock
1 tablespoon fish sauce
185 ml (6 fl oz/¾ cup) light soy sauce
Steamed white rice and sliced fresh red chilli, to serve (optional)

Cucumber and ginger salad
1 Lebanese (short) cucumber, shaved lengthways into thin ribbons
1 spring onion (scallion), thinly sliced diagonally
1 cm (½ inch) piece of fresh ginger, peeled and cut into thin matchsticks
1 tablespoon peanut oil
2 teaspoons rice vinegar

1 Cut the pork belly into 5 cm (2 inch) dice. Heat the oil in the insert pan of a 5.5 litre (192 fl oz/22 cup) slow cooker or a frying pan over medium–high heat. Add the pork in batches and fry for 5 minutes, or until golden, turning to brown all over, removing each batch to a plate.

2 Return the insert pan, if using, to the slow cooker. Add all the pork to the slow cooker. Sprinkle the pork with the sugar and five-spice and gently mix to coat.

3 Add the star anise, then pour in the stock, fish sauce and soy sauce. Cover and cook on low for 6 hours, or until the pork is tender.

4 Near serving time, make the cucumber and ginger salad. Combine the cucumber, spring onion and ginger in a salad bowl. Whisk together the peanut oil and vinegar, pour over the salad and gently toss together.

5 Divide the pork among serving plates and drizzle with the cooking juices. Sprinkle with sliced chilli, if desired, and serve with the cucumber and ginger salad and steamed rice.

⚙ *This dish is from Vietnam, where it is known as 'thit heo kho tieu'. It is also delicious served with thick rice noodles.*

Slow-cooked fennel and rosemary-scented pork belly

Serves **4**   Preparation time **20 minutes**   Cooking time **7 hours 5 minutes**

2 teaspoons fennel seeds, coarsely crushed
2 teaspoons chopped rosemary
½–1 teaspoon chilli flakes
1 teaspoon sea salt flakes
½ teaspoon freshly ground black pepper
1 kg (2 lb 4 oz) piece of pork belly
2 x 400 g (14 oz) tins butterbeans (lima beans), drained and rinsed
Finely grated zest of 1 lemon
1 tablespoon lemon juice
1 tablespoon extra virgin olive oil

1 Mix together the fennel seeds, rosemary, chilli flakes, salt and pepper. Rub the mixture over the pork belly and press it on firmly to crust the pork with the spices.

2 Place a trivet, saucer or upturned cereal bowl in a 5.5 litre (192 fl oz/22 cup) slow cooker, then rest the pork on top.

3 Cover and cook on low for 5–7 hours, or until the pork is very tender. The pork will have a slight pink blush inside when perfectly cooked.

4 Remove the pork to a warm platter and cover loosely with foil. Leave to rest in a warm place.

5 Skim the cooking juices from the slow cooker and reserve about 80 ml (2½ fl oz/⅓ cup). Place the reserved cooking liquid in a food processor with the beans, lemon zest, lemon juice and oil, supplementing with a little stock or hot water if necessary. Purée for 4–5 minutes, or until the mixture is smooth, scraping down the bowl with a spatula to mix well. Season to taste with sea salt and freshly ground black pepper.

6 Gently heat the bean purée in a small saucepan, stirring regularly (or reheat, covered, in a microwave oven).

7 Carve the pork and serve with the butterbean purée.

⚙ *Tip: If you're in a hurry you can cook the pork on high, reducing the cooking time to 2½–3½ hours.*

Pork neck with star anise

Serves **6**   Preparation time **10 minutes**   Cooking time **8 hours 25 minutes**

1.5 kg (3 lb 5 oz) pork neck
1 tablespoon olive oil
2 tablespoons brown sugar
2 fresh bay leaves
1 cinnamon stick
4 whole cloves
2 star anise
500 ml (17 fl oz/2 cups) good-quality
    chicken stock
1 tablespoon cornflour (cornstarch)
Mashed potato, to serve

Braised red cabbage
20 g (¾ oz) butter
1 tablespoon olive oil
1 granny smith apple, peeled,
    cored and thinly sliced
½ small red cabbage, finely shredded
60 ml (2 fl oz/¼ cup) apple juice
½ teaspoon caraway seeds (optional)

1 Season the pork with sea salt and freshly ground black pepper. Heat the olive oil in the insert pan of a 5.5 litre (192 fl oz/22 cup) slow cooker or a frying pan over medium–high heat. Add the pork and cook, turning, for 10 minutes, or until browned all over.

2 Return the insert pan, if using, to the slow cooker, or transfer the pork to the slow cooker. Sprinkle with the sugar, then add the bay leaves, cinnamon stick, cloves and star anise. Pour in the stock. Cover and cook on low for 8 hours, or until the pork is tender.

3 Remove the pork to a warm platter. Cover loosely with foil and keep in a warm place while finishing the sauce.

4 Blend the cornflour with 1 tablespoon water until smooth. Add to the sauce in the slow cooker and stir in well. Cover and cook for a further 15 minutes, or until the sauce has thickened.

5 Near serving time, prepare the braised red cabbage. Heat the butter and olive oil in a large non-stick frying pan over medium heat. Add the apple and cook, turning often, for 3–4 minutes, or until light golden. Add the cabbage, apple juice and caraway seeds, if using. Cook, stirring, for another 5 minutes, or until the cabbage has just wilted. Season to taste.

6 Carve the pork into thick slices. Serve with the braised red cabbage and mashed potato.

Slow-braised rabbit with shallots, cider and thyme

Serves **4**   Preparation time **25 minutes**   Cooking time **4 hours 15 minutes**

60 ml (2 fl oz/¼ cup) olive oil
1 large rabbit, about 1.5 kg
    (3 lb 5 oz), jointed
Plain (all-purpose) flour, seasoned
    with sea salt and freshly ground
    black pepper, for dusting
150 g (5½ oz) pancetta, roughly
    chopped
8 red Asian shallots, finely diced
1 leek, white part only, thinly sliced
4 garlic cloves, crushed
200 ml (7 fl oz) apple cider
125 ml (4 fl oz/½ cup) good-quality
    chicken stock
4 thyme sprigs
60 ml (2 fl oz/¼ cup) thick
    (double/heavy) cream
2 tablespoons coarsely chopped
    flat-leaf (Italian) parsley

Parsnip mash
1 kg (2 lb 4 oz) parsnips, peeled
    and coarsely chopped
150 ml (5 fl oz) pouring cream
1 garlic clove, crushed
4 thyme sprigs
30 g (1 oz) butter, coarsely chopped

1 Heat most of the oil in a 5 litre (175 fl oz/20 cup) slow cooker or a frying pan over medium–high heat. Dust the rabbit in flour, shaking off the excess. Brown on each side for 2–3 minutes, or until golden. Remove to a plate.

2 Heat the remaining oil in the pan. Add the pancetta and cook, stirring, for 4–5 minutes, or until golden. Add the shallot, leek and garlic and cook, stirring occasionally, for 3–4 minutes, or until starting to turn golden. Stir in the cider and simmer for 2 minutes to reduce the sauce slightly, then add the stock and thyme sprigs.

3 Return the insert pan, if using, to the slow cooker, or transfer the mixture to the slow cooker. Add the rabbit and gently mix together. Cover and cook for 3–3½ hours, or until the rabbit is tender.

4 Meanwhile, make the parsnip mash. Boil the parsnip for 20–25 minutes, or until tender. Drain well, return to the pan and mash. Meanwhile, gently heat the cream, garlic, thyme sprigs and butter in a small saucepan; strain half the cream into the mashed parsnip and stir to combine. Add the remaining cream a little at a time until desired consistency is reached. Season to taste and keep warm.

5 Carefully transfer the rabbit to a warm plate using a slotted spoon. Cover with foil and keep warm. Remove the thyme sprigs. Heat the cooking juices in the insert pan or in a saucepan over medium–high heat. Add the cream and cook for 5–10 minutes, to make a light sauce. Season to taste.

6 Gently mix the rabbit back into the sauce with the parsley. Serve with the parsnip mash.

Braised squid with lemon, rice and chorizo

Serves 6   Preparation time **30 minutes**   Cooking time **2 hours 50 minutes**

3 red onions
60 ml (2 fl oz/¼ cup) olive oil
4 garlic cloves, finely chopped
2 chorizo sausages, finely diced
100 g (3½ oz/½ cup) long-grain
   white rice
1 tablespoon thyme leaves
Finely grated zest of 2 lemons
Juice of ½ lemon
12 squid tubes, about 60 g (2¼ oz)
   each, cleaned
1 teaspoon smoked paprika
2 x 400 g (14 oz) tins chopped
   or cherry tomatoes
150 ml (5 fl oz) white wine
1 tablespoon sherry vinegar, or to
   taste
2 tablespoons coarsely chopped
   flat-leaf (Italian) parsley
Crusty baguette, to serve

1   Finely dice one of the onions. Cut the remaining onions into wedges and set aside.

2   Heat 1 tablespoon of the olive oil in the insert pan of a 5 litre (175 fl oz/20 cup) slow cooker or a frying pan over medium heat. Add the chopped onion and half the garlic and cook for 5–7 minutes, or until the onion has softened.

3   Tip the mixture into a bowl and allow to cool. Add the chorizo, rice, thyme and lemon zest and juice. Season with sea salt and freshly ground black pepper and mix well.

4   Carefully spoon the mixture into the squid tubes until they are three-quarters full. Secure the end of each tube with a toothpick. Set aside.

5   Heat the remaining oil in the pan and add the onion wedges and remaining garlic. Cook for 5–7 minutes, or until tender. Add the paprika, stir to combine, then add the tomatoes and wine and season with salt and pepper.

6   Return the insert pan, if using, to the slow cooker, or transfer the sauce mixture to the slow cooker. Carefully add the squid, pressing them gently into the sauce. Cover and cook on high for 2–2½ hours, stirring occasionally, until the squid is tender.

7   Gently stir the vinegar and parsley through. Season to taste and serve with a crusty baguette.

Tip: Be careful not to overstuff the squid as the rice will expand during cooking and needs room to do so.

Seafood fideos

Serves **4–6**   Preparation time **30 minutes (+ 10 minutes soaking)**   Cooking time **3 hours**

300 g (10½ oz) raw prawns (shrimp)
300 g (10½ oz) firm white fish fillets
200 g (7 oz) squid tubes
1 kg (2 lb 4 oz) mussels
1 brown onion, finely chopped
1 garlic clove, finely chopped
½ teaspoon chilli flakes
2 tablespoons chopped oregano
400 g (14 oz) tin whole tomatoes,
    strained (use the juice only)
125 g (4½ oz) fideos or vermicelli
    pasta (see Tip)
Chopped flat-leaf (Italian) parsley,
    to serve

1 First, prepare the seafood. Peel the prawns, leaving the heads and tails intact. Gently pull out the dark vein from the back of each prawn, starting at the head end. Cut the fish into 3 cm (1¼ inch) chunks, and the squid tubes into 1 cm (½ inch) rings. Scrub the mussels with a stiff brush and pull out the hairy beards. Discard any broken mussels or open ones that don't close when tapped on the bench.

2 Place the prawns, fish, squid and mussels in a 4.5 litre (157 fl oz/18 cup) slow cooker. Add the onion, garlic, chilli flakes, oregano and strained tomato juice and gently mix together. Cover and cook on high for 2 hours.

3 Meanwhile, towards the end of the first 2 hours of cooking time, break the noodles into 5 cm (2 inch) lengths and place in a large heatproof bowl. Cover with boiling water and set aside to soften for 10 minutes.

4 Drain the softened noodles and place on top of the seafood in the slow cooker. Turn the slow cooker setting to low, then cover and cook for a further 1 hour.

5 Serve the fideos sprinkled with chopped parsley.

⚙ *Tip: Fideos is a traditional Spanish dish. The word refers to the noodle that is used, which is a very thin, vermicelli-like pasta. If you can't find fideos noodles, use vermicelli or capellini pasta. When the mussels are cooked, discard any unopened mussels.*

Salmon with horseradish crust and puy lentils

Serves **4**   Preparation time **25 minutes**   Cooking time **4 hours 10 minutes**

400 g (14 oz/2 cups) puy lentils
   or tiny blue-green lentils
500 ml (17 fl oz/2 cups)
   good-quality vegetable stock
Finely grated zest and juice of
   1 lemon
1 small fresh green chilli, finely
   chopped
80 g (2¾ oz/1 cup, firmly packed)
   fresh sourdough breadcrumbs
   (made from day old bread)
2 tablespoons grated fresh or
   prepared horseradish
⅓ cup chopped dill
10 g (¼ oz) butter, melted
4 x 180 g (6½ oz) salmon fillets
50 g (1¾ oz) English spinach,
   stalks removed, chopped
1 cup coriander (cilantro) leaves
125 g (4½ oz/½ cup) plain yoghurt
Lemon wedges, to serve

1 Put the lentils, stock, lemon zest, lemon juice and chilli in a 4.5 litre (157 fl oz/18 cup) slow cooker. Gently mix together, then cover and cook on high for 3 hours.

2 In a food processor, roughly pulse the breadcrumbs and horseradish until well combined. Stir the dill and butter through until the mixture is fairly moist.

3 Remove any bones from the salmon using your fingers or tweezers, then press the breadcrumb mixture over the top of the salmon fillets.

4 Heat a large non-stick frying pan over medium heat. Add the salmon, crumbed side down. Cook the crust side only for 3 minutes, or until the crumbs are golden. Work in batches if necessary.

5 Mix the spinach through the lentils in the slow cooker, then place the salmon fillets on top, crust side up.

6 Turn the slow cooker setting to low. Cover and cook for 1 hour, or until the fish is cooked through and flakes when tested with a fork. Remove the salmon to serving plates.

7 Mix the coriander through the lentils. Serve the salmon with the lentils, topped with the yoghurt and with lemon wedges on the side.

Octopus braised in red wine vinegar, red wine and oregano

Serves **4**   Preparation time **20 minutes (+ 20 minutes standing)**   Cooking time **5 hours**

2 large red onions, sliced
2 tablespoons lemon juice
1 garlic clove, crushed
2 dried bay leaves
2 teaspoons dried oregano
2 teaspoons brown sugar
1 teaspoon sea salt
60 ml (2 fl oz/¼ cup) red wine
   vinegar
60 ml (2 fl oz/¼ cup) red wine
16 baby octopus, cleaned (see Tip)
1 cup chopped flat-leaf (Italian)
   parsley
2 tablespoons extra virgin olive oil

Orange, spinach and radish salad
1 orange, peel and white pith
   removed, cut into segments
4 radishes, trimmed and thinly
   sliced
45 g (1½ oz/1 cup) baby English
   spinach leaves
2 tablespoons extra virgin olive oil
80 ml (2½ fl oz/⅓ cup) orange juice

1 Put the onion, lemon juice, garlic, bay leaves, oregano, sugar and salt in a 5.5 litre (192 fl oz/22 cup) slow cooker. Pour in the vinegar, wine and 375 ml (13 fl oz/1½ cups) water, then stir to dissolve the sugar.

2 Wash the baby octopus and pat dry with paper towels. Add to the slow cooker and gently mix together.

3 Cover and cook on low for 5 hours, or until it is easy to cut through the thickest part of the octopus tentacles with a sharp knife.

4 Turn off the slow cooker, leave the lid on and allow the octopus to stand for a further 20 minutes, so it becomes very tender.

5 Near serving time, make the orange, spinach and radish salad. Combine the orange segments, radish and spinach in a bowl. Whisk together the oil and orange juice and season to taste with sea salt and freshly ground black pepper. Pour over the salad and gently toss to combine.

6 Strain the octopus into a serving bowl. Add the parsley and olive oil. Season to taste, then mix together well. Serve with the orange, spinach and radish salad.

Tip: To clean octopus, slice off either side of the eyes and discard. Push the beak (the hard mouth) out from between the tentacles and cut it away, then rinse the head.

Casseroles
and Stews

Vegetable and gnocchi stew

Serves 4   Preparation time **15 minutes**   Cooking time **8 hours**

1 brown onion, chopped
3 garlic cloves, chopped
2 zucchini (courgettes), cut into
   2 cm (¾ inch) chunks
1 red capsicum (pepper), cut into
   2 cm (¾ inch) chunks
100 g (3½ oz) button mushrooms
500 g (1 lb 2 oz) fresh gnocchi
600 ml (21 fl oz) tomato passata
   (puréed tomatoes)
500 ml (17 fl oz/2 cups) good-quality
   vegetable stock (see Tip)
125 ml (4 fl oz/½ cup) white wine
2 rosemary sprigs
1 cup chopped basil, plus extra
   sprigs, to garnish
100 g (3½ oz/1 cup) shaved
   parmesan cheese

1 Place the onion, garlic, zucchini, capsicum and mushrooms in a 5.5 litre (192 fl oz/22 cup) slow cooker. Gently mix together. Arrange the gnocchi over the top.

2 In a bowl, mix together the passata, stock and wine. Pour the mixture into the slow cooker, but do not stir as the gnocchi are quite fragile. Add the rosemary sprigs.

3 Cover and cook on low for 8 hours.

4 Season to taste with sea salt and freshly ground black pepper and gently stir the basil through.

5 Ladle into bowls and scatter the parmesan over the top. Garnish with extra basil sprigs and serve.

⚙ *Tips: For a non-vegetarian version of this dish, use chicken stock instead of vegetable stock. You could also gently stir 200 g (7 oz) chopped ham through the stew when adding the basil. To vary the recipe a little, swap the parmesan for dollops of fresh ricotta.*

Moroccan ratatouille

Serves **6**   Preparation time **25 minutes**   Cooking time **4 hours 20 minutes**

80 ml (2½ fl oz/⅓ cup) olive oil,
approximately
2 large red onions, cut into 2 cm
(¾ inch) chunks
2 eggplants (aubergines), about
450 g (1 lb) each, cut into
2.5 cm (1 inch) chunks
2 large red capsicums (peppers),
cut into 2.5 cm (1 inch) chunks
2 tablespoons Moroccan spice mix
2 x 400 g (14 oz) tins chopped
tomatoes
2 tablespoons tomato paste
(concentrated purée)
400 g (14 oz) tin chickpeas,
drained and rinsed
750 g (1 lb 10 oz) butternut
pumpkin (squash), peeled,
seeded and cut into 3 cm
(1¼ inch) chunks
2 tablespoons lemon juice
2½ teaspoons honey
110 g (3¾ oz/⅔ cup) pimento-
stuffed green olives
2 tablespoons chopped coriander
(cilantro) leaves
250 g (9 oz/1 cup) Greek-style
yoghurt
1 tablespoon chopped mint
Steamed rice and harissa, to serve

1 Heat 1 tablespoon of the olive oil in a large heavy-based
frying pan over medium heat. Add the onion and cook,
tossing occasionally, for 4 minutes, or until it starts
to soften. Transfer to a 5.5 litre (192 fl oz/22 cup)
slow cooker.

2 Heat another tablespoon of the oil in the pan. Fry
the eggplant in two batches for 2 minutes on each side,
or until it has softened slightly and is light golden,
adding a little more oil as necessary. Add to the
slow cooker.

3 Heat another tablespoon of the oil in the pan, then add
the capsicum and cook for 3–4 minutes, or until it starts
to soften and brown, turning often. Stir in the Moroccan
spice mix and cook, stirring, for 30 seconds, or until
aromatic, then add one tin of the tomatoes, stirring to
loosen any stuck-on bits from the base of the pan.

4 Transfer the mixture to the slow cooker. Add the
remaining tomatoes, the tomato paste and the chickpeas
and stir to combine well. Arrange the pumpkin on top.

5 Cover and cook on low for 4 hours, or until the vegetables
are very tender but still holding their shape.

6 Gently stir in the lemon juice, honey, olives and coriander.
Season to taste with sea salt and freshly ground black pepper.

7 Combine the yoghurt and mint. Serve the ratatouille on a
bed of steamed rice, with the minted yoghurt and harissa.

Coq au vin

Serves **4**   Preparation time **25 minutes (+ 8 hours marinating)**   Cooking time **4 hours 25 minutes**

2 kg (4 lb 8 oz) whole chicken, cut into 10 pieces, or 2 kg chicken pieces
500 ml (17 fl oz/2 cups) red wine
2 tablespoons olive oil
250 g (9 oz) French shallots (eschalots), peeled
400 g (14 oz) button mushrooms, trimmed
250 g (9 oz) pancetta or bacon, cut into long strips about 5 mm (¼ inch) square, or into 5 mm (¼ inch) dice
3 garlic cloves, chopped
250 ml (9 fl oz/1 cup) good-quality chicken stock
250 g (9 oz) baby carrots, peeled or scrubbed and trimmed
1 tablespoon thyme leaves
1 dried bay leaf
30 g (1 oz) unsalted butter, softened
2 tablespoons plain (all-purpose) flour

1 Place the chicken pieces in a glass or ceramic container. Pour in the wine and mix until well coated. Cover and marinate in the refrigerator for 8 hours, or overnight.

2 Drain the chicken from the wine marinade, reserving the marinade. Heat half the olive oil in the insert pan of a 5 litre (175 fl oz/20 cup) slow cooker or a large frying pan over medium heat. Fry the chicken in two batches for 5–7 minutes, or until browned, turning frequently. Remove to a plate.

3 Heat the remaining oil in the pan. Add the shallots, mushrooms and pancetta and cook for 4 minutes, or until golden. Add the garlic and cook for 1 minute, stirring frequently so it doesn't burn. Pour in the reserved wine marinade and bring to the boil. Allow to boil for 2 minutes.

4 Return the insert pan, if using, to the slow cooker, or transfer the mixture to the slow cooker. Stir in the stock, then add the chicken and any juices, along with the carrots, thyme and bay leaf. Cover and cook on high for 3½ hours, or until the chicken is cooked through.

5 Using a slotted spoon, remove the chicken, shallots, mushrooms and carrots to a warm serving dish. Cover loosely with foil while finishing the sauce.

6 Combine the butter and flour and whisk into the liquid in the slow cooker. Cover and cook for a further 30 minutes, or until the sauce has thickened slightly. Pour over the chicken and serve.

Chicken ratatouille

Serves **4**   Preparation time **25 minutes**   Cooking time **4 hours 30 minutes**

1.8 kg (4 lb) whole chicken,
    cut into 8 pieces, or 1.8 kg
    chicken pieces
80 ml (2½ fl oz/⅓ cup) olive oil
2 red onions, each cut into 8 wedges
300 g (10½ oz) eggplant (aubergine),
    cut into 2.5 cm (1 inch) chunks
2 zucchini (courgettes), sliced 2.5 cm
    (1 inch) thick
250 g (9 oz) squash, cut into wedges
1 red capsicum (pepper), cut into
    2.5 cm (1 inch) chunks
3 garlic cloves, sliced
400 g (14 oz) tin chopped tomatoes
⅓ cup basil leaves, torn

1 Season the chicken pieces with sea salt and freshly ground black pepper.

2 Heat 1 tablespoon of the olive oil in the insert pan of a 7 litre (245 fl oz/28 cup) slow cooker or a large non-stick frying pan over medium heat. Cook the chicken, in two batches if necessary, for 3–4 minutes on each side, or until nicely browned. Remove to a plate.

3 Heat another 2 tablespoons of the oil in the pan. Add the onion and eggplant and cook for 5 minutes, turning occasionally. Remove to a plate.

4 Heat the remaining oil in the pan and cook the zucchini, squash and capsicum for 3 minutes. Stir in the garlic and cook for a further 1 minute.

5 Return the insert pan, if using, to the slow cooker, or transfer the vegetable mixture to the slow cooker. Stir in the tomatoes, then add the chicken pieces and turn to coat.

6 Cover and cook on low for 4 hours, or until the chicken is cooked through. Season to taste with sea salt and freshly ground black pepper. Stir the basil through and serve.

Creamy tomato and chicken stew

Serves **4**   Preparation time **20 minutes**   Cooking time **4 hours**

1.5 kg (3 lb 5 oz) chicken pieces
4 bacon slices, rind and fat removed, coarsely chopped
2 brown onions, chopped
1 garlic clove, crushed
400 g (14 oz) tin chopped tomatoes
300 g (10½ oz) small button mushrooms, halved
250 ml (9 fl oz/1 cup) pouring cream
2 tablespoons chopped flat-leaf (Italian) parsley
2 tablespoons lemon thyme
Mashed potato and steamed green beans, to serve

1 Trim the chicken pieces of any excess fat. Place in a 4.5 litre (157 fl oz/18 cup) slow cooker with the bacon, onion, garlic and tomatoes. Cover and cook on high for 3 hours, or until the chicken is nearly tender.

2 Stir in the mushrooms and cream, then cover and cook for a further 30 minutes.

3 Remove the lid and cook, uncovered, for a final 30 minutes to thicken the sauce.

4 Stir the parsley and lemon thyme through and season to taste with sea salt and freshly ground black pepper. Serve with mashed potato and green beans.

Chicken goulash

Serves **4** Preparation time **20 minutes** Cooking time **4 hours 40 minutes**

700 g (1 lb 9 oz) skinless chicken thigh fillets
1 brown onion, sliced
2 garlic cloves, sliced
2 green capsicums (peppers), sliced
1 tablespoon sweet paprika
125 ml (4 fl oz/½ cup) tomato passata (puréed tomatoes)
1 marjoram sprig
125 ml (4 fl oz/½ cup) white wine
250 ml (9 fl oz/1 cup) good-quality chicken stock
125 g (4½ oz/½ cup) sour cream or crème fraîche
1 tablespoon cornflour (cornstarch)
1 small handful flat-leaf (Italian) parsley
Steamed rice, to serve

1 Trim the chicken of any fat, then cut each thigh into quarters. Place in a 4.5 litre (157 fl oz/18 cup) slow cooker with the onion, garlic, capsicum, paprika, passata and marjoram sprig.

2 Pour in the wine and stock, then gently mix together. Cover and cook on low for 4½ hours, or until the chicken is tender.

3 Combine the sour cream and cornflour in a small bowl. Stir through the chicken mixture, then cover and cook for a further 5–10 minutes, or until the liquid has thickened.

4 Season to taste with sea salt and freshly ground black pepper, then stir the parsley through. Serve with steamed rice.

Chicken casserole with mustard and tarragon

Serves 4–6   Preparation time **20 minutes**   Cooking time **3 hours**

1 kg (2 lb 4 oz) skinless chicken
  thigh fillets
1 brown onion, finely chopped
1 leek, white part only, thinly sliced
1 garlic clove, finely chopped
½ teaspoon dried tarragon
125 ml (4 fl oz/½ cup) good-quality
  chicken stock
350 g (12 oz) button mushrooms,
  sliced
185 ml (6 fl oz/¾ cup) pouring
  cream
2 tablespoons dijon mustard
1½ tablespoons lemon juice
Mashed potato and steamed zucchini
  (courgette) or green beans,
  to serve

1 Trim the chicken of any fat, then cut each thigh into quarters. Place in a 4.5 litre (157 fl oz/18 cup) slow cooker with the onion, leek, garlic, tarragon and stock. Gently mix together, then cover and cook on high for 2½ hours.

2 Stir in the mushroom, cream and mustard. Cover and cook for a further 30 minutes.

3 Stir the lemon juice through and season to taste with sea salt and freshly ground black pepper. Serve with mashed potatoes and steamed zucchini or green beans.

Basque chicken

Serves **4**   Preparation time **25 minutes**   Cooking time **8 hours**

1.8 kg (4 lb) whole chicken, or
   1.8 kg (4 lb) chicken pieces
1 brown onion, cut into 2 cm
   (¾ inch) chunks
1 red capsicum (pepper), cut into
   2 cm (¾ inch) chunks
1 green capsicum (pepper), cut into
   2 cm (¾ inch) chunks
2 garlic cloves, finely chopped
200 g (7 oz) chorizo sausage, sliced
150 ml (5 fl oz) white wine
80 g (2¾ oz) tomato paste
   (concentrated purée)
90 g (3¼ oz/½ cup) black olives
¼ preserved lemon
2 tablespoons chopped basil
2 tablespoons chopped flat-leaf
   (Italian) parsley
Steamed rice, to serve (optional)

1 If using a whole chicken, cut it into eight pieces using a strong sharp knife. To do this, first remove both legs, then cut between the joint of the drumstick and the thigh to separate them. Cut down either side of the backbone and lift it out. Turn the chicken over and cut through the cartilage down the centre of the breastbone. Cut each breast in half, leaving the wing attached to the top half.

2 Place all the chicken pieces in a 4.5 litre (157 fl oz/18 cup) slow cooker. Add the onion, capsicum, garlic, chorizo, wine, tomato paste and olives.

3 Rinse the preserved lemon well, then remove and discard the pulp and membrane. Finely dice the rind, add to the chicken and gently mix together. Cover and cook on low for 8 hours, or until the chicken is cooked through.

4 Stir the basil through and season to taste with sea salt and freshly ground black pepper. Serve sprinkled with the parsley, with steamed rice if desired.

Chicken agrodolce

Serves **6**   Preparation time **30 minutes**   Cooking time **3 hours 30 minutes**

1.2 kg (2 lb 10 oz) chicken pieces, skin removed
1 garlic clove, finely chopped
1 tablespoon dried oregano
2 dried bay leaves
125 ml (4 fl oz/½ cup) red wine vinegar
125 ml (4 fl oz/½ cup) dry white wine
55 g (2 oz/¼ cup, firmly packed) brown sugar
200 g (7 oz/1 cup) pitted prunes
2 tablespoons capers, rinsed
175 g (6 oz/1 cup) green olives
1 cup flat-leaf (Italian) parsley, chopped
Mashed potato, to serve

1 Trim the chicken of any fat, then place in a 4.5 litre (157 fl oz/18 cup) slow cooker. Add the garlic, oregano, bay leaves, vinegar, wine and sugar and gently mix together. Cover and cook on low for 3 hours.

2 Stir in the prunes, capers and olives. Cover and cook for a further 30 minutes, or until the chicken is cooked through.

3 Season with sea salt and freshly ground black pepper and stir the parsley through. Serve with mashed potato.

Chicken and prune tagine

Serves **4**   Preparation time **15 minutes**   Cooking time **3 hours**

800 g (1 lb 12 oz) skinless chicken
   thigh fillets
1 brown onion, chopped
¼ teaspoon ground saffron
½ teaspoon ground ginger
2 cinnamon sticks
4 coriander (cilantro) sprigs,
   tied in a bunch
Zest of ½ lemon, removed in
   wide strips
300 g (10½ oz/1½ cups) pitted
   prunes
2 tablespoons honey
1 tablespoon sesame seeds,
   toasted

1 Trim the chicken of any fat, then cut each thigh into quarters. Place in a 4.5 litre (157 fl oz/18 cup) slow cooker with the onion, saffron, ginger, cinnamon sticks and coriander sprigs. Pour in 250 ml (9 fl oz/1 cup) water and gently mix together.

2 Cover and cook on high for 2½ hours, or until the chicken is tender.

3 Stir in the lemon zest strips, prunes and honey. Cover and cook for a further 30 minutes, or until the chicken is very tender and cooked through.

4 Remove and discard the coriander sprigs. Serve sprinkled with sesame seeds.

Cajun chicken stew

Serves **6**   Preparation time **15 minutes**   Cooking time **6 hours 15 minutes**

1.5 kg (3 lb 5 oz) skinless chicken
  thigh fillets
1 tablespoon cajun seasoning
2 tablespoons olive oil
375 ml (13 fl oz/1½ cups) good-
  quality chicken stock
400 g (14 oz) tin chopped tomatoes
1 green capsicum (pepper), cut into
  1 cm (½ inch) pieces
2 celery stalks, thinly sliced
1 large brown onion, diced
60 ml (2 fl oz/¼ cup) worcestershire
  sauce
3 fresh bay leaves
1 teaspoon sugar
1 garlic clove, crushed
1 teaspoon freshly ground black
  pepper
Steamed basmati rice, to serve

1 Trim the chicken of any fat, then cut each thigh in half. Place in a large bowl, sprinkle with the cajun seasoning and toss until evenly coated.

2 Heat the olive oil in the insert pan of a 5.5 litre (192 fl oz/22 cup) slow cooker or a large frying pan over medium heat. Add the chicken in batches and fry for 3–4 minutes, or until browned, turning occasionally, and removing each batch to a plate.

3 Return the insert pan, if using to the slow cooker. Place all the chicken in the slow cooker. Add all the remaining ingredients, except the rice, and gently mix together.

4 Cover and cook on low for 6 hours, or until the chicken is cooked through.

5 Season with sea salt and freshly ground black pepper and serve with steamed rice.

Spanish chicken

Serves **4**   Preparation time **15 minutes**   Cooking time **3 hours 15 minutes**

750 g (1 lb 10 oz) skinless chicken
   thigh fillets
2 chorizo sausages, chopped
1 red onion, chopped
100 g (3½ oz) roasted red
   capsicum (pepper) pieces
   (from a jar), thinly sliced
4 garlic cloves, finely chopped
1 long fresh green chilli, seeded
   and finely chopped
2 teaspoons smoked paprika
   (see Tip)
1 teaspoon dried oregano
400 g (14 oz) tin chopped tomatoes
375 ml (13 fl oz/1½ cups) good-
   quality chicken stock
150 g (5½ oz/1 cup) fresh or frozen
   peas
Crusty bread, to serve

1 Trim the chicken of any fat, then cut into 3 cm (1¼ inch) chunks. Place in a 5.5 litre (192 fl oz/22 cup) slow cooker.

2 Add the chorizo, onion, capsicum, garlic, chilli, paprika, oregano, tomatoes and stock. Season with sea salt and freshly ground black pepper and gently mix together. Cover and cook on high for 3 hours.

3 Stir the peas through, then cover and cook for a further 15 minutes, or until the peas are warmed through.

4 Ladle into bowls and serve with crusty bread.

⚙ *Tip: A signature spice in Spanish cuisine, smoked paprika is made from capsicums (peppers) that have been slowly smoked, then ground to a fine powder. It is widely available, but if you don't have any, you can use sweet paprika in this recipe.*

African chicken

Serves **4**   Preparation time **20 minutes**   Cooking time **6 hours 30 minutes**

1 tablespoon olive oil
4 chicken drumsticks
4 chicken wings, the wing tips removed and cut into 2 pieces at the joint
2 chicken thigh cutlets, quartered
2 brown onions, thinly sliced
2 tablespoons berbere spice blend (see Tip)
2 garlic cloves, crushed
60 g (2¼ oz/¼ cup) tomato paste (concentrated purée)
400 g (14 oz) tin chopped tomatoes
Coriander (cilantro) sprigs, to garnish
Lemon cheeks, to serve

Herbed couscous
280 g (10 oz/1½ cups) instant couscous
1 cup coriander (cilantro) leaves, chopped
1 tablespoon olive oil

1 Heat the olive oil in a large frying pan over medium–high heat. Brown the chicken pieces in batches for 5 minutes, or until golden all over, turning during cooking. Transfer each batch to a 5.5 litre (192 fl oz/22 cup) slow cooker.

2 Add the onion to the frying pan and cook, stirring occasionally, for 10 minutes, or until softened. Spread the onion over the chicken pieces in the slow cooker.

3 Cook the berbere spice blend in the pan for 1 minute, or until aromatic. Stir in the garlic and tomato paste and cook for 30 seconds. Add the tomatoes and cook, stirring, for 1 minute, or until heated through.

4 Transfer the mixture to the slow cooker and gently mix together. Cover and cook on high for 5–6 hours, or until the chicken is very tender. Season with sea salt to taste.

5 Near serving time, prepare the herbed couscous. Place the couscous in a heatproof bowl and pour in 375 ml (13 fl oz/1½ cups) boiling water. Cover with a tea towel (dish towel) and stand for 5 minutes, or until the liquid has been absorbed. Fluff the grains up with a fork, then stir in the coriander and olive oil. Season to taste.

6 Serve the chicken on a bed of herbed couscous, drizzled with the cooking juices. Garnish with coriander and serve with lemon cheeks for squeezing over.

Tip: Berbere is a blend of ground spices such as salt, cumin, coriander, pepper, ajowan, fenugreek, allspice, ginger, chilli, nutmeg and cloves. If you can't find it, use a Moroccan spice mix from the supermarket.

Chicken Madeira with mushrooms

Serves 6   Preparation time **15 minutes**   Cooking time **6 hours 10 minutes**

2 tablespoons plain (all-purpose) flour
1 kg (2 lb 4 oz) skinless chicken thigh fillets
1 large leek, white part only, thinly sliced
2 teaspoons chopped rosemary
2 fresh bay leaves
250 ml (9 fl oz/1 cup) good-quality chicken stock
125 ml (4 fl oz/½ cup) Madeira
20 g (¾ oz) butter
250 g (9 oz) button mushrooms, halved, or quartered if large
125 ml (4 fl oz/½ cup) pouring cream
3 tablespoons chopped flat-leaf (Italian) parsley
Mashed potato, to serve
Lemon zest slivers, to garnish

1 Place the flour in a flat dish and season well with freshly ground black pepper. Trim the chicken of any fat, then cut each thigh in half. Add the chicken to the flour and toss well to coat, shaking off any excess.

2 Place the chicken in a 5.5 litre (192 fl oz/22 cup) slow cooker. Add the leek, rosemary and bay leaves, then pour in the stock and Madeira and gently mix together. Cover and cook on low for 5 hours.

3 Melt the butter in a large frying pan. Add the mushrooms and cook for 5–10 minutes, or until golden, stirring occasionally. Add the mushrooms to the slow cooker, then stir in the cream.

4 Cover and cook for a further 1 hour, or until the sauce is thick. Stir the parsley through and season to taste with sea salt and freshly ground black pepper.

5 Serve with mashed potato, drizzled with the sauce and garnished with lemon zest.

Lamb shank casserole with root vegetables

Serves **4**   Preparation time **30 minutes**   Cooking time **4 hours 45 minutes**

4 French-trimmed lamb shanks
Plain (all-purpose) flour, for dusting
1 tablespoon olive oil
1 large brown onion, coarsely
   chopped
2 celery stalks, diced
3 garlic cloves, chopped
2 parsnips, peeled and cut into
   wedges
2 carrots, diced
450 g (1 lb) celeriac (about ½ large),
   peeled and diced
330 ml (11¼ fl oz/1⅓ cups)
   good-quality chicken stock
2 tablespoons mint jelly
1½ tablespoons chopped flat-leaf
   (Italian) parsley

1 Season the lamb shanks with sea salt and freshly ground black pepper. Dust with the flour, shaking off any excess.

2 Heat the olive oil in the insert pan of a 5 litre (175 fl oz/ 20 cup) slow cooker, or a large, deep frying pan over medium–high heat. Add the shanks and cook, turning occasionally, for 6 minutes, or until golden. Remove to a plate.

3 Reduce the heat to medium–low. Add the onion, celery and garlic to the pan and cook, stirring occasionally, for 5 minutes, or until softened.

4 Return the insert pan, if using, to the slow cooker, or transfer the onion mixture to the slow cooker. Add the shanks, parsnip, carrot and celeriac. Pour the stock over and gently mix together. Cover and cook on high for 4½ hours, or until the lamb is tender.

5 Transfer the shanks and vegetables to warm plates using a slotted spoon.

6 Stir the mint jelly and parsley through the sauce and season to taste with sea salt and freshly ground black pepper. Ladle the sauce over the shanks and serve.

Lamb tagine with chickpeas and buttered couscous

Serves **6**   Preparation time **35 minutes**   Cooking time **4 hours 15 minutes**

2 tablespoons olive oil
2 small lamb necks, about 1.5 kg (3 lb 5 oz), trimmed of excess fat and cut into 4 pieces
2 brown onions, thickly sliced
3 garlic cloves, crushed
1 tablespoon ground cumin
1 tablespoon ground coriander
2 teaspoons ground ginger
1 teaspoon cayenne pepper
5 cardamom pods
2 cinnamon sticks
400 g (14 oz) pumpkin (winter squash), peeled and coarsely chopped
400 g (14 oz) tin chickpeas, drained and rinsed
2 x 400 g (14 oz) tins whole tomatoes
Chopped preserved lemon and Greek-style yoghurt, to serve
Coriander (cilantro) leaves, to garnish

Buttered couscous
280 g (10 oz/1½ cups) instant couscous
1 tablespoon olive oil
30 g (1 oz) soft butter, diced

1 Heat half the olive oil in the insert pan of a 5 litre (175 fl oz/20 cup) slow cooker or a frying pan over medium heat. Add the lamb necks and cook, turning occasionally, for 4–5 minutes, or until golden. Transfer to a plate.

2 Add the onion and garlic and cook, stirring occasionally, for 3–4 minutes, or until golden. Add the spices and stir for 30 seconds, or until aromatic.

3 Return the insert pan, if using, to the slow cooker, or transfer the onion mixture to the slow cooker. Add the pumpkin, chickpeas, tomatoes and lamb neck.

4 Cover and cook on high for 3–4 hours, or until the lamb is very tender. Season to taste with sea salt and freshly ground black pepper and keep warm. Remove the cinnamon sticks.

5 Near serving time, make the buttered couscous. Place the couscous in a bowl, drizzle with the olive oil and season with sea salt and freshly ground black pepper. Massage the oil into the couscous with your fingertips, then pour over enough boiling water to cover. Cover with plastic wrap and set aside for 7–10 minutes, or until the couscous has softened. Add the butter and fluff the grains with a fork.

6 Serve the tagine with the couscous, topped with some chopped preserved lemon and yoghurt, and garnished with coriander leaves.

Lancashire hotpot

Serves **4**   Preparation time **15 minutes**   Cooking time **4 hours**

4 all-purpose potatoes, sliced
6 baby onions, peeled and left whole
1 tablespoon chopped thyme
1 kg (2 lb 4 oz) lamb shoulder chops
2 tablespoons worcestershire sauce
125 ml (4 fl oz/½ cup) good-quality
   beef stock
1 cup flat-leaf (Italian) parsley,
   chopped
Steamed green vegetables to serve

1 In a large bowl, toss together the potato, onions and thyme. Layer the potato and onions in a 4.5 litre (157 fl oz/18 cup) slow cooker.

2 Trim the lamb chops of excess fat, then place on top of the vegetables. Pour the worcestershire sauce and stock over. Cover and cook on high for 4 hours, or until the lamb is tender and cooked through.

3 Season with sea salt and freshly ground black pepper, stir the parsley through and serve with the steamed green vegetables.

Lamb chops in ratatouille

Serves **4–6**   Preparation time **30 minutes**   Cooking time **7 hours 30 minutes**

1 eggplant (aubergine)
1 red capsicum (pepper)
1 green capsicum (pepper)
1 red onion
2 tablespoons capers
4 anchovy fillets, chopped
80 g (2¾ oz/½ cup) pitted kalamata
   olives, chopped
60 g (2¼ oz/¼ cup) tomato paste
   (concentrated purée)
2 garlic cloves, chopped
400 g (14 oz) tin chopped tomatoes
1 kg (2 lb 4 oz) lamb forequarter
   chops
150 g (5½ oz/¾ cup) Israeli
   couscous (see Tip)
Chopped flat-leaf (Italian) parsley,
   to serve

1 Cut the eggplant and capsicums into 2 cm (¾ inch) chunks, and the onion into 1 cm (½ inch) dice. Place the vegetables in a 4.5 litre (157 fl oz/18 cup) slow cooker. Add the capers, anchovy, olives, tomato paste, garlic and tomatoes and gently mix together.

2 Trim the lamb chops of excess fat, then cut into large pieces and place in the slow cooker. Cover and cook on low for 6–6½ hours, or until the lamb is tender, stirring the mixture occasionally.

3 Stir in the couscous. Cover and cook for a further 1 hour, or until the couscous is cooked through.

4 Season to taste with sea salt and freshly ground black pepper and serve sprinkled with parsley.

Tip: Israeli couscous is larger in size than the more familiar Moroccan couscous, and has a chewier texture. It is sold in most gourmet food shops and health food stores.

Irish stew

Serves **6**   Preparation time **25 minutes**   Cooking time **4 hours 30 minutes**

600 g (1 lb 5 oz) all-purpose
   potatoes, thickly sliced
3 carrots, thickly sliced
1 brown onion, cut into 16 wedges
1 small leek, white part only,
   thickly sliced
150 g (5½ oz) savoy cabbage,
   thinly sliced
4 bacon slices, rind and fat removed,
   cut into strips
8 lamb neck chops
375 ml (13 fl oz/1½ cups) good-
   quality beef stock
2 tablespoons finely chopped
   flat-leaf (Italian) parsley
Crusty bread, to serve

1 Layer half the potato, carrot, onion, leek, cabbage and
   bacon in a 4.5 litre (157 fl oz/18 cup) slow cooker.

2 Trim the lamb chops of excess fat, then place on top
   of the mixture in a single layer. Layer the remaining
   vegetables and bacon over the lamb, then pour the
   stock over.

3 Cover and cook on low for 4½ hours, or until the lamb
   is very tender and the sauce has reduced slightly.

4 Season to taste with sea salt and freshly ground black
   pepper. Sprinkle with the parsley and serve with crusty
   bread to mop up the juices.

Navarin of lamb

Serves **4**   Preparation time **20 minutes**   Cooking time **3 hours 45 minutes**

1 kg (2 lb 4 oz) boneless lamb
　　shoulder
200 g (7 oz) baby turnips
8 bulb spring onions (scallions),
　　trimmed
175 g (6 oz) small new potatoes,
　　unpeeled, halved if large
1 brown onion, chopped
1 garlic clove, crushed
125 ml (4 fl oz/½ cup) good-quality
　　chicken stock
125 ml (4 fl oz/½ cup) red wine
2 tablespoons tomato paste
　　(concentrated purée)
1 large rosemary sprig
2 thyme sprigs
1 dried bay leaf
18 baby carrots
150 g (5½ oz/1 cup) fresh or
　　frozen peas
1 tablespoon redcurrant jelly
1 cup flat-leaf (Italian) parsley,
　　chopped

1 Trim the lamb of any excess fat, then cut into 3 cm
(1¼ inch) chunks. Place in a 4.5 litre (157 fl oz/18 cup)
slow cooker.

2 Add the turnips, spring onions, potatoes, onion, garlic,
stock, wine, tomato paste, rosemary sprig, thyme sprigs
and bay leaf and gently mix together.

3 Cover and cook on high for 3 hours, or until the lamb
is almost tender.

4 Trim the carrots, leaving a little bit of green stalk, then
stir them into the stew. Cover and cook for a further
40 minutes, or until the carrots are tender.

5 Stir in the peas, redcurrant jelly and parsley and cook
for a further 5 minutes, or until the peas are tender.

6 Season to taste with sea salt and freshly ground black
pepper and serve.

Lamb with green olives and preserved lemon

Serves **4**   Preparation time **30 minutes**   Cooking time **3 hours**

1 kg (2 lb 4 oz) lamb forequarter
  chops
½ preserved lemon
1 brown onion, sliced
2 garlic cloves, crushed
2 cm (¾ inch) piece fresh ginger,
  finely diced
1 teaspoon ground cumin
½ teaspoon ground turmeric
130 g (4½ oz/¾ cup) green olives
625 ml (21½ fl oz/2½ cups) good-
  quality chicken stock
400 g (14 oz) all-purpose potatoes,
  cut into 2 cm (¾ inch) chunks
2 tablespoons chopped flat-leaf
  (Italian) parsley
2 tablespoons chopped coriander
  (cilantro) leaves
Steamed rice, to serve

1 Trim the lamb of any excess fat, then cut each chop
  in half. Place in a 4.5 litre (157 fl oz/18 cup) slow cooker.

2 Rinse the preserved lemon well, then remove and discard
  the pulp and membrane. Finely dice the rind and add
  to the slow cooker with the onion, garlic, ginger, cumin,
  turmeric, olives and stock. Gently mix together.

3 Cover and cook on high for 2 hours.

4 Stir in the potato and half the parsley and coriander.
  Cover and cook for a further 1 hour, or until the lamb
  is tender and the potato is cooked through.

5 Stir in the remaining parsley and coriander and season
  to taste with sea salt and freshly ground black pepper.
  Serve with steamed rice.

African-style lamb and peanut stew

Serves **4–6**   Preparation time **30 minutes**   Cooking time **6 hours**

1 kg (2 lb 4 oz) boneless
   lamb leg steaks
3 teaspoons purchased curry powder
1 teaspoon dried oregano
A pinch of cayenne pepper
1 large brown onion, chopped
1 large carrot, chopped
1 red capsicum (pepper), chopped
500 g (1 lb 2 oz) orange sweet
   potato, cut into 2 cm (¾ inch)
   chunks
4 garlic cloves, chopped
1 long fresh red or green chilli,
   seeded and finely chopped
400 g (14 oz) tin chopped tomatoes
125 ml (4 fl oz/½ cup) tomato
   sauce (ketchup)
2 dried bay leaves
90 g (3¼ oz/⅓ cup) crunchy or
   smooth peanut butter
1 tablespoon lemon juice
165 ml (5½ fl oz) tin coconut milk
150 g (5½ oz/1 cup) fresh or frozen
   peas
Steamed rice or couscous, to serve

1 Trim the lamb of any fat, then cut into 2 cm (¾ inch) chunks. Place in a large bowl and sprinkle with the curry powder, oregano and cayenne pepper. Season with sea salt and freshly ground black pepper and toss well to coat the lamb.

2 Add the onion, carrot, capsicum, sweet potato, garlic, chilli, tomatoes, tomato sauce and bay leaves. Toss well to thoroughly combine all the ingredients.

3 Transfer the mixture to a 4.5 litre (157 fl oz/18 cup) slow cooker. Cover and cook on high for 4–6 hours, or until the lamb and vegetables are tender and cooked through.

4 Meanwhile, combine the peanut butter, lemon juice and coconut milk in a small bowl. During the last 30 minutes of cooking, add the peanut butter mixture to the slow cooker and stir to combine the ingredients.

5 Add the peas and cook for 5 minutes, or until tender. Remove the bay leaves and serve with steamed rice or couscous.

Moroccan spiced lamb with pumpkin

Serves **6**   Preparation time **20 minutes**   Cooking time **5 hours**

1.5 kg (3 lb 5 oz) boneless lamb
  shoulder
1 large brown onion, diced
1 teaspoon ground coriander
½ teaspoon ground ginger
½ teaspoon cayenne pepper
¼ teaspoon ground saffron
1 cinnamon stick
500 g (1 lb 2 oz) pumpkin (winter
  squash), cut into 2 cm (¾ inch)
  chunks
500 ml (17 fl oz/2 cups) good-quality
  chicken stock
100 g (3½ oz) dried apricots
Coriander (cilantro) sprigs, to garnish
Steamed rice or couscous, to serve

1 Trim the lamb of excess fat, then cut into 3 cm (1¼ inch) chunks. Place in a 4.5 litre (157 fl oz/18 cup) slow cooker with the onion, spices and pumpkin. Gently mix together, then pour in the stock. Cover and cook on low for 4 hours.

2 Stir in the apricots, then cover and cook for a further 1 hour.

3 Season to taste with sea salt and freshly ground black pepper. Garnish with coriander sprigs and serve with steamed rice or couscous.

Spiced lamb with red lentils

Serves **4**   Preparation time **30 minutes**   Cooking time **6 hours**

750 g (1 lb 10 oz) boneless lamb
   leg or shoulder
1 large brown onion, diced
1 carrot, diced
2 celery stalks, including a few
   leaves, diced
125 g (4½ oz) green beans,
   trimmed and cut into 4 cm
   (1½ inch) lengths
1 tablespoon finely grated fresh
   ginger
2 garlic cloves, chopped
500 ml (17 fl oz/2 cups)
   good-quality beef stock
250 ml (9 fl oz/1 cup) tomato
   passata (puréed tomatoes) or
   tomato pasta sauce
1 tablespoon lemon juice
200 g (7 oz/1 cup) red lentils
Coriander (cilantro) leaves, to garnish
Steamed basmati rice or warmed
   flat bread, to serve

Spice mix
2 teaspoons ground cumin
1 teaspoon ground coriander
½ teaspoon ground turmeric
A pinch of chilli flakes

1 Combine the spice mix ingredients in a large bowl.

2 Trim the lamb of excess fat, then cut into 2 cm (¾ inch) chunks. Add the lamb to the spice mix and toss well to thoroughly coat in the spices. Add the onion, carrot, celery, beans, ginger and garlic and toss to combine.

3 Transfer the mixture to a 4.5 litre (157 fl oz/18 cup) slow cooker. Stir in the stock, passata, lemon juice and lentils and season well with sea salt and freshly ground black pepper.

4 Cover and cook on high for 4–6 hours, or until the lamb is very tender and the lentils are cooked. The mixture will become thicker the longer it is cooked, so add a little extra stock or water to thin it if necessary.

5 Season to taste and garnish with coriander leaves. Serve with steamed basmati rice or warmed flat bread.

Persian lamb with chickpeas

Serves **4–6** Preparation time **30 minutes** Cooking time **6 hours**

750 g (1 lb 10 oz) boneless lamb
    leg or shoulder
1 teaspoon ground cinnamon
1 teaspoon ground allspice
1 teaspoon freshly grated nutmeg
1 teaspoon sea salt
1 large red onion, chopped
2 garlic cloves, chopped
200 g (7 oz) eggplant (aubergine),
    cut into 2 cm (¾ inch) chunks
1 carrot, chopped
1 zucchini (courgette), chopped
400 g (14 oz) tin chopped tomatoes
60 ml (2 fl oz/¼ cup) lemon juice
1 tablespoon tomato paste
    (concentrated purée)
400 g (14 oz) tin chickpeas, drained
    and rinsed (see Tip)
130 g (4½ oz/¾ cup) raisins
65 g (2¼ oz/½ cup) slivered
    almonds, toasted
Mint sprigs, to garnish
Steamed basmati rice and
    yoghurt, to serve

1 Trim the lamb of excess fat, then cut into 2 cm (¾ inch) chunks. Place in a 4.5 litre (157 fl oz/18 cup) slow cooker and sprinkle with the cinnamon, allspice, nutmeg and salt. Season with freshly ground black pepper and gently mix to coat the lamb in the spices.

2 Stir in the onion, garlic, eggplant, carrot and zucchini. Add the tomatoes and lemon juice and stir the tomato paste through. Stir in the chickpeas and raisins.

3 Cover and cook for 4–6 hours, or until the lamb is very tender.

4 Serve scattered with the almonds and garnished with mint sprigs, with steamed rice and yoghurt on the side.

⚙ *Tip: You can replace the chickpeas with a 400 g (14 oz) tin of red kidney beans, if you prefer.*

Rosemary-infused lamb and lentil casserole

Serves **6**   Preparation time **20 minutes**   Cooking time **5 hours**

1 kg (2 lb 4 oz) boneless lamb leg
1 brown onion, thinly sliced
2 garlic cloves, crushed
1 small carrot, finely chopped
2 teaspoons finely chopped fresh
    ginger
2 teaspoons rosemary leaves,
    plus extra rosemary sprigs,
    to garnish
500 ml (17 fl oz/2 cups) good-quality
    lamb or chicken stock
215 g (7½ oz/1 cup) green or brown
    lentils
1 tablespoon brown sugar
2 teaspoons balsamic vinegar

1 Trim the lamb of excess fat, then cut into 4 cm (1½ inch) chunks. Place in a 4.5 litre (157 fl oz/18 cup) slow cooker with the onion, garlic, carrot, ginger, rosemary leaves, stock and lentils. Gently mix together.

2 Cover and cook on high for 4 hours.

3 Stir in the sugar and vinegar. Cover and cook for a further 1 hour, or until the lentils are cooked and the lamb is tender.

4 Season to taste with sea salt and freshly ground black pepper. Serve garnished with extra rosemary sprigs.

Greek lamb with risoni and feta

Serves **4–6**   Preparation time **15 minutes**   Cooking time **7 hours 40 minutes**

1 kg (2 lb 4 oz) diced lamb
2 small red onions, finely chopped
2 garlic cloves, crushed
2 dried bay leaves
2 x 400 g (14 oz) tins chopped
  tomatoes
125 ml (4 fl oz/½ cup) good-quality
  chicken stock
125 ml (4 fl oz/½ cup) white wine
220 g (7¾ oz/1 cup) risoni (see Tip)
65 g (2¼ oz/½ cup) crumbled feta
  cheese
1 tablespoon finely grated
  lemon zest
2 tablespoons small oregano leaves
Crusty bread, to serve

Greek salad
1 Lebanese (short) cucumber
4 vine-ripened tomatoes, cut into
  wedges
10 kalamata olives
200 g (7 oz/1½ cups) crumbled
  feta cheese
60 ml (2 fl oz/¼ cup) extra virgin
  olive oil
1 tablespoon lemon juice

1 Put the lamb in a 5.5 litre (192 fl oz/22 cup) slow cooker with the onion, garlic, bay leaves and tomatoes. Pour in the stock and wine and gently mix together.

2 Cover and cook on low for 7 hours, or until the lamb is very tender.

3 Sprinkle the risoni over the lamb and mix it in well. Cover and cook for a further 40 minutes, or until the risoni is tender.

4 Near serving time, make the Greek salad. Cut the cucumber in half lengthways, discard the seeds, then cut into bite-sized pieces. Place in a serving bowl with the tomato, olives and feta. Whisk together the olive oil and lemon juice, pour over the salad and gently toss together.

5 Season the stew generously with freshly ground black pepper. Sprinkle with the feta, lemon zest and oregano and serve with the Greek salad and crusty bread.

⚙ *Tip: Risoni, also known as orzo, is a small rice-shaped pasta. You'll find it in continental delicatessens and larger supermarkets. If unavailable, you can use macaroni in this recipe instead.*

Lebanese lamb stew

Serves **6**   Preparation time **20 minutes**   Cooking time **7 hours 10 minutes**

2 tablespoons plain (all-purpose) flour
2 teaspoons sea salt
½ teaspoon freshly ground black pepper
1 tablespoon baharat (see Tip)
1.5 kg (3 lb 5 oz) boneless lamb shoulder
2 tablespoons tomato paste (concentrated purée)
125 ml (4 fl oz/½ cup) tomato passata (puréed tomatoes)
1 brown onion, finely chopped
2 garlic cloves, crushed
400 g (14 oz) tin white beans, drained and rinsed
3 tablespoons chopped flat-leaf (Italian) parsley
Steamed basmati rice and lemon cheeks, to serve

1 Place the flour, salt, pepper and baharat in a large bowl. Trim the lamb of excess fat, then cut into 3 cm (1¼ inch) chunks. Add to the flour mixture and toss until evenly coated.

2 Transfer the lamb to a 5.5 litre (192 fl oz/22 cup) slow cooker. Add the tomato paste, passata, onion, garlic and 125 ml (4 fl oz/½ cup) water and gently mix until well combined.

3 Cover and cook on low for 6–7 hours, or until the lamb is very tender and falls apart when stirred.

4 Gently stir the beans into the lamb mixture. Cover and cook for a further 10 minutes to heat through.

5 Sprinkle with the parsley and serve with steamed rice and lemon cheeks, for squeezing over.

⚙ *Tips: Baharat is a spice mixture used in Middle Eastern cooking. It is available in speciality food stores and Middle Eastern supermarkets. Although there is no direct substitute, you can use any Middle Eastern spice mix in this stew. Instead of rice, you could also serve this stew with steamed couscous.*

Lamb shanks with puy lentils

Serves **4** Preparation time **25 minutes** Cooking time **5 hours 15 minutes**

1 brown onion, chopped
1 celery stalk, chopped
1 carrot, peeled and chopped
1 parsnip, peeled and chopped
100 g (3½ oz) button mushrooms, halved
50 g (1¾ oz) pancetta or bacon, chopped
2 garlic cloves, chopped
2 anchovy fillets, finely chopped
4 French-trimmed lamb shanks
250 ml (9 fl oz/1 cup) good-quality chicken stock
250 ml (9 fl oz/1 cup) red wine
200 g (7 oz/1 cup) puy lentils or tiny blue-green lentils (see Tip)
1 tablespoon cornflour (cornstarch)
Chopped flat-leaf (Italian) parsley and horseradish cream, to serve

1 Put the vegetables in a 5.5 litre (192 fl oz/22 cup) slow cooker with the pancetta, garlic and anchovy. Gently mix together.

2 Arrange the lamb shanks over the vegetables. Season well with sea salt and freshly ground black pepper, then pour the stock and wine over the shanks.

3 Cover and cook on high for 4 hours.

4 Using tongs, turn the shanks in the cooking liquid. Mix the lentils through the liquid, then cover and cook for a further 1 hour, or until the lamb and lentils are tender and cooked through.

5 Remove the shanks to a warm platter, cover loosely with foil and keep in a warm place while finishing the sauce.

6 Blend the cornflour with 1 tablespoon water until smooth, then stir into the sauce and vegetables. Cover and cook for a further 15 minutes, or until the sauce has thickened slightly.

7 Sprinkle with parsley and serve with horseradish cream.

Tip: Puy lentils are small blue-green lentils originating from the Puy region of France. They hold their shape well and don't turn mushy during cooking. They should be rinsed before using.

Country beef stew

Serves **6–8**   Preparation time **30 minutes**   Cooking time **5 hours 30 minutes**

1 kg (2 lb 4 oz) chuck, blade or
   skirt steak
1 small eggplant (aubergine), cut
   into 1.5 cm (⅝ inch) chunks
250 g (9 oz) small new potatoes,
   unpeeled, halved
2 celery stalks, sliced
3 carrots, chopped
2 red onions, sliced
6 ripe tomatoes, chopped
2 garlic cloves, crushed
1 teaspoon ground coriander
½ teaspoon allspice
¾ teaspoon sweet paprika
2 dried bay leaves
2 tablespoons tomato paste
   (concentrated purée)
250 ml (9 fl oz/1 cup) red wine
500 ml (17 fl oz/2 cups) good-quality
   beef stock
3 tablespoons chopped flat-leaf
   (Italian) parsley

1 Trim the beef of excess fat, then cut into 4 cm (1½ inch) chunks. Place in a 4.5 litre (157 fl oz/18 cup) slow cooker along with the vegetables, garlic, spices, bay leaves and tomato paste.

2 Pour in the wine and stock and gently mix together. Cover and cook on low for 5½ hours, or until the beef is tender.

3 Season to taste with sea salt and freshly ground black pepper. Stir the parsley through and serve.

Italian beef ribs with crushed potatoes

Serves **4**   Preparation time **30 minutes**   Cooking time **8 hours 50 minutes**

2 tablespoons olive oil
4 beef short ribs, about 450 g (1 lb)
   each
2 brown onions, finely diced
5 garlic cloves, chopped
1 carrot, finely diced
2 tablespoons tomato paste
   (concentrated purée)
300 ml (10½ fl oz) red wine
200 ml (7 fl oz) good-quality
   beef stock
4 rosemary sprigs
2 tablespoons brown sugar
1 tablespoon balsamic vinegar,
   or to taste

Crushed potatoes
600 g (1 lb 5 oz) small new potatoes,
   unpeeled
60 ml (2 fl oz/¼ cup) olive oil
3 tablespoons chopped flat-leaf
   (Italian) parsley

1 Heat half the olive oil in the insert pan of a 5 litre (175 fl oz/20 cup) slow cooker or a large frying pan over high heat. Season the ribs with sea salt and freshly ground black pepper, then cook, turning occasionally, for 2–3 minutes, or until sealed on each side. Set aside.

2 Reduce the heat to medium. Heat the remaining oil in the pan and add the onion, garlic and carrot. Cook for 5–6 minutes, or until tender. Stir in the tomato paste and cook for 1–2 minutes, or until the paste becomes darker. Add the wine and simmer for 2–3 minutes, or until slightly reduced.

3 Return the insert pan, if using, to the slow cooker, or transfer the onion mixture to the slow cooker. Add the stock, rosemary sprigs and sugar. Add the ribs to the mixture and gently turn to coat. Cover and cook on low for 8 hours, or until the meat is tender. Remove the ribs to a warm platter, cover loosely with foil and keep in a warm place while finishing the sauce.

4 Transfer the sauce to a saucepan, or the insert pan to the stovetop. Remove the rosemary sprigs. Cook over medium–high heat for 20–30 minutes, or until the sauce has reduced. Stir in the vinegar and season to taste. Stir the ribs through.

5 Meanwhile, prepare the crushed potatoes. Boil the potatoes for 20–25 minutes, or until tender. Drain well, transfer to a bowl and roughly crush with a fork. Drizzle with the oil, add the parsley and season to taste. Stir to combine.

6 Serve the ribs with the crushed potatoes, drizzled with the sauce.

Ragu bolognese

Serves **8** Preparation time **20 minutes** Cooking time **3 hours 20 minutes**

3 tablespoons olive oil
2 kg (4 lb 8 oz) minced (ground) beef
250 g (9 oz) bacon, rind and fat
  removed and chopped
250 g (9 oz) chicken livers, trimmed
  and finely chopped (optional)
3 brown onions, finely chopped
4 garlic cloves, finely chopped
185 ml (6 fl oz/¾ cup) red wine
2 x 400 g (14 oz) tins chopped
  tomatoes
350 ml (12 fl oz) tomato passata
  (puréed tomatoes)
90 g (3¼ oz/⅓ cup) tomato paste
  (concentrated purée)
1 teaspoon sea salt
1 teaspoon sugar
¼ teaspoon freshly ground black
  pepper
3 tablespoons basil leaves, torn
Hot cooked spaghetti or tagliatelle
  and shaved parmesan cheese,
  to serve

1 Heat half the olive oil in the insert pan of a 5 litre (175 fl oz/20 cup) slow cooker or a large frying pan over medium–high heat. Add half the beef and cook for 3–4 minutes, breaking up any lumps with a wooden spoon as it browns. Remove the meat to a large bowl using a slotted spoon. Repeat with the remaining beef.

2 Brown the bacon and livers, if using, in the pan for 2 minutes. Remove with a slotted spoon and add to the beef. Reduce the heat to medium, add the remaining oil and cook the onion for 3 minutes, or until softened. Add the garlic and cook, stirring, for a further 1 minute.

3 Stir in the wine, using a wooden spoon to loosen any cooked-on bits from the base of the pan. Cook for 3 minutes, or until almost all the wine has evaporated.

4 Return the insert pan, if using, to the slow cooker, or transfer the onion mixture to the slow cooker. Add the beef and bacon mixture, the tomatoes, passata and tomato paste. Gently mix together.

5 Cover and cook on high for 3 hours. Stir in the salt, sugar and pepper, then adjust the seasoning if necessary.

6 Stir the basil through. Serve spooned over hot spaghetti or tagliatelle, scattered with shaved parmesan.

⚙ Tips: *This is an easy way to cook a large batch of bolognese! It's a good idea to freeze half the sauce for another meal. Adding chicken liver to this dish may not appeal to everyone, but it does add a wonderful depth of flavour.*

Beef, pancetta and pea pie

Serves 6   Preparation time **40 minutes (+ cooling time)**   Cooking time **7 hours**

1.2 kg (2 lb 10 oz) beef chuck steak, cut into 3 cm (1¼ inch) pieces
Plain (all-purpose) flour, seasoned with sea salt and freshly ground black pepper, for dusting
2 tablespoons olive oil
150 g (5½ oz) pancetta, diced
6 French shallots (eschalots), finely diced
5 garlic cloves, thinly sliced
250 ml (9 fl oz/1 cup) red wine
250 ml (9 fl oz/1 cup) good-quality beef stock
4 thyme sprigs, plus 1 tablespoon thyme leaves
215 g (7½ oz/1½ cups) frozen peas, thawed
1 sheet frozen puff pastry, thawed
1 egg, lightly beaten
Relish, to serve

1 Trim the beef of excess fat, then cut into 3 cm (1¼ inch) chunks. Dust the beef in the flour, shaking off any excess.

2 Heat the olive oil in the insert pan of a 5 litre (175 fl oz/ 20 cup) slow cooker or a frying pan over medium– high heat. Brown the beef in batches for 3–4 minutes, transferring each batch to a plate.

3 Reduce the heat to low. Add the pancetta, shallot and garlic and cook for 4–6 minutes, or until the shallot is tender. Stir in the wine and simmer for 2–3 minutes, or until reduced slightly. Add the stock, thyme sprigs and beef, bring to a simmer and season to taste.

4 Return the insert pan, if using, to the slow cooker, or transfer the beef mixture to the slow cooker. Cover and cook on low for 4–5 hours, or until the beef is tender.

5 Turn the slow cooker setting to high. Remove the lid and cook for a further 45–60 minutes, or until the sauce has thickened. Stir in the peas and thyme leaves. Remove the thyme sprigs. Transfer the beef mixture to a 1 litre (35 fl oz/4 cup) pie or baking dish and set aside to cool.

6 Preheat the oven to 180°C (350°F/Gas 4). Brush the edges of the baking dish with the egg. Cut the pastry to fit the top of the pie, with a 2 cm (¾ inch) overhang. Place the pastry over the beef mixture and gently press the edges with a fork to seal. Pierce a small hole in the centre of the pastry to allow steam to escape, then brush with the egg wash. Bake for 35–40 minutes, or until the pastry is golden and cooked through. Serve hot, with relish if desired.

Osso bucco bianco

Serves **4**   Preparation time **30 minutes**   Cooking time **6 hours 20 minutes**

4 veal osso bucco pieces, about 1 kg
  (2 lb 4 oz)
Plain (all-purpose) flour, seasoned
  with sea salt and freshly ground
  black pepper, for dusting
2 tablespoons olive oil
1 brown onion, finely chopped
3 garlic cloves, finely chopped
2 bacon slices, rind and fat removed,
  finely chopped
1 celery stalk, finely chopped
1 carrot, finely chopped
1 teaspoon dried thyme
1 dried bay leaf
250 ml (9 fl oz/1 cup) white wine
2 teaspoons dried fennel seeds
375 ml (13 fl oz/1½ cups) good-
  quality chicken stock

Polenta
185 ml (6 fl oz/¾ cup) good-quality
  chicken stock
190 g (6¾ oz/1 cup) instant polenta
60 g (2¼ oz) butter
70 g (2½ oz/½ cup) finely grated
  parmesan cheese

Gremolata
3 tablespoons finely chopped
  flat-leaf (Italian) parsley
Finely grated zest of 1 lemon
1 garlic clove, finely chopped

1 Coat the veal in the flour and shake off the excess.

2 Heat the olive oil in the insert pan of a 5 litre (175 fl oz/
20 cup) slow cooker or a large frying pan over medium–
high heat. Cook the veal for 2 minutes on each side, or
until golden. Remove to a plate.

3 Reduce the heat to medium. Add the onion, garlic, bacon,
celery, carrot, thyme and bay leaf to the pan and cook,
stirring occasionally, for 8–10 minutes, or until the
vegetables are soft.

4 Increase the heat to high, add the wine and boil until
the liquid has reduced by two-thirds.

5 Return the insert pan, if using, to the slow cooker, or
transfer the onion mixture to the slow cooker. Add the
fennel seeds, then stir in the stock. Season lightly with
sea salt and freshly ground black pepper and add the veal.
Cover and cook on low for 6 hours, or until the meat is
almost falling off the bone.

6 Near serving time, prepare the polenta. Heat the stock
and 125 ml (4 fl oz/½ cup) water in a saucepan until
simmering. Add the polenta in a thin stream and whisk
until combined. Cook for 4–5 minutes, then stir in the
butter and parmesan. Season with black pepper.

7 Meanwhile, combine all the gremolata ingredients
in a small bowl.

8 Serve the veal on a bed of polenta, drizzled with the
braising liquid and sprinkled with the gremolata.

Beef stroganoff with mixed mushrooms

Serves **4** Preparation time **40 minutes** Cooking time **4 hours 10 minutes**

350 g (12 oz) small new potatoes, unpeeled, sliced 1.5 cm (⅝ inch) thick

300 g (10½ oz) mixed mushrooms, such as oyster and Swiss brown, thickly sliced

1 brown onion, sliced into thin rings

2–3 garlic cloves, chopped

1 teaspoon dried oregano

750 g (1 lb 10 oz) round or sirloin steak

35 g (1¼ oz/¼ cup) plain (all-purpose) flour

½ teaspoon paprika

2 tablespoons olive oil

125 ml (4 fl oz/½ cup) good-quality beef stock

125 ml (4 fl oz/½ cup) white wine

2 tablespoons tomato paste (concentrated purée)

125 g (4½ oz/½ cup) sour cream

1 cup chopped flat-leaf (Italian) parsley

1 Layer the potato slices in a 4.5 litre (157 fl oz/18 cup) slow cooker.

2 Place the mushrooms and onion in a large bowl. Sprinkle with the garlic and oregano and season well with sea salt and freshly ground black pepper.

3 Trim the beef of excess fat, then cut it into thin strips across the grain. Pat dry with paper towels. Combine the flour and paprika in a flat dish.

4 Heat 2 teaspoons of the olive oil in a large frying pan over high heat. Working with one-quarter of the meat at a time, dust the beef with the flour, shake off the excess, then add to the pan and toss for 1–2 minutes, or until the meat is browned all over. Add to the mushroom and onion mixture. Repeat with the remaining oil, beef and flour.

5 Add any remaining flour to the frying pan, then pour in the stock, wine and tomato paste and whisk together until hot. Pour over the meat mixture in the bowl and toss well to combine. Transfer to the slow cooker, placing the mixture over the sliced potato.

6 Cover and cook on high for 3–4 hours, or until the beef is tender and the potato slices are cooked.

7 Just before serving, stir the sour cream and half the parsley through. Spoon the stroganoff onto serving plates, sprinkle with the remaining parsley and serve with the potato.

Portuguese beef

Serves **6**   Preparation time **20 minutes**   Cooking time **5 hours 10 minutes**

1.25 kg (2 lb 12 oz) beef chuck steak
2 garlic cloves, thinly sliced
175 g (6 oz) smoked bacon slices,
    rind and fat removed, chopped
1 tablespoon sweet paprika
¾ teaspoon smoked paprika
2 dried bay leaves
2 teaspoons dried oregano
250 ml (9 fl oz/1 cup) red wine
250 ml (9 fl oz/1 cup) good-quality
    beef stock
20 g (¾ oz) butter, at room
    temperature
2 tablespoons plain (all-purpose)
    flour
175 g (6 oz/1 cup) green olives
35 g (1¼ oz/¼ cup) slivered almonds
Mashed potato or steamed rice,
    to serve

1 Trim the beef of excess fat, then cut into 4 cm (1½ inch) chunks. Place in a 4.5 litre (157 fl oz/18 cup) slow cooker with the garlic, bacon, sweet and smoked paprika, bay leaves and oregano.

2 Pour in the wine and stock and gently mix together. Cover and cook on low for 5 hours, or until the beef is tender.

3 Mix together the butter and flour and gradually whisk through the beef mixture. Cook, uncovered, for a further 10 minutes, or until the sauce has thickened.

4 Stir the olives and almonds through and season to taste with sea salt and freshly ground black pepper. Serve with mashed potato or steamed rice.

Beef with root vegetables and broad beans

Serves **4**   Preparation time **20 minutes**   Cooking time **4 hours**

1.2 kg (2 lb 10 oz) beef chuck steak
½ teaspoon dried thyme
2 garlic cloves, chopped
1 leek, white part only, cut into
   1 cm (½ inch) thick slices
1 celery stalk, sliced
2 parsnips, peeled and quartered
300 g (10½ oz) orange sweet potato,
   cut into 8 wedges
1 swede (rutabaga), peeled and cut
   into 8 wedges
60 ml (2 fl oz/¼ cup) tomato sauce
   (ketchup)
250 ml (9 fl oz/1 cup) red wine
1 tablespoon cornflour (cornstarch)
175 g (6 oz) frozen broad (fava)
   beans
Crusty bread, to serve

1 Trim the beef of excess fat, then cut into 4 cm (1½ inch) chunks. Place in a 4.5 litre (157 fl oz/18 cup) slow cooker, sprinkle with the thyme and season well with sea salt and freshly ground black pepper.

2 Add the garlic, vegetables and tomato sauce, then pour in the wine and gently mix together. Cover and cook on high for 4 hours, or until the beef is tender.

3 About 20 minutes before the end of cooking, combine the cornflour with a little water to make a smooth paste. Stir it through the stew, along with the broad beans. Continue to cook until the broad beans are tender.

4 Ladle into bowls and serve with crusty bread.

Beef casserole

Serves **6**   Preparation time **20 minutes**   Cooking time **7 hours 20 minutes**

1 kg (2 lb 4 oz) beef chuck steak
80 ml (2½ fl oz/⅓ cup) olive oil
350 g (12 oz) eggplant (aubergine),
    cut into 5 cm (2 inch) chunks
1 brown onion, thinly sliced
3 garlic cloves, chopped
1 teaspoon fennel seeds
2 dried bay leaves
1 tablespoon thyme leaves
2 tablespoons tomato paste
    (concentrated purée)
1 tablespoon plain (all-purpose)
    flour
250 ml (9 fl oz/1 cup) good-quality
    beef stock
1 fennel bulb, about 400 g (14 oz),
    sliced into 3 cm (1¼ inch) wedges
400 g (14 oz) all-purpose potatoes,
    such as desiree, peeled and
    cut into large chunks
2 tomatoes, chopped
400 g (14 oz) tin chickpeas, drained
    and rinsed
⅓ cup chopped flat-leaf (Italian)
    parsley
Crusty bread, to serve

1 Trim the beef of excess fat, then cut into 4 cm (1½ inch) chunks. Season the beef with sea salt and freshly ground black pepper and set aside.

2 Heat 2 tablespoons of the olive oil in the insert pan of a 7 litre (245 fl oz/28 cup) slow cooker or a large frying pan over high heat. Add the eggplant and cook for 5–6 minutes, or until golden on all sides. Remove to a plate.

3 Reduce the heat to medium–high. Heat the remaining oil in the pan and add the onion, garlic, fennel seeds, bay leaves and half the thyme. Cook, stirring, for 5 minutes, or until the onion has softened.

4 Increase the heat to high and add the beef. Cover and cook for 5 minutes, or until the beef is brown. Add the tomato paste, sprinkle with the flour and cook for 2 minutes, stirring occasionally. Stir in the stock.

5 Return the insert pan, if using, to the slow cooker, or transfer the beef mixture to the slow cooker. Add the fennel wedges and potato and season with freshly ground black pepper. Cover and cook on low for 6½ hours, or until the beef is tender.

6 Stir in the tomatoes, chickpeas, remaining thyme and half the parsley. Cover and cook for a further 30 minutes.

7 Season to taste, sprinkle with remaining parsley and serve with crusty bread.

Italian beef casserole with dumplings

Serves **4–6** Preparation time **30 minutes** Cooking time **4 hours 30 minutes**

1 kg (2 lb 4 oz) beef chuck, blade
  or skirt steak
1 brown onion, sliced
2 garlic cloves, crushed
2 x 400 g (14 oz) tins chopped
  tomatoes
450 g (1 lb) jar roasted red
  capsicums (peppers), drained
  and thickly sliced
1 tablespoon chopped oregano
250 ml (9 fl oz/1 cup) good-quality
  beef stock
Purchased pesto, to serve

Dumplings
50 g (1¾ oz/⅓ cup) plain
  (all-purpose) flour
50 g (1¾ oz/¼ cup) instant polenta
1 teaspoon baking powder
½ teaspoon sea salt
1 egg white
2 tablespoons milk
1 tablespoon olive oil

1 Trim the beef of excess fat, then cut into 3 cm (1¼ inch) chunks. Place in a 4.5 litre (157 fl oz/18 cup) slow cooker with the onion, garlic, tomatoes, capsicum and oregano.

2 Pour in the stock, season with sea salt and freshly ground black pepper and gently mix together. Cover and cook on high for 4 hours, or until the beef is tender.

3 Meanwhile, make the dumplings. Combine the flour, polenta, baking powder and salt in a large bowl. Make a well in the centre, add the egg white, milk and olive oil and stir well to combine. Form teaspoonfuls of the mixture into small balls.

4 Add the dumplings to the slow cooker. Cover and cook for a further 30 minutes, or until the dumplings are cooked through.

5 Check the seasoning and add extra salt and pepper if needed. Serve topped with a dollop of pesto.

Stifado

Serves **4**   Preparation time **20 minutes**   Cooking time **4 hours 15 minutes**

1 kg (2 lb 4 oz) beef chuck steak
500 g (1 lb 2 oz) whole baby onions
1 garlic clove, cut in half lengthways
1 cinnamon stick
4 whole cloves
1 dried bay leaf
1 tablespoon red wine vinegar
2 tablespoons tomato paste
    (concentrated purée)
125 ml (4 fl oz/½ cup) red wine
125 ml (4 fl oz/½ cup) good-quality
    beef stock
2 tablespoons currants
Steamed rice, potatoes or crusty
    bread, to serve

1 Trim the beef of excess fat, then cut into 5 cm (2 inch) chunks. Place in a 4.5 litre (157 fl oz/18 cup) slow cooker with the onions, garlic, cinnamon stick, cloves, bay leaf, vinegar and tomato paste.

2 Pour in the wine and stock, season with sea salt and freshly ground black pepper and gently mix together. Cover and cook on high for 4 hours, or until the beef is tender.

3 Stir the currants through. Cover and cook for a further 15 minutes.

4 Discard the cinnamon stick. Check the seasoning and add extra salt and pepper if needed. Serve with steamed rice, potatoes or crusty bread.

Creamy beef with cherry tomatoes and sun-dried tomatoes

Serves **6**   Preparation time **25 minutes**   Cooking time **6 hours 30 minutes**

35 g (1¼ oz/¼ cup) plain (all-purpose) flour
2 teaspoons sea salt
½ teaspoon freshly ground black pepper
1 teaspoon sweet paprika
1.5 kg (3 lb 5 oz) beef chuck steak
1½ tablespoons tomato paste (concentrated purée)
60 ml (2 fl oz/¼ cup) white wine
1 brown onion, finely chopped
2 garlic cloves, crushed
500 g (1 lb 2 oz) cherry tomatoes, halved
110 g (3¾ oz/½ cup) semi-dried (sun-blushed) tomatoes, chopped
245 g (9 oz/1 cup) sour cream
400 g (14 oz) fresh pappardelle pasta
Toasted pine nuts, for sprinkling
Small basil leaves, to garnish
Shaved parmesan cheese, to serve

1 Combine the flour, salt, pepper and paprika in a large bowl. Trim the beef of excess fat, then cut into 3 cm (1¼ inch) chunks. Add the beef to the flour mixture and toss until evenly coated. Shake off any excess flour, then place in a 5.5 litre (192 fl oz/22 cup) slow cooker.

2 Mix the tomato paste with the wine, then add to the beef with the onion, garlic, cherry tomatoes and semi-dried tomatoes. Gently mix together.

3 Cover and cook on low for 5–6 hours, or until the beef is very tender.

4 Stir in the sour cream, then cover and cook for another 30 minutes, or until heated through.

5 Near serving time, add the pasta to a large saucepan of rapidly boiling salted water and cook according to the packet instructions until al dente. Drain well.

6 Divide the pasta among serving bowls, then spoon the beef mixture over the top. Serve sprinkled with pine nuts, basil and parmesan.

Sichuan and anise beef stew

Serves **4**   Preparation time **20 minutes**   Cooking time **3 hours**

1½ tablespoons plain (all-purpose)
    flour
1 kg (2 lb 4 oz) beef chuck steak
1 large red onion, thickly sliced
2 garlic cloves, crushed
3 tablespoons tomato paste
    (concentrated purée)
2 dried bay leaves, crushed
3 long orange zest strips, about
    1.5 cm (⅝ inch) wide
2 star anise
1 teaspoon sichuan peppercorns
1 teaspoon chopped thyme
1 tablespoon chopped rosemary
250 ml (9 fl oz/1 cup) red wine
250 ml (9 fl oz/1 cup) good-quality
    beef stock
3 tablespoons chopped coriander
    (cilantro) leaves
Steamed rice, to serve

1 Put the flour in a flat dish and season with sea salt and freshly ground black pepper. Trim the beef of excess fat, then cut into 3 cm (1¼ inch) chunks. Add the beef to the flour mixture and toss until evenly coated. Shake off any excess flour, then place in a 4.5 litre (157 fl oz/18 cup) slow cooker.

2 Add the onion, garlic, tomato paste, bay leaves, orange zest, star anise, peppercorns, thyme and rosemary. Pour in the wine and stock and gently mix together. Cover and cook on high for 3 hours, or until the beef is tender.

3 Season to taste with sea salt and freshly ground black pepper. Stir in most of the coriander leaves and garnish with the remainder. Serve with steamed rice.

Chilli beef with avocado salsa

Serves **6**   Preparation time **30 minutes**   Cooking time **6 hours 5 minutes**

800 g (1 lb 12 oz) beef chuck steak
2 x 400 g (14 oz) tins chopped
  tomatoes
1 red capsicum (pepper), diced
100 g (3½ oz) mushroom flats,
  finely chopped
2 brown onions, chopped
2 garlic cloves, crushed
4 medium–hot fresh green chillies,
  seeded and finely chopped,
  or to taste
2 teaspoons ground cumin
½ teaspoon ground cinnamon
1 teaspoon caster (superfine) sugar
2 dried bay leaves
200 ml (7 fl oz) good-quality
  beef stock
½ cup coriander (cilantro) leaves
400 g (14 oz) tin red kidney beans,
  drained and rinsed
25 g (1 oz) bitter dark chocolate
  (Mexican if possible), grated
250 g (9 oz/1 cup) sour cream

Avocado salsa
1 firm, ripe avocado, diced
½ red onion, chopped
½ cup coriander (cilantro) leaves

1   Trim the beef of excess fat, then cut into 3 cm (1¼ inch) chunks. Place in a 4.5 litre (157 fl oz/18 cup) slow cooker.

2   Add the tomatoes, capsicum, mushroom, onion, garlic, chilli, cumin, cinnamon, sugar and bay leaves. Pour in the stock and gently mix together. Cover and cook on low for 6 hours, or until the beef is tender.

3   Stir in the coriander, kidney beans and chocolate. Season with sea salt and extra chopped chilli if desired. Cover and cook for a further 5 minutes, or until the beans are warmed through.

4   Just before serving, combine the avocado salsa ingredients in a small bowl.

5   Serve the chilli beef topped with a spoonful of the sour cream and the avocado salsa.

Beef and vegetable stew

Serves **4**   Preparation time **25 minutes**   Cooking time **4 hours**

1 kg (2 lb 4 oz) beef blade, skirt
steak or chuck steak
1 brown onion
1 carrot
1 parsnip
1 swede (rutabaga) or turnip
2 all-purpose potatoes
250 g (9 oz) sweet potato
1 celery stalk
100 g (3½ oz) button mushrooms
2 thick bacon slices, rind and fat
removed, coarsely chopped
2 garlic cloves, chopped
1 teaspoon dried oregano
400 g (14 oz) tin chopped tomatoes
2 tablespoons tomato paste
(concentrated purée)
60 ml (2 fl oz/¼ cup) red wine
400 ml (14 fl oz) good-quality beef
or chicken stock
1 cup flat-leaf (Italian) parsley,
chopped

1 Trim the beef of excess fat, then cut into 4 cm (1½ inch) chunks. Place in a 5.5 litre (192 fl oz/22 cup) slow cooker.

2 Peel the onion, carrot, parsnip, swede, potatoes and sweet potato and cut into 4 cm (1½ inch) chunks. Cut the celery into 4 cm (1½ inch) chunks. Wipe the mushrooms clean and slice in half. Add the vegetables to the slow cooker.

3 Scatter the bacon, garlic and oregano over the vegetables and add the tomatoes and tomato paste. Pour in the wine and stock, season well with sea salt and freshly ground black pepper and gently mix together.

4 Cover and cook on high for 4 hours, or until the beef and vegetables are tender.

5 Check the seasoning and add extra salt and pepper if needed. Serve sprinkled with the parsley.

Tip: This stew is delicious served with steamed green or yellow beans and good crusty bread.

Spanish beef with chorizo

Serves 4   Preparation time **10 minutes**   Cooking time **6 hours 20 minutes**

2 tablespoons extra virgin olive oil
1 kg (2 lb 4 oz) beef chuck steak,
    trimmed of excess fat and cut
    into 3 cm (1¼ inch) chunks
1 red onion, sliced
2 chorizo sausages, thickly sliced
2 garlic cloves, crushed
1 tablespoon smoked paprika
2 tablespoons tomato paste
    (concentrated purée)
2 x 400 g (14 oz) tins chopped
    tomatoes
1 red capsicum (pepper), cut into
    3 cm (1¼ inch) chunks
Sliced fresh green chilli and crusty
    bread, to serve

Bean and orange salad
400 g (14 oz) tin borlotti beans,
    drained and rinsed
1 small red onion, thinly sliced
1 cup flat-leaf (Italian) parsley
Finely grated zest of 1 orange
1 orange
2 tablespoons olive oil
1 tablespoon dijon mustard

1   Heat the olive oil in the insert pan of a 5.5 litre
    (192 fl oz/22 cup) slow cooker or a large frying pan
    over medium–high heat. Add the beef in batches and
    cook for 5 minutes, turning to brown all over and
    transferring each batch to a plate.

2   Add the onion and chorizo to the pan and cook, stirring,
    for 2–3 minutes. Add the garlic, paprika and tomato paste
    and cook for 1 minute. Stir in the tomatoes and capsicum,
    using a wooden spoon to scrape up any cooked-on bits.

3   Return the insert pan, if using, to the slow cooker, or
    transfer the mixture to the slow cooker. Add the beef
    and gently mix together. Cover and cook on high for
    5–6 hours, or until the beef is very tender.

4   Near serving time, make the bean and orange salad.
    Combine the beans, onion, parsley and orange zest in a
    large bowl. Peel the orange, removing all the white pith.
    Holding the orange over a bowl to catch any juices, cut
    along each side of the white membranes to remove the
    segments. Add the orange segments to the salad. Whisk
    the olive oil and mustard into the reserved orange juice
    and season with sea salt and freshly ground black pepper.
    Pour the dressing over the salad and gently toss together.

5   Sprinkle the beef with chopped green chilli. Serve with
    crusty bread and the bean and orange salad.

*Tip: If you have more time you can cook the beef on low, increasing
the cooking time to 8–10 hours.*

Osso bucco with green olives

Serves **4–6**   Preparation time **25 minutes**   Cooking time **8 hours 30 minutes**

35 g (1¼ oz/¼ cup) plain
   (all-purpose) flour
8 osso bucco pieces, about
   1.5 kg (3 lb 5 oz)
2 tablespoons olive oil
1 brown onion, finely chopped
1 celery stalk, finely chopped
1 carrot, finely chopped
400 g (14 oz) tin chopped tomatoes
2 dried bay leaves
2 rosemary sprigs
185 ml (6 fl oz/¾ cup) white wine
375 ml (13 fl oz/1½ cups) good-
   quality chicken stock
100 g (3½ oz/½ cup) green olives
3 tablespoons chopped flat-leaf
   (Italian) parsley, plus extra, to
   garnish

Soft polenta
500 ml (17 fl oz/2 cups) milk
190 g (6¾ oz/1 cup) white or yellow
   polenta
40 g (1½ oz) butter
40 g (1½ oz/⅓ cup) coarsely grated
   parmesan cheese

1 Put the flour in a flat dish and season with sea salt and freshly ground black pepper. Dust the veal with the flour, shaking off any excess.

2 Heat the olive oil in the insert pan of a 5.5 litre (192 fl oz/22 cup) slow cooker or a large frying pan over medium–high heat. Add the veal in batches and cook for 5 minutes on each side, or until golden brown all over, transferring each batch to a plate.

3 Return the insert pan, if using to the slow cooker. Place the onion, celery, carrot, tomatoes, bay leaves and rosemary sprigs in the slow cooker, then pour in the wine and stock and gently mix together.

4 Add the veal, then cover and cook on low for 8 hours, or until the veal is very tender.

5 Near serving time, make the soft polenta. Bring the milk and 250 ml (9 fl oz/1 cup) water to the boil in a saucepan. Stirring continuously, add the polenta in a thin stream. Cook over low heat, stirring often, for 30–35 minutes, or until the polenta is thick and soft. Remove from the heat and stir in the butter and parmesan.

6 Stir the olives and parsley through the stew and season to taste. Serve the osso bucco on a bed of soft polenta, sprinkled with extra parsley.

Oxtail with marmalade

Serves **4**   Preparation time **20 minutes (+ overnight marinating)**   Cooking time **4 hours 15 minutes**

160 g (5½ oz/½ cup) marmalade
100 ml (3½ fl oz) dry sherry
1.5 kg (3 lb 5 oz) oxtail
2 tablespoons olive oil
4 all-purpose potatoes, peeled and
    cut into 3 cm (1¼ inch) chunks
2 carrots, sliced
1 brown onion, thinly sliced
2 dried bay leaves
1 cinnamon stick
Mashed potato, to serve
1 orange, peeled and segmented,
    to garnish

1 Mix the marmalade and sherry together in a large bowl. Cut the oxtail into sections, then add to the marmalade mixture and turn to coat all over. Cover and marinate in the refrigerator overnight.

2 Heat the olive oil in a large frying pan over high heat. Add the oxtail in batches and cook for 4 minutes on each side, or until nicely browned, transferring each batch to a plate.

3 Place the potato, carrot, onion, bay leaves and cinnamon stick in a 4.5 litre (157 fl oz/18 cup) slow cooker. Sit the oxtail pieces on top. Cover and cook on high for 4 hours, or until the oxtail is tender.

4 Season to taste with sea salt and freshly ground black pepper. Serve with mashed potato, garnished with the orange segments.

Beef cheeks with onion, mushrooms and thyme

Serves **4**   Preparation time **25 minutes**   Cooking time **8 hours**

1 kg (2 lb 4 oz) beef cheeks
100 g (3½ oz) bacon pieces or speck, trimmed and chopped
2 celery stalks, finely chopped
1 carrot, finely chopped
1 brown onion, finely chopped
¼ cup thyme leaves
3 garlic cloves, chopped
250 ml (9 fl oz/1 cup) red wine
250 ml (9 fl oz/1 cup) good-quality beef stock
40 g (1½ oz) butter
12 baby onions, peeled and trimmed, halved lengthways if large
1½ tablespoons sugar
1½ tablespoons sherry vinegar
16 button mushrooms, halved
Mashed potato and steamed green vegetables, to serve

1 Trim the beef cheeks of excess fat and sinew, then cut each cheek into four portions. Place in a 4.5 litre (157 fl oz/18 cup) slow cooker along with the bacon, celery, carrot, onion, thyme and garlic.

2 Pour in the wine and stock and gently mix together. Cover and cook on low for 7 hours, or until the meat is almost falling apart. (The cooking time may vary slightly, depending on the thickness of the beef.)

3 Meanwhile, melt half the butter in a heavy-based frying pan. Add the onions and cook over medium–low heat for 8 minutes, or until golden. Add the sugar and cook until caramelised, shaking the pan occasionally to ensure the sugar caramelises evenly. Stir in half the vinegar, using a wooden spoon to scrape up any cooked-on bits from the base of the pan. Transfer the mixture to the slow cooker.

4 Increase the heat to medium. Melt the remaining butter in the pan and cook the mushrooms for 5–6 minutes, or until golden. Pour in the remaining vinegar and stir to scrape up any cooked-on bits.

5 Add the mushrooms to the slow cooker. Cook, uncovered, for a further 1 hour, or until the beef is tender and the sauce has reduced and thickened slightly.

6 Serve the beef cheeks drizzled with the sauce, with mashed potato and steamed green vegetables.

Sweet paprika veal goulash

Serves **4**   Preparation time **20 minutes**   Cooking time **4 hours 5 minutes**

1 kg (2 lb 4 oz) boneless veal
   shoulder
1 brown onion, sliced
2 garlic cloves, crushed
2 all-purpose potatoes, peeled
   and diced
1 tablespoon sweet paprika
½ teaspoon caraway seeds
2 dried bay leaves
625 ml (21½ fl oz/2½ cups) tomato
   passata (puréed tomatoes)
125 ml (4 fl oz/½ cup) red wine
125 ml (4 fl oz/½ cup) good-quality
   chicken stock
275 g (9¾ oz) jar roasted red
   capsicums (peppers), drained
375 g (13 oz) fresh fettuccine
Sour cream, to serve

1 Cut the veal into 3 cm (1¼ inch) chunks. Place in a 4.5 litre (157 fl oz/18 cup) slow cooker with the onion, garlic, potato, paprika, caraway seeds and bay leaves.

2 Pour in the passata, wine and stock and gently mix together. Cover and cook on high for 4 hours, or until the veal is tender.

3 Stir in the capsicum, then cover and cook for a further 5 minutes, or until warmed through. Season to taste with sea salt and freshly ground black pepper.

4 Near serving time, add the fettuccine to a large saucepan of rapidly boiling salted water and cook according to the packet instructions until al dente. Drain well.

5 Serve the goulash on a bed of fettuccine, topped with a dollop of sour cream.

Veal with sweet potato, tomato and olives

Serves **4**   Preparation time **15 minutes**   Cooking time **4 hours 10 minutes**

1 kg (2 lb 4 oz) piece of veal rump
350 g (12 oz) orange sweet potato
1 large red onion, chopped
1 celery stalk, chopped
2 garlic cloves, chopped
1 rosemary sprig
2 tablespoons tomato paste
   (concentrated purée)
400 g (14 oz) tin chopped tomatoes
60 ml (2 fl oz/¼ cup) white wine
1 tablespoon cornflour (cornstarch)
12 pitted or stuffed green olives
2 tablespoons chopped parsley
Finely grated zest of 1 small lemon

1 Cut the veal into 4 cm (1½ inch) chunks and place in a 4.5 litre (157 fl oz/18 cup) slow cooker. Peel the sweet potato, cut into 4 cm (1½ inch) chunks and add to the slow cooker.

2 Add the onion, celery, garlic, rosemary sprig and tomato paste. Add the tomatoes and wine, season with sea salt and freshly ground black pepper and gently mix together.

3 Cover and cook on high for 4 hours, or until the veal is tender. Remove the rosemary sprig.

4 Combine the cornflour with a little water to make a smooth paste, then stir it into the stew. Cook for a further 5–10 minutes to thicken the juices a little.

5 Stir the olives through. Serve sprinkled with the parsley and lemon zest.

Veal, lemon and caper casserole

Serves **4**   Preparation time **25 minutes**   Cooking time **4 hours**

300 g (10½ oz) French shallots
   (eschalots)
1 kg (2 lb 4 oz) boneless veal
   shoulder
2 garlic cloves, crushed
3 leeks, white part only, cut into
   large chunks
2 tablespoons plain (all-purpose)
   flour
2 dried bay leaves
1 teaspoon finely grated lemon zest
80 ml (2½ fl oz/⅓ cup) lemon juice
500 ml (17 fl oz/2 cups) good-quality
   chicken stock
2 tablespoons capers, rinsed well
Chopped flat-leaf (Italian) parsley,
   to serve

1 Place the shallots in a heatproof bowl. Pour enough boiling water over to cover, then set aside for 5 minutes to soften. Drain the shallots, peel them and place in a 4.5 litre (157 fl oz/18 cup) slow cooker.

2 Cut the veal into 4 cm (1½ inch) chunks. Add to the slow cooker along with the garlic, leek, flour, bay leaves and lemon zest. Pour in the lemon juice and stock and gently mix together.

3 Cover and cook on high for 4 hours, or until the veal is tender. During the last 30 minutes of cooking, remove the lid to allow the sauce to reduce a little.

4 Stir in the capers and season to taste with sea salt and freshly ground black pepper. Serve sprinkled with parsley.

Veal cacciatore

Serves **6**   Preparation time **20 minutes**   Cooking time **4 hours 30 minutes**

1½ tablespoons plain (all-purpose) flour
6 veal osso bucco pieces, about 1 kg (2 lb 4 oz)
1 brown onion, chopped
2 garlic cloves, crushed
1 red capsicum (pepper), cut into 2 cm (¾ inch) chunks
1 dried bay leaf
2 anchovy fillets, chopped
1 tablespoon tomato paste (concentrated purée)
125 ml (4 fl oz/½ cup) good-quality chicken stock
400 g (14 oz) tin chopped tomatoes
125 ml (4 fl oz/½ cup) white wine
75 g (2½ oz/½ cup) pitted kalamata olives
400 g (14 oz/2 cups) risoni
30 g (1 oz) butter
1 cup basil leaves, to garnish

1   Place the flour in a bowl and season with sea salt and freshly ground black pepper. Toss the veal lightly in the flour to coat, then place in a 5.5 litre (192 fl oz/22 cup) slow cooker. Sprinkle with any remaining flour and add the onion, garlic, capsicum and bay leaf.

2   In a small bowl, mash the anchovy to a paste using the back of a spoon. Blend with the tomato paste and stock and add to the slow cooker.

3   Add the tomatoes and wine and gently mix together. Cover and cook on high for 4 hours, or until the veal is tender.

4   Remove the lid and cook, uncovered, for a further 30 minutes to thicken the sauce a little. Season with sea salt and freshly ground black pepper. Stir in the olives.

5   Near serving time, add the risoni to a large saucepan of rapidly boiling salted water and cook according to the packet instructions until al dente. Drain well and stir the butter through.

6   Spoon the risoni into wide shallow bowls, then ladle the veal mixture over the top. Garnish with the basil.

Spanish-style pork and vegetable stew

Serves **4–6** Preparation time **25 minutes** Cooking time **4 hours**

1 kg (2 lb 4 oz) boneless pork
   shoulder
2 hot chorizo sausages, sliced
600 g (1 lb 5 oz) all-purpose
   potatoes, peeled and diced
1 red onion, diced
2 garlic cloves, chopped
2 red capsicums (peppers),
   chopped
A pinch of saffron threads
1 tablespoon sweet paprika
10 large thyme sprigs
1 dried bay leaf
60 g (2¼ oz/¼ cup) tomato paste
   (concentrated purée)
125 ml (4 fl oz/½ cup) good-quality
   chicken stock
400 g (14 oz) tin chopped tomatoes
125 ml (4 fl oz/½ cup) white wine
2 tablespoons sherry
1 cup flat-leaf (Italian) parsley,
   chopped

1 Trim the pork of excess fat, then cut into 4 cm
   (1½ inch) chunks. Place in a 4.5 litre (157 fl oz/18 cup)
   slow cooker with the chorizo, potato, onion, garlic,
   capsicum, saffron threads, paprika, thyme sprigs and
   bay leaf.

2 Blend the tomato paste with the stock and add to the
   slow cooker. Add the tomatoes, wine and sherry and
   gently mix together. Cover and cook on high for 4 hours,
   or until the pork is tender.

3 Season to taste with sea salt and freshly ground black
   pepper. Stir the parsley through and serve.

Sausage and bean casserole

Serves **6**   Preparation time **20 minutes (+ 8 hours soaking)**   Cooking time **7 hours 45 minutes**

300 g (10½ oz/1½ cups) dried
  cannellini beans
300 g (10½ oz) dried black-eyed
  beans
6 bacon slices, rind and fat removed,
  cut into 6 cm (2½ inch) lengths
4 small brown onions, quartered
10 garlic cloves, peeled
3 long thin carrots, cut into
  3 cm (1¼ inch) pieces
3 dried bay leaves
1 small fresh red chilli, halved
  and seeded
7 oregano sprigs, leaves picked
500 ml (17 fl oz/2 cups) good-quality
  chicken stock
2 tablespoons tomato paste
  (concentrated purée)
6 thick pork sausages

1 Soak the cannellini beans and black-eyed beans for
8 hours or overnight in plenty of cold water. Drain
the beans, discarding the water, then place in a large
saucepan. Cover with fresh water and bring to the
boil. Boil rapidly for 10 minutes. Rinse the beans
and drain again.

2 Layer the bacon in a 4.5 litre (157 fl oz/18 cup) slow
cooker. Add the onion, garlic, carrot, bay leaves, chilli and
half the oregano. Season well with freshly ground black
pepper and add the cannellini beans and black-eyed beans.

3 Combine the stock and tomato paste and pour over
the beans. Cover and cook on high for 6 hours.

4 Add the sausages, then cover and cook for a further
1½ hours, or until the beans are tender and the sausages
are cooked through.

5 Check the seasoning and add extra salt and pepper if
needed. Serve sprinkled with the remaining oregano.

Cassoulet

Serves **4**   Preparation time **20 minutes**   Cooking time **8 hours**

600 g (1 lb 5 oz) pork spare ribs
4 thick beef or lamb sausages
6 French shallots (eschalots),
    peeled and chopped
1 carrot, diced
1 celery stalk, diced
3–4 garlic cloves, chopped
½ teaspoon paprika
1 large rosemary sprig
2 tablespoons tomato paste
    (concentrated purée)
60 ml (2 fl oz/¼ cup) white wine
400 g (14 oz) tin chopped tomatoes
2 x 400 g (14 oz) tins white beans,
    such as cannellini, haricot or
    butterbeans (lima beans),
    drained and rinsed
1 cup flat-leaf (Italian) parsley,
    chopped
Crusty bread, to serve

1 Trim the rind and excess fat from the spare ribs, then cut each piece into three thick chunks. Cut the sausages in half and place in a 4.5 litre (157 fl oz/18 cup) slow cooker with the pork.

2 Add the shallot, carrot, celery and garlic. Sprinkle the paprika over and tuck in the rosemary sprig. Season with sea salt and freshly ground black pepper.

3 Blend the tomato paste with the wine, then add to the slow cooker with the tomatoes. Add the beans and gently mix together. Cover and cook on low for 6–8 hours, or until the meat is tender.

4 Remove the rosemary sprig and stir the parsley through. Serve with crusty bread.

Fabada

Serves **8–10**   Preparation time **20 minutes (+ 8 hours soaking)**   Cooking time **4 hours 15 minutes**

500 g (1 lb 2 oz) dried butterbeans
  (lima beans)
60 ml (2 fl oz/¼ cup) extra virgin
  olive oil
1 tablespoon smoked paprika
1 fresh bay leaf
1 ham hock, about 500 g (1 lb 2 oz)
1 brown onion
1 whole garlic bulb
3 chorizo sausages
2 morcilla (blood sausages)
400 g (14 oz) piece of speck or
  bacon, trimmed
¼ cup flat-leaf (Italian) parsley,
  chopped and crusty bread,
  to serve

1 Soak the beans for 8 hours or overnight in plenty of cold water. Drain the beans, discarding the water, then place in a large saucepan. Cover with fresh water and bring to the boil. Boil rapidly for 10 minutes. Rinse the beans and drain again.

2 Place the beans in a 7 litre (245 fl oz/28 cup) slow cooker with the olive oil, paprika, bay leaf and ham hock.

3 Peel the onion and the papery skin from the garlic bulb, then cut the onion and garlic bulb in half horizontally and add to the slow cooker.

4 Pour in 1.5 litres (52 fl oz/6 cups) water, making sure the ham hock is covered with water by at least 4 cm (1½ inches). Gently mix together, then cover and cook on high for 1 hour.

5 Stir in the chorizo, morcilla and speck. Cover and cook for a further 2–3 hours, or until the beans are tender.

6 Using tongs, carefully remove the ham hock, speck and sausages. Discard the bay leaf, onion and garlic.

7 Shred the meat from the ham hock, discarding the skin and bones, then return the ham to the beans. Roughly chop the speck and sausages and stir through the stew.

8 Season to taste with sea salt and freshly ground black pepper. Sprinkle with parsley and serve with crusty bread.

Rabbit ragu

Serves **6**   Preparation time **30 minutes**   Cooking time **5 hours 40 minutes**

80 ml (2½ fl oz/⅓ cup) olive oil
1 large rabbit, about 1 kg
    (2 lb 4 oz), jointed
1½ carrots, finely diced
1 celery stalk, diced
1 brown onion, finely diced
3 garlic cloves, thinly sliced
1 tablespoon chopped rosemary
300 ml (10½ fl oz) white wine
300 ml (10½ fl oz) good-quality
    chicken stock
40 g (1½ oz) butter, chopped
2 tablespoons chopped flat-leaf
    (Italian) parsley
Finely grated parmesan cheese
    and hot cooked pasta, such as
    linguine or pappardelle, to serve

1 Heat half the olive oil in the insert pan of a 5 litre (175 fl oz/20 cup) slow cooker or a large frying pan over high heat. Add the rabbit and cook, in batches if necessary, for 2–3 minutes each side, or until golden. Remove to a plate.

2 Heat the remaining oil over medium heat. Sauté the carrot, celery and onion for 5–6 minutes, or until softened. Stir in the garlic and rosemary. Add the wine, bring to a simmer, then add the stock and rabbit. Bring back to a simmer and season with sea salt and freshly ground black pepper.

3 Return the insert pan, if using, to the slow cooker, or transfer the mixture to the slow cooker. Cover and cook on low for 4–5 hours, or until the rabbit is very tender.

4 Remove the rabbit using a slotted spoon. Set aside to cool slightly, then coarsely shred the meat. In the insert pan of the slow cooker or a saucepan, reduce the braising liquid over medium–high heat for 15–20 minutes, until thickened.

5 Stir in the butter, parsley and shredded rabbit. Sprinkle with parmesan and serve with hot cooked pasta.

Tip: This ragu is fabulous with handmade pasta. Combine 200 g (7 oz/ 1⅓ cups) '00' flour or plain (all-purpose) flour and 1 teaspoon fine sea salt in a bowl. Make a well in the centre. Stir in 2 large eggs with a fork. Knead on a floured work surface for 6–7 minutes, or until smooth; cover and refrigerate for 1 hour. Feed half the dough through a pasta machine, reducing the settings and folding the dough as you go, until 2 mm (¹⁄₁₆ inch) thick. Place on a tray lined with baking paper and sprinkled with semolina. Repeat with the remaining dough. Cut the pasta into strips and cook in boiling salted water for 1–2 minutes, until al dente.

Moroccan fish tagine

Serves **4**   Preparation time **20 minutes**   Cooking time **3 hours 30 minutes**

1 red onion, sliced
8 new potatoes, unpeeled, halved
4 roma (plum) tomatoes, quartered
6 garlic cloves
1 red capsicum (pepper), sliced
100 g (3½ oz) pitted black olives
125 ml (4 fl oz/½ cup) good-quality
   fish stock
A pinch of saffron threads
4 x 200 g (7 oz) firm white skinless
   fish fillets (such as ling)
2 tablespoons chopped preserved
   lemon rind (see Tip)
Flat-leaf (Italian) parsley, to garnish
Steamed couscous, to serve

Chermoula
1 tablespoon olive oil
2 garlic cloves, crushed
½ cup coriander (cilantro)
   leaves, chopped
2 teaspoons ground cumin
2 teaspoons ground paprika
60 ml (2 fl oz/¼ cup) lemon juice
1 teaspoon sea salt

1 Place the onion, potato, tomato, garlic, capsicum and olives in a 5.5 litre (192 fl oz/22 cup) slow cooker.

2 Blend all the chermoula ingredients in a small food processor until a smooth paste forms. Mix 1 tablespoon of the chermoula into the stock until smooth, reserving the remainder for rubbing over the fish. Stir the saffron threads into the stock, then pour over the vegetables in the slow cooker and gently mix together.

3 Cover and cook on high for 3 hours, or until the potato halves are tender.

4 About 15 minutes before the vegetables are cooked, spread the remaining chermoula over both sides of each fish fillet and set aside for the flavours to be absorbed.

5 Add the fish to the slow cooker, then cover and cook for a further 30 minutes, or until the fish flakes when tested with a fork.

6 Stir the preserved lemon through the tagine. Garnish with parsley and serve with steamed couscous.

🔅 Tip: *Preserved lemon is a condiment used in North African cooking. It is prepared by pickling lemons in salt. Only the rind of the lemons is used — the flesh of the lemon is discarded as it is very salty.*

Pasta, Noodles and Rice

Macaroni cheese

Serves **4–6**   Preparation time **25 minutes (+ 10 minutes soaking)**   Cooking time **3 hours**

300 g (10½ oz/2 cups) macaroni
Olive oil or softened butter,
    for brushing
375 ml (13 fl oz/1½ cups) milk
375 ml (13 fl oz/1½ cups)
    evaporated milk
3 eggs, lightly beaten
½ teaspoon freshly grated nutmeg
3 spring onions (scallions), chopped
125 g (4½ oz) tin corn kernels,
    drained
60 g (2¼ oz) ham, chopped
100 g (3½ oz/1 cup) finely grated
    parmesan cheese
150 g (5½ oz/1½ cups, loosely
    packed) grated cheddar cheese
Snipped chives, to garnish
Green salad, to serve

1 Put the macaroni in a large heatproof bowl. Cover with boiling water and set aside to soften, stirring occasionally, for 10 minutes. Drain.

2 Meanwhile, spray the bowl of a 4.5 litre (157 fl oz/ 18 cup) slow cooker with cooking oil spray, or grease well with olive oil or softened butter.

3 Pour the milk and evaporated milk into the slow cooker. Gently whisk in the egg and nutmeg and season with sea salt and freshly ground black pepper. Stir in the drained macaroni, spring onion, corn, ham, parmesan and 100 g (3½ oz/1 cup) of the cheddar. Sprinkle with the remaining cheddar.

4 Cover and cook on low for 2 hours. After 2 hours, start checking the pasta — it needs to be cooked until it is al dente, and the sauce needs to be thick and still a little wet in the centre. It may take a further 1 hour to reach this point, but take care not to overcook the mixture or the sauce will curdle.

5 Sprinkle with chives and serve with a green salad.

⚙ *Tip: Cook this recipe on low heat only. For a vegetarian meal, simply leave out the ham.*

Zucchini and ricotta cannelloni

Serves **4–6**   Preparation time **20 minutes**   Cooking time **3 hours**

2 zucchini (courgettes), grated
500 g (1 lb 2 oz) fresh ricotta cheese
2 teaspoons chopped rosemary
200 g (7 oz) dried cannelloni
(about 20 tubes)
700 g (1 lb 9 oz) purchased tomato
pasta sauce
190 g (6¾ oz/1½ cups, loosely
packed) grated mozzarella cheese
1 cup basil, chopped
Green salad, to serve

1 Place the zucchini, ricotta and rosemary in a bowl. Season with sea salt and freshly ground black pepper and mix together well. Using a teaspoon, fill the cannelloni tubes with the ricotta mixture.

2 Place half the cannelloni in a 4.5 litre (157 fl oz/18 cup) slow cooker. Cover with half the tomato pasta sauce, then sprinkle with half the cheese and half the basil. Top with another layer of cannelloni, then the remaining pasta sauce, cheese and basil.

3 Cover and cook on high for 3 hours, or until the pasta is al dente and the cheese has melted. Serve with a green salad.

Greek lamb with macaroni

Serves **4–6**   Preparation time **30 minutes (+ 10 minutes soaking)**   Cooking time **2 hours 15 minutes**

1 kg (2 lb 4 oz) boneless lamb leg
1 large brown onion, chopped
2 garlic cloves, crushed
1 tablespoon brown sugar
1 teaspoon dried oregano
60 g (2¼ oz/¼ cup) tomato paste
   (concentrated purée)
2 tablespoons red wine vinegar
400 g (14 oz) tin chopped tomatoes
500 ml (17 fl oz/2 cups) good-quality
   beef stock
300 g (10½ oz/2 cups) macaroni
125 g (4½ oz/1¼ cups) grated
   pecorino cheese

1 Trim the lamb of excess fat, then cut into 3 cm (1¼ inch) chunks. Place in a 4.5 litre (157 fl oz/18 cup) slow cooker with the onion and garlic and sprinkle with the sugar and oregano.

2 Blend the tomato paste with the vinegar, then add to the slow cooker. Add the tomatoes and stock and gently mix together. Cover and cook on high for 1¾ hours, or until the lamb is tender.

3 Meanwhile, put the macaroni in a large heatproof bowl. Cover with boiling water and set aside to soften, stirring occasionally, for 10 minutes.

4 Drain the macaroni and add to the slow cooker. Mix well, then cover and cook for a further 30 minutes, or until the macaroni is tender and the liquid has been absorbed.

5 Season to taste with sea salt and freshly ground black pepper and serve sprinkled with the cheese.

Lasagne with ham, lemon and basil

Serves **4–6**   Preparation time **25 minutes (+ 10 minutes resting)**   Cooking time **3 hours**

Olive oil, for brushing
690 ml (24 fl oz) tomato passata
    (puréed tomatoes)
2 garlic cloves, crushed
150 g (5½ oz/1½ cups, loosely
    packed) grated cheddar cheese
50 g (1¾ oz/½ cup) finely grated
    parmesan cheese
1 egg
300 ml (10½ fl oz) thick (double/
    heavy) cream
1 cup basil, chopped
1 teaspoon finely grated lemon zest
150 g (5½ oz) shaved ham,
    shredded
250 g (9 oz) packet instant lasagne
    sheets
Green salad, to serve

1 Lightly brush the bowl of a 5.5 litre (192 fl oz/22 cup) slow cooker with olive oil.

2 Mix together the passata and garlic. In a separate bowl, mix together 125 g (4½ oz/1 cup) of the cheddar, the parmesan, egg, cream, basil and lemon zest. Season to taste with sea salt and freshly ground black pepper.

3 Spoon one-third of the passata mixture into the slow cooker. Top with one-third of the ham and one-quarter of the cheese mixture. Arrange one-third of the lasagne sheets over the top in a single layer, breaking them to fit the shape of the slow cooker.

4 Spoon another one-third of the passata mixture over the lasagne sheets, then top with another one-third of the ham and one-quarter of the cheese mixture. Layer another one-third of the lasagne sheets over the top.

5 Repeat with the remaining passata, ham, another one-quarter of the cheese mixture and the remaining lasagne sheets to make a third layer.

6 Spread the remaining cheese mixture over the top. (Ensure all the pasta is covered, otherwise it won't cook through properly.) Sprinkle with the remaining cheddar. Cover and cook on low for 3 hours, or until the pasta is al dente.

7 Allow to sit for 10 minutes, then serve with a green salad.

⚙ *Tip: Instead of shredded ham, try using chopped prosciutto, and replace the cheddar cheese with mozzarella.*

Braised teriyaki beef with udon noodles

Serves **4**   Preparation time **20 minutes**   Cooking time **8 hours**

Olive oil, for brushing
1 small brown onion, chopped
375 ml (13 fl oz/1½ cups) teriyaki
    marinade
125 ml (4 fl oz/½ cup) good-quality
    beef stock
1 garlic clove, crushed
1.25 kg (2 lb 12 oz) budget rump
    steaks, cut into 4 cm (1½ inch)
    chunks
440 g (15½ oz) fresh udon noodles
3 spring onions (scallions), thinly
    sliced, plus extra, to garnish

Asian salad
¼ cup coriander (cilantro) leaves
1 red capsicum (pepper), cut into
    matchsticks
1 large carrot, cut into matchsticks
1 Lebanese (short) cucumber,
    seeded and cut into matchsticks
2 tablespoons light soy sauce
1 tablespoon peanut oil
2 tablespoons lime juice
1 teaspoon white sesame seeds

1 Lightly brush the bowl of a 5.5 litre (192 fl oz/22 cup)
   slow cooker with olive oil. Scatter the onion over the base.

2 In a large bowl, mix together the teriyaki marinade,
   stock and garlic. Add the beef and toss until well coated.
   Thread the beef onto 12 small bamboo skewers and place
   them in the slow cooker.

3 Cover and cook on low for 7½ hours, turning the skewers
   over at least once, if possible.

4 Place the noodles in a heatproof bowl and cover with
   boiling water. Leave to soak for a few minutes, until the
   noodles have softened.

5 Remove the skewers from the slow cooker. Drain the
   noodles and add to the slow cooker with the spring
   onion. Stir to coat the noodles with the sauce.

6 Sit the skewers on top of the noodles, then cover and
   cook for a further 30 minutes, or until the noodles are
   heated through.

7 Near serving time, make the Asian salad. Put the
   coriander, capsicum, carrot and cucumber in a bowl and
   toss to combine. Whisk together the soy sauce, peanut
   oil and lime juice, then pour over the salad. Toss gently
   and sprinkle with the sesame seeds.

8 Serve the skewers on a bed of noodles, sprinkled with
   extra spring onion, with the Asian salad on the side.

Chinese chicken and rice with chilli ginger dressing

Serves **4**   Preparation time **15 minutes (+ 2 hours marinating)**   Cooking time **2 hours 10 minutes**

1 kg (2 lb 4 oz) chicken thighs, with the skin and bones
2 tablespoons soy sauce
1 tablespoon Chinese rice wine or dry sherry
1 teaspoon sesame oil
1 teaspoon sugar
A pinch of ground white pepper
1½ tablespoons peanut oil
1 tablespoon finely chopped fresh ginger
3 garlic cloves, finely chopped
4 spring onions (scallions), finely sliced, white and green parts separated
400 g (14 oz/2 cups) long-grain white rice, washed and very well drained
1 teaspoon sea salt
500 ml (17 fl oz/2 cups) good-quality chicken stock

Chilli ginger dressing
2 long fresh red chillies, seeded
1 tablespoon chopped fresh ginger
2 tablespoons lime juice
2 teaspoons peanut oil
1 teaspoon sea salt
1 teaspoon soy sauce
60 ml (2 fl oz/¼ cup) good-quality chicken stock

1 Trim the chicken of any fat, then place in a glass or ceramic bowl. Stir in the soy sauce, Chinese rice wine, sesame oil, sugar and white pepper and mix until well coated. Cover and marinate in the refrigerator for 2 hours, or overnight.

2 Heat the peanut oil in the insert pan of a 5 litre (175 fl oz/ 20 cup) slow cooker or a large frying pan over high heat. Brown the chicken, in batches if necessary, for 3–4 minutes, or until golden on all sides. Remove to a plate.

3 Add the ginger, garlic and white spring onion slices to the pan and cook for 30 seconds. Add the rice and salt and stir for 1–2 minutes, or until the rice is coated in the oil.

4 Return the insert pan, if using, to the slow cooker, or transfer the rice mixture to the slow cooker. Pour in the stock, then add the chicken, pushing the pieces down into the rice. Cover and cook on high for 1 hour.

5 Lift the lid, then quickly but gently stir the mixture to free the rice underneath. Cover and cook for a further 30 minutes.

6 Lift the lid and stir gently again. Turn the slow cooker setting to low and leave the lid ajar so steam can escape. Leave for 30 minutes to steam. The rice will dry a little and there will be a slight crust on the bottom.

7 Meanwhile, blend the chilli ginger dressing ingredients in a small food processor until smooth.

8 Garnish the chicken rice with the green spring onion slices and serve with the chilli ginger dressing.

Lamb biryani with mixed vegetables

Serves **4**   Preparation time **10 minutes**   Cooking time **2 hours 15 minutes**

¼ teaspoon saffron threads
600 g (1 lb 5 oz) lamb shoulder
2 teaspoons ground turmeric
60 g (2¼ oz) ghee
2 brown onions, finely chopped
2 garlic cloves, finely chopped
1 tablespoon finely chopped fresh
　ginger
2 long fresh green chillies, seeded
　and finely chopped
2 teaspoons sea salt
1 teaspoon ground coriander
300 g (10½ oz/1½ cups) basmati
　rice, washed well and drained
A pinch of cayenne pepper (optional)
375 ml (13 fl oz/1½ cups) good-
　quality chicken stock
2 tablespoons currants
½ teaspoon garam masala
2 tablespoons chopped coriander
　(cilantro) leaves
Yoghurt, to serve (optional)

1 Place the saffron threads in a cup, cover with 80 ml (2½ fl oz/ ⅓ cup) hot water and leave to infuse for 10 minutes.

2 Meanwhile, trim the lamb of excess fat, then cut into 1 cm (½ inch) dice and place in a bowl. Sprinkle with half the turmeric and toss well to coat. Set aside.

3 Heat 40 g (1½ oz) of the ghee in the insert pan of a 5 litre (175 fl oz/20 cup) slow cooker or a large frying pan over high heat. Add the onion and cook, stirring, for 7–8 minutes, or until it begins to caramelise. Add the lamb and cook for 3–4 minutes, or until browned on all sides. Remove the mixture to a plate.

4 Heat the remaining ghee in the pan. Cook the garlic, ginger, chilli, salt and ground coriander for 1 minute, or until aromatic. Add the rice, remaining turmeric and the cayenne pepper, if using. Cook, stirring, for 2 minutes, or until the rice is well coated in the ghee and spices.

5 Return the insert pan, if using, to the slow cooker, or transfer the rice mixture to the slow cooker. Add the lamb mixture, pour in the stock and the saffron liquid and gently mix together. Cover and cook on high for 1 hour.

6 Remove the lid, quickly and gently stir the lamb mixture, then cover and cook for a further 45 minutes. Stir in the currants, then leave the lid ajar and cook for a further 15 minutes, or until the rice dries a little and the lamb is tender. (The rice will continue to dry as it cools.)

7 Stir the garam masala through. Scatter with chopped coriander and serve with yoghurt, if desired.

Kedgeree

Serves **4**   Preparation time **15 minutes**   Cooking time **3 hours**

500 g (1 lb 2 oz/2½ cups)
   par-cooked long-grain white rice
1 brown onion, finely chopped
1 teaspoon ground cumin
2 dried bay leaves
2 tablespoons purchased mild Indian
   curry paste
500 ml (17 fl oz/2 cups) good-quality
   chicken or fish stock
500 g (1 lb 2 oz) boneless, skinless
   salmon fillets
125 ml (4 fl oz/½ cup) pouring
   cream
50 g (1¾ oz) butter
140 g (5 oz/1 cup) frozen peas
2 tablespoons chopped flat-leaf
   (Italian) parsley
2 tablespoons lemon juice

1 Put the rice, onion, cumin and bay leaves in a 4.5 litre (157 fl oz/18 cup) slow cooker. Blend the curry paste with 250 ml (9 fl oz/1 cup) water and pour into the slow cooker with the stock. Gently mix together.

2 Cover and cook on low for 2½ hours, or until the rice is almost tender.

3 Remove any bones from the salmon using your fingers or tweezers. Cut the salmon into 3 cm (1¼ inch) chunks and place on top of the rice. Add the cream, butter and peas and cook for a further 30 minutes, or until the rice is tender and the fish flakes easily when tested with a fork.

4 Stir the parsley and lemon juice through. Season to taste with sea salt and freshly ground black pepper and serve.

Armenian chicken with rice pilaff

Serves **4**   Preparation time **25 minutes**   Cooking time **5 hours**

Cooking oil spray, olive oil or
  softened butter, for brushing
1.2 kg (2 lb 10 oz) whole chicken
1 lemon, quartered (see Tip)
2 garlic cloves, lightly crushed
3 thyme sprigs
2 teaspoons extra virgin olive oil
¼ teaspoon paprika
Green salad or steamed vegetables,
  to serve

Rice pilaff
200 g (7 oz/1 cup) par-cooked
  long-grain white rice
50 g (1¾ oz) rice vermicelli, noodles
  broken into small lengths
40 g (1½ oz/¼ cup) pine nuts
30 g (1 oz) butter, melted
1 teaspoon finely grated lemon zest
500 ml (17 fl oz/2 cups) good-quality
  chicken stock

1 Spray the bowl of a 4.5 litre (157 fl oz/18 cup) slow cooker with cooking oil spray, or grease well with olive oil or softened butter.

2 Wash the chicken and pat dry with paper towels. Place the lemon, garlic and thyme sprigs inside the cavity of the chicken. Skewer the legs and wings together, or tie with kitchen string. Place the chicken, breast side up, in the slow cooker. Brush the breast and legs with the olive oil, then sprinkle with the paprika, some sea salt and freshly ground black pepper. Cover and cook on high for 1 hour.

3 To make the rice pilaff, put the rice, noodles and pine nuts in a large bowl. Stir the butter and lemon zest through, then stir in the stock. Carefully pour the rice mixture around the chicken in the slow cooker, distributing it evenly and mixing the rice and noodles into the liquid.

4 Cover and cook on high for a further 3–4 hours, or until the rice is cooked and the chicken is tender and the juices run clear when the thigh is pierced with a skewer. During the cooking time, stir the rice once or twice with a fork.

5 Lift the chicken carefully from the slow cooker and place on a board. Remove the skewers or string.

6 Cut or pull the chicken apart into large pieces. Serve with the rice pilaff and a green salad or steamed vegetables.

⚙ *Tip: Before cutting the lemon into quarters, grate enough zest to get 1 tablespoon to use in the rice pilaff.*

Mexican chicken rice

Serves **4** Preparation time **10 minutes** Cooking time **4 hours**

Cooking oil spray, olive oil or
  softened butter, for brushing
600 g (1 lb 5 oz) skinless chicken
  thigh fillets
330 g (11½ oz/1½ cups) par-cooked
  short-grain white rice
400 g (14 oz) tin red kidney
  beans, drained and rinsed
400 g (14 oz) jar spicy taco sauce
250 ml (9 fl oz/1 cup) good-quality
  chicken stock
200 g (7 oz/2 cups, loosely packed)
  grated cheddar cheese
125 g (4½ oz/½ cup) sour cream
1 cup coriander (cilantro) leaves,
  chopped

1 Spray the bowl of a 4.5 litre (157 fl oz/18 cup) slow
   cooker with cooking oil spray, or grease well with olive
   oil or softened butter.

2 Trim the chicken of any fat, then cut each thigh in half.

3 Put the rice in the slow cooker, then top with the chicken,
   kidney beans, taco sauce, stock and cheese. Cover and
   cook on low for 4 hours, or until the chicken and rice
   are tender.

4 Serve topped with a dollop of sour cream and sprinkled
   with coriander.

Arroz con pollo

Serves **6**   Preparation time **20 minutes**   Cooking time **9 hours 5 minutes**

4 very ripe tomatoes

2 kg (4 lb 8 oz) chicken pieces, skin removed

100 g (3½ oz) chorizo sausage, sliced

1 large brown onion, finely chopped

1 green capsicum (pepper), diced

1 tablespoon sweet paprika

1 long fresh red chilli, seeded and finely chopped

2 garlic cloves, crushed

A pinch of saffron threads (optional)

2½ tablespoons tomato paste (concentrated purée)

80 ml (2½ fl oz/⅓ cup) dry sherry

250 ml (9 fl oz/1 cup) good-quality chicken stock

400 g (14 oz/2 cups) par-cooked long-grain white rice

100 g (3½ oz/⅔ cup) frozen peas

3 tablespoons finely chopped flat-leaf (Italian) parsley

60 g (2¼ oz/⅓ cup) stuffed green olives (optional)

1 Score a cross in the base of each tomato. Put the tomatoes in a heatproof bowl and cover with boiling water. Leave for 30 seconds, then transfer to cold water, drain and peel the skin away from the cross. Cut the tomatoes in half, scoop out the seeds and coarsely chop the flesh. Place in a 4.5 litre (157 fl oz/18 cup) slow cooker.

2 Trim the chicken of excess fat and add to the slow cooker with the chorizo, onion and capsicum. Sprinkle with the paprika, chilli, garlic and saffron threads, if using.

3 Blend the tomato paste with the sherry, then pour into the slow cooker with the stock and gently mix together. Cover and cook on low for 8 hours.

4 Add the rice to the slow cooker and stir to coat well. Cover and cook for a further 1 hour, or until the liquid has been absorbed.

5 Stir in the peas, then cover and cook for a further 5 minutes, or until the rice, peas and chicken are tender and cooked through.

6 Stir in the parsley and olives, if using. Season to taste with sea salt and freshly ground black pepper and serve.

Brown rice and barley risotto with pumpkin and chicken

Serves **4** Preparation time **20 minutes (+ 8 hours soaking)** Cooking time **3 hours 35 minutes**

330 g (11½ oz/1½ cups) short-grain brown rice
100 g (3½ oz/½ cup) pearl barley
1 tablespoon olive oil
1 skinless chicken breast fillet
1 red onion, finely chopped
350 g (12 oz) pumpkin (winter squash), peeled, seeded and cut into 1 cm (½ inch) dice
12 sage leaves, plus extra sage leaves, to garnish
1 teaspoon vegetable or chicken stock (bouillon) powder (optional)
60 ml (2 fl oz/¼ cup) white wine
140 g (5 oz/1 cup) frozen peas
50 g (1¾ oz/½ cup) finely grated parmesan, cheese plus extra, to serve

1 Place the rice and barley in a bowl and cover with 1 litre (35 fl oz/4 cups) water. Leave to soak for 8 hours, or overnight.

2 Pour the olive oil into the bowl of a 4.5 litre (157 fl oz/18 cup) slow cooker bowl and spread the oil over the base and side. Pour the rice and barley, along with the soaking water, into the slow cooker.

3 Trim the chicken of any fat, then cut into bite-sized chunks. Add to the slow cooker with the onion, pumpkin and sage. Mix the stock powder, if using, with the wine, then stir it through the mixture. Season well with sea salt and freshly ground black pepper.

4 Cover and cook on high for 3 hours, or until all the liquid has been absorbed and the rice and barley are tender, stirring occasionally during cooking. If the grains are not quite cooked after 3 hours, cook for a further 20–30 minutes, or until tender.

5 Beat the grains with a fork to thoroughly mix in the pumpkin until the risotto looks 'creamy'. Stir in the peas and parmesan. Cover and cook for a further 5 minutes, or until the peas are cooked through.

6 Season to taste with sea salt and freshly ground black pepper. Serve sprinkled with extra parmesan and garnished with extra sage leaves.

Tip: For a vegetarian version, leave out the chicken and use vegetable stock rather than chicken stock.

Jambalaya

Serves **4**   Preparation time **30 minutes**   Cooking time **3 hours**

4 vine-ripened tomatoes
½ teaspoon saffron threads
1 red onion, sliced
3 bacon slices, rind and fat removed, chopped
2 chorizo sausages, cut diagonally into 1 cm (½ inch) slices
1 small red capsicum (pepper), sliced
1 small green capsicum (pepper), sliced
2 garlic cloves, finely chopped
1–2 teaspoons seeded and finely chopped jalapeño chilli
1 teaspoon smoked paprika
3 teaspoons cajun spice mix
400 g (14 oz/2 cups) par-cooked long-grain white rice, rinsed
250 ml (9 fl oz/1 cup) beer
500 ml (17 fl oz/2 cups) good-quality chicken stock
2 skinless chicken breast fillets
16 raw prawns (shrimp)

1 Score a cross in the base of each tomato. Put the tomatoes in a heatproof bowl and cover with boiling water. Leave for 30 seconds, then transfer to cold water, drain and peel the skin away from the cross. Cut the tomatoes into quarters, scoop out the seeds and set aside.

2 Place the saffron threads in a small bowl, cover with 1 tablespoon hot water and leave to infuse for 10 minutes.

3 Put the onion, bacon, chorizo and capsicum in a 4.5 litre (157 fl oz/18 cup) slow cooker. Sprinkle with the garlic, chilli, paprika and cajun spice mix. Scatter the rice over the top. Add the tomato quarters, then pour in the beer, stock and the saffron liquid.

4 Cover and cook on low for 2 hours, or until the rice is tender and the liquid has been absorbed.

5 Meanwhile, prepare the chicken and prawns. Trim the chicken of any fat, then cut into strips about 1.5 cm (⅝ inch) wide and 6 cm (2½ inches) long. Peel the prawns, leaving the tails intact. Gently pull out the dark vein from the back of each prawn, starting at the head end.

6 Add the chicken and prawns to the slow cooker, mixing them in well. Cover and cook for a further 1 hour, or until the chicken and prawns are cooked.

Pork and rice hotpot

Serves **4**   Preparation time **20 minutes**   Cooking time **3 hours**

500 g (1 lb 2 oz) lean pork fillet
15 g (½ oz) dried Chinese mushrooms, sliced
140 g (5 oz) tin straw mushrooms, drained and rinsed
125 g (4½ oz) tin sliced bamboo shoots, drained
300 g (10½ oz/1½ cups) long-grain white rice
2 teaspoons finely grated fresh ginger
3 garlic cloves, crushed
1 cinnamon stick
2 star anise
1½ tablespoons hoisin sauce
2 tablespoons dark soy sauce
1 tablespoon light soy sauce
2 tablespoons Chinese rice wine
500 ml (17 fl oz/2 cups) good-quality chicken stock
Shredded spring onions (scallions), to garnish
Steamed Asian greens, to serve

1 Cut the pork into 2 cm (¾ inch) chunks, then place in a 4.5 litre (157 fl oz/18 cup) slow cooker.

2 Add the dried mushrooms, straw mushrooms, bamboo shoots and rice. Sprinkle with the ginger and garlic and add the cinnamon stick and star anise.

3 Blend the hoisin sauce with the dark and light soy sauces, then pour into the slow cooker with the Chinese rice wine and stock.

4 Cover and cook on low for 3 hours, or until the rice and pork are tender and the liquid has been absorbed.

5 Garnish with spring onion and serve with steamed Asian greens.

Sides

Braised root vegetable salad with chickpeas and couscous

Serves 6   Preparation time **30 minutes**   Cooking time **3 hours 5 minutes**

400 g (14 oz) cauliflower,
cut into large florets

1 large desiree potato, peeled and
cut into 3 cm (1¼ inch) chunks

1 sweet potato, cut into 3 cm
(1¼ inch) chunks

1 large beetroot (beet), peeled and
cut into 2 cm (¾ inch) wedges

2 carrots, halved lengthways and cut
into 3 cm (1¼ inch) chunks

1 whole garlic bulb, cloves separated
and peeled

Finely grated zest and juice of
1 lemon

60 ml (2 fl oz/¼ cup) extra virgin
olive oil

500 ml (17 fl oz/2 cups) good-quality
chicken stock

400 g (14 oz) tin chickpeas, drained
and rinsed

240 g (8½ oz/1¼ cups) instant
couscous

40 g (1½ oz) butter, at room
temperature, chopped

⅓ cup mint, torn

⅓ cup coriander (cilantro) leaves

25 g (1 oz/¼ cup) flaked almonds,
lightly toasted

1 Place all the vegetables in a 7 litre (245 fl oz/28 cup) slow cooker. Add the garlic and lemon zest. Pour in the olive oil and stock, season with sea salt and freshly ground black pepper and gently mix together. Cover and cook on high for 2½ hours.

2 Stir in the chickpeas, then cover and cook for a further 30 minutes, or until the vegetables are tender, but still retain some bite.

3 Pour the braising liquid into a large bowl and measure out 310 ml (10¾ fl oz/1¼ cups), making up any difference with extra stock or water. Turn the slow cooker setting to low, then cover and keep cooking the vegetables while preparing the couscous.

4 Bring the braising liquid to the boil in a saucepan. Remove from the heat, add the lemon juice and couscous and stir with a fork for 20 seconds. Cover and allow to soften for 5 minutes, then return the saucepan to low heat. Add the butter and fluff the couscous grains with a fork until the butter melts through.

5 Add the couscous and half the herbs to the slow cooker and gently mix to combine. Spoon onto a large platter, scatter with the remaining herbs and toasted almonds and serve.

⚙ *Tip: This salad goes well with grilled or roasted meats. It is also delicious sprinkled with crumbled feta cheese and served with crusty bread.*

Warm lentil salad

Serves **6**   Preparation time **15 minutes**   Cooking time **3 hours 30 minutes**

370 g (13 oz/1¾ cup) puy lentils
   or tiny blue-green lentils
1 teaspoon thyme
2 garlic cloves, halved
Finely grated zest of 1 lemon
500 ml (17 fl oz/2 cups) good-quality
   chicken or vegetable stock

Dressing
½ cup flat-leaf (Italian) parsley
   leaves
½ cup mint leaves
1 tablespoon salted capers, rinsed
2 anchovy fillets, drained and
   chopped
1 garlic clove, finely chopped
80 ml (2½ fl oz/⅓ cup) olive oil
2 tablespoons lemon juice

1 Rinse the lentils and drain well, then place in a 5 litre (175 fl oz/20 cup) slow cooker with the thyme, garlic and lemon zest. Pour in the stock and 200 ml (7 fl oz) water.

2 Cover and cook on low for 3½ hours, or until the lentils are soft but not mushy, and all the liquid has been absorbed. If the lentils are cooked but some stock remains, drain it before adding the dressing.

3 To make the dressing, place the parsley, mint, capers, anchovy and garlic in a small food processor and blend until combined. With the motor running, slowly add the olive oil and continue processing until emulsified. Stir in the lemon juice.

4 Add the dressing to the lentils in the slow cooker. Season with sea salt and freshly ground black pepper. Gently mix to combine, adding more lemon juice or olive oil to the lentils if needed to balance the flavour.

⊙ *Tip: Serve with grilled chicken or sausages, or with crumbled feta cheese and crusty bread.*

Potato and celery with bagna cauda

Serves **4**   Preparation time **15 minutes**   Cooking time **2 hours 30 minutes**

5 garlic cloves, chopped
10 anchovy fillets, drained and
    chopped
125 ml (4 fl oz/½ cup) olive oil
100 g (3½ oz) butter, at room
    temperature, chopped
800 g (1 lb 12 oz) small desiree
    potatoes, unpeeled, sliced into
    1 cm (½ inch) thick rounds
5 celery stalks, cut into 5 cm
    (2 inch) lengths
½ teaspoon apple cider vinegar

1 In a small food processor, blend the garlic and anchovy fillets with 1 tablespoon of the oil until smooth. Add the remaining oil and butter and blend to form a thick paste.

2 Combine the potato and celery in a bowl and toss with the anchovy paste. Season well with sea salt and freshly ground black pepper.

3 Place the potato and celery in a 5 litre (175 fl oz/20 cup) slow cooker. Cover and cook on high for 2½ hours, or until the vegetables are tender. Using a slotted spoon, gently remove the vegetables to a warmed plate.

4 Stir the sauce to emulsify it (the sauce will have split). Stir in the vinegar and season to taste. Pour the sauce over the vegetables and serve.

Alu bhaji

Serves **4** Preparation time **15 minutes** Cooking time **2 hours 10 minutes**

40 g (1½ oz) ghee
1 kg (2 lb 4 oz) desiree potatoes,
    peeled and cut into 2.5 cm
    (1 inch) chunks
2 brown onions, finely chopped
1–2 long fresh green chillies,
    finely chopped
2 teaspoons finely chopped fresh
    ginger
½ teaspoon mustard seeds
½ teaspoon ground turmeric
½ teaspoon cumin seeds
1 teaspoon sea salt
2 tablespoons chopped coriander
    (cilantro) leaves, to garnish
Lemon wedges, to serve

1 Heat the ghee in the insert pan of a 5 litre (175 fl oz/ 20 cup) slow cooker or a large frying pan over medium– high heat. Add the potato and onion and cook, stirring, for 3–4 minutes, or until the onion starts to soften.

2 Stir in the chilli, ginger, spices and salt and cook for a further 2–3 minutes, or until the potato is golden.

3 Return the insert pan, if using, to the slow cooker, or transfer the mixture to the slow cooker. Sprinkle 2 tablespoons water over the mixture, then cover and cook on high for 2 hours, or until the potato is tender.

4 Garnish with coriander and serve with lemon wedges.

Slow-cooked onions with thyme and parmesan

Serves **8–10**   Preparation time **15 minutes**   Cooking time **8 hours 10 minutes**

10 small onions
250 ml (9 fl oz/1 cup) pouring cream
100 ml (3½ fl oz) good-quality
  chicken stock
5 thyme sprigs
3 garlic cloves, crushed
30 g (1 oz) butter, chopped
50 g (1¾ oz/⅓ cup) finely grated
  parmesan cheese, to serve

1 Peel the onions, then use a sharp knife to score a cross into the top of each one. Place the onions in a 5 litre (175 fl oz/ 20 cup) slow cooker, with the scored side facing up.

2 Pour the cream and stock over the onions, then scatter with the thyme sprigs, garlic and butter. Season with sea salt and freshly ground black pepper.

3 Cover and cook on low, stirring occasionally, for 8 hours, or until the onions are very tender.

4 Carefully strain the cream mixture into a saucepan. Allow to reduce over medium–high heat for 7–10 minutes, or until the sauce has thickened.

5 Pour the sauce over the onions and season to taste. Serve sprinkled with the parmesan.

Braised fennel with a sourdough and prosciutto crust

Serves **6** Preparation time **15 minutes** Cooking time **2 hours 40 minutes**

125 ml (4 fl oz/½ cup) olive oil
4 small fennel bulbs, trimmed and
    cut into 6 wedges
5 thyme sprigs
250 ml (9 fl oz/1 cup) milk
125 ml (4 fl oz/½ cup) good-quality
    chicken stock
50 g (1¾ oz/⅓ cup) finely grated
    parmesan cheese
125 g (4½ oz/2 cups, lightly packed)
    coarse day-old sourdough
    breadcrumbs
50 g (1¾ oz) prosciutto, diced

1 Heat one-third of the olive oil in the insert pan of a
   5 litre (175 fl oz/20 cup) slow cooker or a large frying
   pan over medium–high heat. Add the fennel and cook,
   stirring occasionally, for 5–6 minutes, or until golden.

2 Return the insert pan, if using, to the slow cooker,
   or transfer the fennel to the slow cooker. Add the
   thyme sprigs, milk and stock and season with sea salt
   and freshly ground black pepper. Cover and cook on
   high for 2–2½ hours, or until the fennel is very tender.
   Season to taste, sprinkle with the parmesan and
   keep warm.

3 Meanwhile, heat the remaining oil in a frying pan over
   medium heat. Add the breadcrumbs and prosciutto and
   cook, stirring occasionally, for 2–3 minutes, or until
   golden and crisp.

4 Serve the fennel topped with the crisp breadcrumbs
   and prosciutto.

Braised artichokes with potatoes, garlic and sage

Serves **6–8**   Preparation time **40 minutes**   Cooking time **2 hours 30 minutes**

Juice of 1 lemon
8 globe artichokes
1 kg (2 lb 4 oz) desiree potatoes, peeled and coarsely chopped
1 fresh bay leaf
750 ml (26 fl oz/3 cups) good-quality vegetable stock
1 tablespoon sage, coarsely chopped
Extra virgin olive oil, for drizzling

1 Add the lemon juice to a bowl of water. Using a large knife, cut off and discard the top 4–5 cm (1½–2 inches) of each artichoke. Remove the tough outer leaves, then cut each artichoke into quarters and scrape away the hairy choke inside the artichokes. As you're working, add artichokes to the lemon water so they don't discolour.

2 Drain the artichokes and place in a 7 litre (245 fl oz/ 28 cup) slow cooker with the potato and bay leaf. Pour in enough stock to just cover the vegetables.

3 Cover and cook on high for 2–2½ hours, stirring occasionally, until the artichokes and potato are tender. Stir in the sage during the last 30 minutes of cooking.

4 Transfer the vegetables to a warm serving dish using a slotted spoon. Drizzle with a little of the braising liquid and some olive oil. Season to taste with sea salt and freshly ground black pepper and serve.

Dhal

Serves **4–6**   Preparation time **15 minutes**   Cooking time **4 hours**

305 g (10¾ oz/1½ cups) red lentils
 or 325 g (11½ oz/1½ cups)
 brown lentils
2 tomatoes, finely chopped
2 garlic cloves, crushed
2 teaspoons finely chopped fresh
 ginger
1 long fresh green chilli, finely
 chopped
2 tablespoons coriander (cilantro),
 leaves, chopped, plus extra,
 to garnish
2 teaspoons ground turmeric
½ teaspoon ground cinnamon
¼ teaspoon ground cardamom
500 ml (17 fl oz/2 cups) good-quality
 vegetable stock
40 g (1½ oz) ghee
1 brown onion, thinly sliced
1 teaspoon garam masala
½ teaspoon mustard seeds
½ teaspoon cumin seeds
Warm naan bread, to serve

1 Rinse and drain the lentils. Place in a 5 litre (175 fl oz/ 20 cup) slow cooker with the tomato, garlic, ginger, chilli, coriander, turmeric, cinnamon and cardamom.

2 Pour in the stock and 500 ml (17 fl oz/2 cups) water and gently mix together. Cover and cook on low for 4 hours, or until the lentils are soft.

3 Meanwhile, heat 30 g (1 oz) of the ghee in a frying pan over high heat. Add the onion and cook, stirring, for 8–10 minutes, or until dark brown. Remove to a plate.

4 Heat the remaining ghee in the pan until it is almost smoking, then add the garam masala, mustard seeds and cumin seeds. Cook, stirring, for 30 seconds, then add the spices to the lentils and stir them through. Season to taste with sea salt.

5 Serve the lentils scattered with the fried onion and extra coriander leaves, with naan bread to the side.

Italian-style beans

Serves **10–12** Preparation time **20 minutes (+ 8 hours soaking)** Cooking time **4 hours 25 minutes**

800 g (1 lb 12 oz) dried white beans,
  such as cannellini
2 tablespoons olive oil
2 brown onions, cut into thin wedges
4 garlic cloves, crushed
2 x 400 g (14 oz) tins whole
  tomatoes, roughly crushed
1 litre (35 fl oz/4 cups) good-quality
  vegetable or chicken stock
400 g (14 oz) piece of pancetta,
  skin removed, cut into 5 mm
  (¼ inch) thick slices
Extra virgin olive oil, for drizzling

1 Soak the beans for 8 hours or overnight in plenty of cold water. Drain the beans, discarding the water, then place in a large saucepan. Cover with fresh water and bring to the boil. Boil rapidly for 10 minutes. Rinse the beans and drain again.

2 Heat the olive oil in the insert pan of a 7 litre (245 fl oz/28 cup) slow cooker or a frying pan over medium heat. Add the onion and garlic and cook, stirring, for 5–7 minutes, or until softened.

3 Return the insert pan, if using, to the slow cooker, or transfer the onion mixture to the slow cooker. Add the beans, tomatoes, stock and pancetta and gently mix together.

4 Cover and cook on high for 3½–4 hours, or until the beans are tender.

5 Season to taste with sea salt and freshly ground black pepper. Serve drizzled with extra virgin olive oil.

Braised chickpeas with onion and silverbeet

Serves **8–10**   Preparation time **15 minutes (+ 8 hours soaking)**   Cooking time **4 hours 20 minutes**

375 g (13 oz) dried chickpeas
2 tablespoons olive oil
20 g (¾ oz) butter
1 brown onion, sliced into wedges
4 garlic cloves, crushed
500 g (1 lb 2 oz/½ bunch) silverbeet
    (Swiss chard), stalks thinly sliced,
    leaves coarsely chopped
1 litre (35 fl oz/4 cups) good-quality
    chicken stock
Extra virgin olive oil, for drizzling

1 Soak the chickpeas for 8 hours or overnight in plenty of cold water. Drain the chickpeas, discarding the water, then place in a large saucepan. Cover with fresh water and bring to the boil. Boil rapidly for 10 minutes. Rinse the chickpeas and drain again.

2 Heat the olive oil and butter in the insert pan of a 5 litre (175 fl oz/20 cup) slow cooker or a frying pan over medium heat. Add the onion, garlic and silverbeet stalks and cook, stirring, for 5–6 minutes, or until softened.

3 Return the insert pan, if using, to the slow cooker, or transfer the mixture to the slow cooker. Add the stock and chickpeas and gently mix together. Cover and cook on high for 3 hours, or until the chickpeas are almost cooked through.

4 Stir in the silverbeet leaves, then cover and cook a further 1 hour, or until the chickpeas are very tender.

5 Season to taste with sea salt and freshly ground black pepper. Serve drizzled with extra virgin olive oil.

Herb pilaff with roasted almonds

Serves **6–8**   Preparation time **20 minutes**   Cooking time **1 hour 25 minutes**

1 tablespoon olive oil
20 g (¾ oz) butter
1 brown onion, diced
3 garlic cloves, finely chopped
500 g (1 lb 2 oz/2½ cups) long-grain
   white rice
850 ml (29 fl oz) good-quality
   chicken or vegetable stock
1 cinnamon stick
1 preserved lemon
Juice of 1 lemon
1 cup flat-leaf (Italian) parsley,
   coarsely torn
1 cup mint, coarsely torn
80 g (2¾ oz/½ cup) roasted almonds,
   coarsely chopped, to garnish
Greek-style yoghurt, to serve

1 Heat the olive oil and butter in the insert pan of a 5 litre (175 fl oz/20 cup) slow cooker or a frying pan over medium heat. Add the onion and garlic and cook, stirring, for 5–7 minutes, or until softened.

2 Return the insert pan, if using, to the slow cooker, or transfer the onion mixture to the slow cooker. Add the rice, stirring to coat the grains in the oil, then add the stock and cinnamon stick.

3 Cover and cook on high, stirring occasionally, for 1–1¼ hours, or until the rice is tender and fluffy, adding a little extra stock or water if the rice seems to be drying out.

4 Rinse the preserved lemon well, then remove and discard the pulp and membrane. Finely dice the rind, then stir it through the pilaff with the lemon juice and herbs.

5 Garnish with the almonds and serve with yoghurt.

Fontina and rosemary risotto

Serves **4–6**   Preparation time **15 minutes**   Cooking time **1 hour**

2 tablespoons olive oil
1 brown onion, finely diced
3 garlic cloves, finely chopped
2 tablespoons rosemary leaves,
  coarsely chopped
440 g (15½ oz/2 cups) arborio rice
  (see Tip)
200 ml (7 fl oz) white wine
1.4 litres (49 fl oz) good-quality
  chicken or vegetable stock,
  heated
120 g (4¼ oz/1 cup) roughly grated
  fontina cheese
50 g (1¾ oz/⅓ cup) finely grated
  parmesan cheese, plus extra, to
  serve
40 g (1½ oz) butter, chopped

1 Heat the olive oil in the insert pan of a 5 litre (175 fl oz/ 20 cup) slow cooker or a frying pan over medium–low heat. Add the onion and garlic and cook, stirring, for 4–6 minutes, or until softened.

2 Add the rosemary and rice and stir for 1–2 minutes, or until the rice is hot. Pour in the wine and stir for 2–3 minutes, or until it has slightly reduced. Stir in the hot stock and bring to a simmer.

3 Return the insert pan, if using, to the slow cooker, or transfer the rice mixture to the slow cooker. Cover and cook on high, stirring occasionally, for 35–45 minutes, or until the rice is tender.

4 Stir the fontina cheese, parmesan and butter through the risotto until creamy and combined. Season to taste with sea salt and freshly ground black pepper and serve sprinkled with extra parmesan.

Tip: Arborio rice is a short-grain rice perfect for making risotto. You can find arborio in the rice section at the supermarket.

Desserts and Puddings

Stuffed apples with vanilla cream

Serves **4**   Preparation time **20 minutes**   Cooking time **6 hours**

1 tablespoon desiccated coconut

4 granny smith apples, about 200 g
(7 oz) each

60 g (2¼ oz/⅓ cup, lightly packed)
brown sugar

60 g (2¼ oz/⅓ cup) raisins, coarsely
chopped

2 tablespoons chopped walnuts

½ teaspoon ground cinnamon,
plus extra, to serve

¼ teaspoon ground ginger

A pinch of ground cloves

1 tablespoon honey

185 ml (6 fl oz/¾ cup) thick
(double/heavy) cream

¼ teaspoon freshly grated nutmeg

20 g (¾ oz) unsalted butter

1 Lightly grease the base of a 5 litre (175 fl oz/20 cup)
slow cooker and sprinkle with the coconut.

2 Core the apples, then slice the bottom off each one so
they will sit flat. Make a small incision in the skin around
the middle of each apple to allow steam to escape during
cooking. Peel off a 1 cm (½ inch) ring from around the
top of each apple.

3 In a bowl, mix together the sugar, raisins, walnuts,
cinnamon, ginger, cloves and honey. Pack the mixture
into the middle of each apple where the core has been
removed. Place the apples in the slow cooker, pour the
cream over them and dust the tops with nutmeg. Dot
the apples with the butter.

4 Cover and cook on low for 6 hours, or until the apples
are tender but not mushy. Carefully remove each apple
to a warm bowl.

5 Stir the cream sauce to recombine it, then pour over
the apples. Serve warm, sprinkled with extra cinnamon.

Sago pudding with caramelised pineapple and toasted coconut

Serves **4**   Preparation time **20 minutes**   Cooking time **3 hours**

100 g (3½ oz/½ cup) sago or
  tapioca pearls
100 g (3½ oz/½ cup, lightly packed)
  brown sugar
¼ teaspoon ground cinnamon
½ teaspoon natural vanilla extract
Finely grated zest of 1 lemon
300 ml (10½ fl oz) milk
2 x 400 ml (14 fl oz) tins coconut
  milk
2 egg yolks
160 g (5¾ oz/1 cup) chopped fresh
  pineapple pieces
25 g (1 oz/⅓ cup) shredded coconut,
  lightly toasted

1 Place the sago in a 5 litre (175 fl oz/20 cup) slow cooker with 2 tablespoons of the sugar, the cinnamon, vanilla, lemon zest and a pinch of salt. Pour in the milk and coconut milk and gently mix together.

2 Cover and cook on low for 2½ hours, or until the sago is tender, stirring once during cooking.

3 In a bowl, whisk the egg yolks with 2 tablespoons of the remaining sugar until thick. Slowly whisk 250 ml (9 fl oz/1 cup) of the hot sago mixture into the eggs until well combined. Pour the egg mixture back into the slow cooker and stir well to combine. Cover and cook for a further 20–25 minutes, or until thickened.

4 Meanwhile, add the pineapple pieces to a cold frying pan and sprinkle with the remaining 2 tablespoons sugar. Place over medium heat and shake gently until the sugar melts and the pineapple releases its juice. Increase the heat to medium–high and cook for a further for 4–5 minutes, shaking the pan until the pineapple is lightly caramelised. Transfer to a bowl.

5 Serve the pudding topped with the pineapple and coconut.

Vanilla and cinnamon rice pudding with baked strawberries and rhubarb

Serves **6**   Preparation time **20 minutes**   Cooking time **1 hour 40 minutes**

750 ml (26 fl oz/3 cups) milk

250 ml (9 fl oz/1 cup) pouring cream

140 g (5 oz/⅔ cup) raw caster (superfine) sugar

1 cinnamon stick

½ vanilla bean, split in half lengthways, seeds scraped

220 g (7¾ oz/1 cup) white short-grain or medium-grain rice

3 egg yolks

20 g (¾ oz) butter, chopped

Baked strawberries and rhubarb

750 g (1 lb 10 oz) rhubarb, trimmed and cut into 4 cm (1½ inch) lengths

250 g (9 oz) strawberries, hulled and halved

90 g (3¼ oz/½ cup) raw caster (superfine) sugar

Juice of ½ orange

½ vanilla bean, split in half lengthways, seeds scraped

1   Combine the milk, cream, sugar, cinnamon stick and the vanilla bean and seeds in the insert pan of a 5 litre (175 fl oz/20 cup) slow cooker or a saucepan. Bring to a simmer over medium heat.

2   Return the insert pan, if using, to the slow cooker, or transfer the mixture to the slow cooker. Stir in the rice, then cover and cook on high for 1–1½ hours, or until the rice is tender.

3   Meanwhile, bake the rhubarb and strawberries. Preheat the oven to 180°C (350°F/Gas 4). Combine the rhubarb, strawberries, sugar, orange juice and the vanilla bean and seeds in a baking dish. Cover with foil and roast for 15–20 minutes, stirring once, or until the rhubarb is tender. Remove the vanilla bean.

4   Remove the vanilla bean from the rice pudding, then stir the egg yolks and butter through until well combined. Top with the baked rhubarb and strawberries and serve.

Self-saucing chocolate and hazelnut pudding

Serves **8–10**   Preparation time **20 minutes**   Cooking time **2 hours**

250 g (9 oz/1⅔ cups) plain
(all-purpose) flour
250 g (9 oz/1⅓ cups) raw caster
(superfine) sugar
1 tablespoon baking powder
55 g (2 oz/½ cup) unsweetened
cocoa powder
500 ml (17 fl oz/2 cups) milk
180 g (6 oz) butter, melted
4 eggs, lightly beaten
150 g (5½ oz/1 cup) coarsely
chopped dark chocolate
75 g (2½ oz/½ cup) toasted
hazelnuts, chopped
Vanilla or hazelnut ice cream,
to serve

Topping
200 g (7 oz) brown sugar
30 g (1 oz/¼ cup) unsweetened
cocoa powder

1 Sift the flour, sugar, baking powder, cocoa powder and a pinch of sea salt into a bowl. Add the milk, butter and eggs and stir until smooth. Fold the chocolate and hazelnuts through, then pour the batter into a 5 litre (175 fl oz/20 cup) slow cooker.

2 Combine the topping ingredients in a bowl, then sprinkle over the pudding batter. Pour 400 ml (14 fl oz) hot water over the top.

3 Cover and cook on high for 2 hours, or until the pudding is just cooked through.

4 Serve with vanilla or hazelnut ice cream.

Poached quince with cinnamon custard and pistachios

Serves **8–10** Preparation time **20 minutes (+ 30 minutes infusing)**
Cooking time **8 hours 10 minutes**

1 kg (2 lb 4 oz) caster (superfine)
   sugar
2 cinnamon sticks
2 star anise
1 vanilla bean, split in half
   lengthways, seeds scraped
Juice of 1 lemon
6 quinces
40 g (1½ oz/⅓ cup) toasted
   pistachio nuts, coarsely chopped

Cinnamon custard
500 ml (17 fl oz/2 cups) milk
400 ml (14 fl oz) pouring cream
1 teaspoon ground cinnamon
6 egg yolks
150 g (5½ oz/¾ cup) raw caster
   (superfine) sugar

1 Place the sugar, cinnamon sticks, star anise and vanilla bean and seeds in the insert pan of a 5 litre (175 fl oz/ 20 cup) slow cooker or a saucepan. Pour in 1.2 litres (42 fl oz) water. Bring to a simmer over medium–high heat, stirring occasionally, for 5–7 minutes, or until the sugar has dissolved. Return the insert pan, if using, to the slow cooker, or transfer the syrup to the slow cooker.

2 Add the lemon juice to a bowl of water. Peel, core and quarter the quinces, adding them to the lemon water to prevent browning. Place the quince cores and peel in a piece of muslin (cheesecloth), gather the ends and tie them together to form a pouch. Add the pouch to the sugar syrup. Drain the quince and add to the sugar syrup. Cover and cook on low for 7–8 hours, or until the quince is tender. Remove muslin pouch.

3 About 45 minutes before serving time, make the cinnamon custard. First, combine the milk, cream and cinnamon in a saucepan over medium heat. Bring just to the boil, then set aside to infuse for 30 minutes.

4 Whisk together the egg yolks and sugar. Bring the milk mixture back to just below a simmer. Strain the egg yolk mixture into the milk mixture, whisking continuously to combine. Transfer the custard to a clean saucepan and cook over medium heat, stirring continuously, for 5–7 minutes, or until the custard thickly coats the back of a wooden spoon. Remove from the heat and stir until just warm. Cover and keep warm.

5 Serve the quince with the cinnamon custard, sprinkled with the pistachios.

Pears poached in ginger wine

Serves **6**   Preparation time **15 minutes**   Cooking time **3 hours**

750 ml (26 fl oz/3 cups) green
    ginger wine
660 g (1 lb 7 oz/3 cups) caster
    (superfine) sugar
1 lime
6 beurre bosc pears, peeled,
    with the stems left intact
Vanilla ice cream, to serve

1 Pour the ginger wine and 750 ml (26 fl oz/3 cups) water into a 5 litre (175 fl oz/20 cup) slow cooker. Stir in the sugar.

2 Remove thick strips of zest from the lime using a vegetable peeler, being careful to avoid the bitter white pith. Squeeze and strain the juice from the lime and add it to the slow cooker with the zest strips.

3 Add the pears to the liquid (they will float). Cover and cook on high for 3 hours, or until the pears are tender.

4 Serve warm with a scoop of vanilla ice cream, drizzled with some of the syrup.

⚙ *Tips: This is also delicious with the coconut rice pudding on page 268. You could make the dessert more substantial by serving the pears with some purchased sponge cake, sprinkled with chopped pistachio nuts.*

Coconut rice pudding

Serves **6**   Preparation time **10 minutes**   Cooking time **4 hours**

625 ml (21½ fl oz/2½ cups)
coconut milk
625 ml (21½ fl oz/2½ cups) milk
110 g (3¾ oz/½ cup) caster
(superfine) sugar
6 makrut (kaffir lime) leaves
220 g (7¾ oz/1 cup) medium-grain
white rice
Grated palm sugar (jaggery) or
brown sugar, for sprinkling

1 Place the coconut milk, milk, sugar, lime leaves and rice in a 5 litre (175 fl oz/20 cup) slow cooker and gently mix together. Cover and cook on low for 4 hours.

2 Serve warm, sprinkled with palm sugar or brown sugar.

⚙ *Tips: This easy dessert is wonderful served with the pears poached in ginger wine on page 267. In warmer months, you could simply serve it cold with some sliced fresh mango.*

Lemon pudding

Serves 4 Preparation time **15 minutes (+ 10 minutes cooling)** Cooking time **2 hours 35 minutes**

60 g (2¼ oz) unsalted butter,
  chopped, plus some softened
  butter, for greasing
3 eggs, separated
165 g (5¾ oz/¾ cup) white
  granulated sugar
Finely grated zest of 1 lemon
60 ml (2 fl oz/¼ cup) strained
  lemon juice
375 ml (13 fl oz/1½ cups) milk
35 g (1¼ oz/¼ cup) plain
  (all-purpose) flour
Ice cream, to serve

1 Melt the butter in a very small saucepan over low heat. Set aside to cool for 10 minutes. Meanwhile, grease the bowl of a 5 litre (175 fl oz/20 cup) slow cooker with the softened butter.

2 Place the egg yolks, sugar, lemon zest and lemon juice in a bowl. Beat until combined, using electric beaters.

3 Add the melted butter and beat until combined, then add the milk and beat until combined. Beat in the flour.

4 Using clean electric beaters, beat the egg whites in a bowl until stiff peaks form. Gently fold the egg whites through the lemon mixture.

5 Pour the batter into the slow cooker, then cover and cook on high for 2½ hours, or until the pudding is set.

6 Serve warm, with ice cream.

Apple, rhubarb and strawberry cobbler

Serves **6**   Preparation time **25 minutes**   Cooking time **3 hours 45 minutes**

330 g (11½ oz/1½ cups) white granulated sugar
1 teaspoon ground cinnamon
1 vanilla bean, split in half lengthways, seeds scraped
1 kg (2 lb 4 oz) granny smith apples, peeled and cut into 3 cm (1¼ inch) chunks
500 g (1 lb 2 oz) rhubarb, trimmed and cut into 3 cm (1¼ inch) lengths
250 g (9 oz) strawberries, hulled and halved
2 teaspoons lemon juice

Batter
150 g (5½ oz/1 cup) plain (all-purpose) flour
1½ teaspoons baking powder
55 g (2 oz/¼ cup) white granulated sugar
60 g (2¼ oz) unsalted butter, chopped and slightly softened
125 ml (4 fl oz/½ cup) milk
1 teaspoon natural vanilla extract
2 tablespoons cornflour (cornstarch)

1   Place the sugar, cinnamon and vanilla seeds in a large bowl and mix to combine. Add the apple, rhubarb and strawberries and toss to combine.

2   Transfer the mixture to a 5 litre (175 fl oz/20 cup) slow cooker, adding the scraped vanilla bean. Drizzle the lemon juice and 125 ml (4 fl oz/½ cup) water over. Cover and cook on low for 2½ hours.

3   To make the batter, sift the flour and baking powder into a bowl, add the sugar and mix to combine. Work in the butter using your fingertips until combined. Stir in the milk and vanilla until just smooth.

4   Blend the cornflour with 2 tablespoons water until smooth. Working as quickly as possible, so the slow cooker doesn't lose too much heat, remove the lid and stir the cornflour mixture through the fruit. Quickly dollop the batter over the top, using a large spoon.

5   Cover and cook on high for 1¼ hours, or until the batter is cooked. Serve warm.

Marmalade bread and butter pudding

Serves **8**   Preparation time **20 minutes**   Cooking time **4 hours**

600 g (1 lb 5 oz) thickly sliced fruit loaf, with the crust on

60 g (2¼ oz) butter, softened, plus extra, for greasing

225 g (8 oz/⅔ cup) good-quality marmalade, plus an extra 115 g (4 oz/⅓ cup), for brushing (see Tip)

6 eggs

165 g (5¾ oz/¾ cup) white granulated sugar, plus an extra 1½ teaspoons, for sprinkling

250 ml (9 fl oz/1 cup) milk

500 ml (17 fl oz/2 cups) pouring cream

2 teaspoons natural vanilla extract

Vanilla ice cream, to serve

1 Spread half the fruit loaf slices with the butter, then spread the remaining slices with the marmalade. Sandwich together and cut in half.

2 Grease a 7 litre (245 fl oz/28 cup) slow cooker and arrange the bread slices inside it on a slight angle, covering the base.

3 In a bowl, whisk together the eggs, sugar, milk, cream and vanilla. Pour over the bread and gently press the bread down with your hands to help the liquid to soak into the bread. Sprinkle with the extra sugar.

4 Cover and cook on low for 4 hours.

5 Brush the pudding with the extra marmalade and serve warm, with vanilla ice cream.

Tip: It's good to use marmalade with citrus zest in it, or even a bitter English-style marmalade, as a contrast to the sweetness of this dish.

Index

Published in 2012 by Murdoch Books Pty Limited

Reprinted 2012

Murdoch Books Australia
Pier 8/9
23 Hickson Road
Millers Point NSW 2000
Phone: +61 (0) 2 8220 2000
Fax: +61 (0) 2 8220 2558
www.murdochbooks.com.au
info@murdochbooks.com.au

Murdoch Books UK Limited
Erico House, 6th Floor
93–99 Upper Richmond Road
Putney, London SW15 2TG
Phone: +44 (0) 20 8785 5995
Fax: +44 (0) 20 8785 5985
www.murdochbooks.co.uk
info@murdochbooks.co.uk

For Corporate Orders & Custom Publishing contact Noel Hammond,
National Business Development Manager Murdoch Books Australia

Publisher: Anneka Manning
Designer: Katy Wall
Cover Designer: Adam Walker
Illustrator: Heather Menzies
Project Editor: Martina Vascotto
Editor: Katri Hilden
Food Editor: Michelle Earl
Recipe Developers: Alice Storey, Brett Sargent, Sonia Greig and the Murdoch Books Test Kitchen
Production: Alexandra Gonzalez
Photographers: Jared Fowler and Natasha Milne

Front cover images L to R: Chicken braised with ginger and star anise (pg 97), Chilli beef with avocado salsa (pg 214) and Chicken and prune tagine (pg 181).

Back cover images L to R: Thai chicken and galangal soup (pg 30), Lasagne with ham, lemon and basil (pg 235) and Bouillabaisse (pg 52).

National Library of Australia Cataloguing-in-Publication Data
Title: 250 must-have slow cooker recipes
ISBN 978-1-74266-679-2 (pbk.)
Notes: Includes index.
Subjects: Electric cooking, Slow
Dewey Number: 641.5884

Printed by Hang Tai Printing Company Limited, China

IMPORTANT: Those who might be at risk from the effects of salmonella poisoning (the elderly, pregnant women, young children and those suffering from immune deficiency diseases) should consult their doctor with any concerns about eating raw eggs.

OVEN GUIDE: You may find cooking times vary depending on the oven you are using. For fan-forced ovens, as a general rule, set the oven temperature to 20°C (35°F) lower than indicated in the recipe. We have used 20 ml (4 teaspoon) tablespoon measures. If you are using a 15 ml (3 teaspoon) tablespoon add an extra teaspoon of the ingredient for each tablespoon specified.